THE

EVERYTHING®

JEWISH
WEDDING
BOOK

The Everything Series:

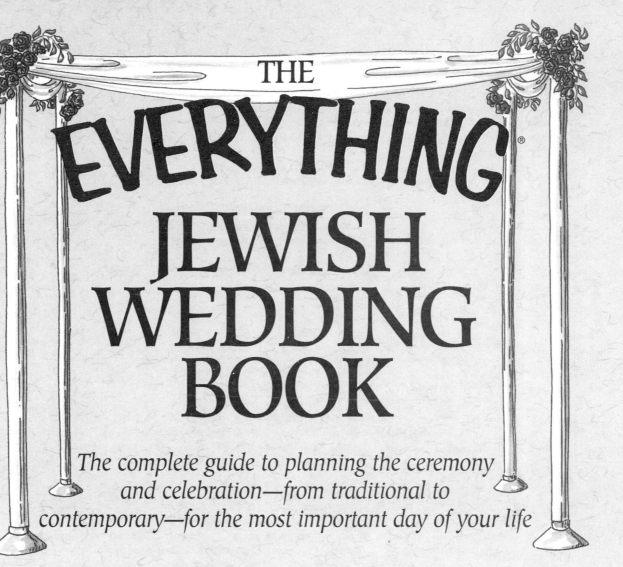

THE
EVERYTHING®
JEWISH WEDDING BOOK

*The complete guide to planning the ceremony
and celebration—from traditional to
contemporary—for the most important day of your life*

Helen Latner

Adams Media Corporation
Holbrook, Massachusetts

An Everything® Series Book.
The Everything® Series is a registered trademark of Adams Media Corporation.

Published by
Adams Media Corporation
260 Center Street, Holbrook, MA 02343

ISBN: 1-55850-801-5

Printed in the United States of America.

J   I   H   G   F   E   D   C

Library of Congress Cataloging-in-Publication Data
The everything Jewish wedding book / Helen Latner.
        p.   cm.
Includes index.
ISBN 1-55850-801-5
1. Marriage customs and rites, Jewish. 2. Wedding etiquette. I. Title.
        BM713.L39   1998
        296.4'44—dc21   97-43502
                                          CIP

This publication is designed to provide accurate and authoritative information with regard to the subject matter covered. It is sold with the understanding that the publisher is not engaged in rendering legal, accounting, or other professional advice. If legal advice or other expert assistance is required, the services of a competent professional person should be sought.
—From a *Declaration of Principles* jointly adopted by a Committee of the American Bar Association and a Committee of Publishers and Associations

Interior illustrations by Barry Littmann, Joanna Hodgens, and Mary Nagin

This book is available at quantity discounts for bulk purchases.
For information, call 1-800-872-5627 (in Massachusetts, call 781-767-8100).

Visit our home page at http://www.adamsmedia.com

CONTENTS

CONTENTS

CONTENTS

מש מח

INTRODUCTION

Mazel tov! You're engaged, soon to be married, and you, your future husband and your parents are doubly blessed. Everyone should be married, according to Jewish thought, because it is the ideal state of existence, ordained since the Creation. Starry-eyed, you agree. And your parents, when they lead you to the wedding canopy (*huppah*), will be realizing their fondest dream for you. The very first blessing they said over you as babies when they gave you your names expressed the hope to one day see you as radiant bride and groom.

Underlying that happy glow is the knowledge that arranging a wedding is a complicated business, too often defined by the three P's—parties, plans—and panic. In the midst of happiness, you and your fiancé may find yourselves involved in a tense standoff between two families. You will have to deal with the mind-set of at least two generations and face a range of choices that can escalate from a no-frills ceremony at City Hall to the all-out splendor of a Hollywood extravaganza—and cope with details, details, details—most of which spell either expense or perplexity.

The perfect wedding, whatever its scale, does not create itself. There is a great deal of preliminary planning, much of it long in advance of the great day. This book is designed to help you understand the traditions that make a wedding Jewish, to point the way through the bewildering array of choices, to suggest solutions to the problems that can be caused by divorces in the family, deceased parents, differences of religion, or getting married in an unfamiliar community. It will help you deal with all those little nagging worries that wake you in the middle of the night as the wedding day draws closer.

You will learn how to work with your providers—whether they are caterers, florists, or musicians—as allies instead of adversaries, because you will know what to demand and what to expect. This book will help you to reach your goal—a beautiful, smoothly run wedding.

Weddings can be overwhelmingly expensive, but they need not be. I have indicated ways to economize, ways to share the cost, ways to spare yourself needless tension and exhaustion. There's a detailed countdown to the wedding day, a planning calendar to help

Made In Heaven

THERE IS A LEGEND (*MIDRASH*) THAT TELLS US THAT FORTY DAYS BEFORE YOU WERE BORN, ANGELS ANNOUNCED THE NAME OF YOUR ORDAINED MATE (YOUR *ZIVUK*) IN HEAVEN.

HOWEVER...ANOTHER COMMENTARY IN THE TALMUD REMARKS THAT THE PERFECT MARRIAGE OCCURS AS OFTEN AS THE PARTING OF THE RED SEA.

WHICHEVER WAY YOU REGARD MARRIAGE, STILL ANOTHER COMMENTARY HOLDS THAT THE VERY FIRST QUESTIONS YOU WILL BE ASKED ON JUDGMENT DAY WILL BE: "ARE YOU MARRIED?" AND "HAVE YOU CREATED A FAMILY?"

Made In Heaven

THERE IS A LEGEND (*MIDRASH*) THAT TELLS US THAT FORTY DAYS BEFORE YOU WERE BORN, ANGELS ANNOUNCED THE NAME OF YOUR ORDAINED MATE (YOUR *ZIVUK*) IN HEAVEN.

HOWEVER…ANOTHER COMMENTARY IN THE TALMUD REMARKS THAT THE PERFECT MARRIAGE OCCURS AS OFTEN AS THE PARTING OF THE RED SEA.

WHICHEVER WAY YOU REGARD MARRIAGE, STILL ANOTHER COMMENTARY HOLDS THAT THE VERY FIRST QUESTIONS YOU WILL BE ASKED ON JUDGMENT DAY WILL BE: "ARE YOU MARRIED?" AND "HAVE YOU CREATED A FAMILY?"

you set up a timetable and keep track of your appointments, and expense charts for watching your costs. Use the worksheets, checklists and "panic-stoppers" to stay on top of the flood of details coming at you.

With the help of this book you can stay calm, avoid most of the frayed tempers and tiffs that tension creates, and arrange a truly Jewish wedding that is distinctive and emotionally fulfilling.

A NOTE TO THE BRIDE

Yes, it *is* your wedding and you have the right to the last word in all decisions, but bear in mind—you are marrying into another family. They have rights, too! Try to consult your fiancé's wishes and those of his parents before you make those big decisions.

Remember that parents and grandparents have a special role to play in Jewish wedding ceremonies. Be a wise bride and take them all into account in your plans.

Planning equals lists and notebooks. The more you write down, the less you have to worry about remembering. Use the questions in the checklists in this book, the pages for your guest and gift records, the calendar for your appointments and "do now" memos. All this attention to detail will make it possible for you to approach your wedding day with less confusion. It's the way to walk down the aisle serene, radiant and happy.

As they say in traditional congratulations: *Mazel tov and siman tov!*

PART ONE

A REAL JEWISH WEDDING

CHAPTER 1

WHAT MAKES A WEDDING JEWISH?

HUPPAH

RABBI

YARMULKE

WINE

WINE GLASS

HALLAH

GROOM

BRIDE

משמח

It's a Mitzvah!

A WEDDING, SINCE BIBLICAL TIMES, HAS BEEN REGARDED AS THE "BUILDING OF JOY" AND WAS CELEBRATED WITH GREAT FESTIVITIES. MUSIC, FEASTING, PROCESSIONS, SPECIAL DRESS AND CROWNS FOR THE BRIDE AND GROOM WERE THE ORDER OF THE DAY, TOGETHER WITH ALL THE HILARIOUS REVELRY AND MERRYMAKING THE GUESTS COULD COME UP WITH, EVEN TUMBLING, CLOWNING, JUGGLING AND COMIC VERSIFYING. BRIDE AND GROOM WERE REGARDED AS KING AND QUEEN; THEIR EVERY WISH WAS GRANTED; THEY WERE SEATED ON THRONELIKE CHAIRS AT THE RECEPTION AND WERE RAISED ALOFT ON THE CHAIRS DURING THE JOYFUL DANCING. THE BELIEF WAS THAT ALL THEIR PAST SINS WERE FORGIVEN AND THEY WERE STARTING THEIR LIFE TOGETHER WITH A "CLEAN SLATE." THE ENTIRE COMMUNITY, INCLUDING THE POOR, JOINED IN THE CELEBRATION AND TOOK PART IN THE MITZVAH OF HELPING THE COUPLE MARRY AND START A NEW HOUSEHOLD. IT WAS ALSO A SPECIAL MITZVAH TO INCREASE THE REJOICING OF THE BRIDE AND GROOM ON THEIR WEDDING DAY. THIS REMAINS A MITZVAH TO THIS DAY.

What occasion in Jewish life is more joyous than a wedding? How parents and guests *kvell* (rejoice) that two who were separate and alone will now be one and together! You are becoming part of a basic social institution—founding a home and a family. Getting married, in Jewish tradition, is a holy act, since it results in the creation of life—the fulfillment of the commandment (a *mitzvah*) to increase and multiply.

THE JUDAIC CONCEPT OF MARRIAGE

The bride and groom entering this ideal state are regarded as a new Adam and Eve, coming into a new Garden of Eden. The purpose of their marriage is not only founding a family but also enjoying true companionship. The ceremony that unites them is designed to surround a legal contract entered into publicly (the *ketubah*) with blessings that sanctify the relationship, which is why the ceremony is called *kiddushin*—sanctification. A wedding used to be marked with feasting for seven days—and you think planning for the one big day is mind-boggling!

Forget about the weddings you see in the movies and on TV, where the groom materializes at the altar as though he had been let out of a box and the bride is "given away" by her father, while the mothers of both watch from the sidelines, relegated to the front pews. The Jewish tradition is that both sets of parents are bringing their children to be consecrated to each other under the *huppah*—wedding canopy—and the parents' rightful place is also there, alongside them, during the marriage service. The grandparents, who, after all, started the line, are also honored with a special place in the procession.

The Orthodox regard the wedding day almost as a minor Yom Kippur (Day of Atonement) since all the past sins of the bride and groom have been forgiven. That's why the Orthodox bride and groom fast before the wedding, the bride dresses in white as a symbol of spiritual purity and the groom dons a white *kittel* (the ceremonial gown worn on Yom Kippur) for the *huppah*.

משמח

Lavish hospitality has always been a Jewish tradition. Some rabbis have even ruled that one may pledge or sell a Torah scroll (the holiest of books) to provide a wedding for a daughter. But to complicate matters even further, others have held that the splendor of the wedding should not be so far beyond the family's means that it becomes an impossible burden. (Your father will be happy to hear that!) Whether it's a wedding in the thirteenth century or one in the twenty-first, you can see that the golden mean is the rule.

SPECIAL NEW RELATIONSHIPS

MEHUTONIM

The two sets of parents enter into a new degree of relationship created by the marriage of their children. No English word really exists to describe it. The word "in-laws" is only an approximate translation of the Hebrew *mehutonim* (plural). The mothers are each given the title of *machteniste* (singular) and the fathers, *mehuton*. In the old, tight-knit families the relationship meant specific social and familial obligations. In today's far-flung families, these can be as close and cordial (or as distant) as you choose to make them.

Use tact and consideration in the early days when the families are becoming acquainted with each other, and take care to avoid friction in planning. That will help make this relationship genuinely warm and lead to a pleasurable extended family. And you don't have to flounder about, deciding how to do it. There are certain rules of etiquette that help in creating harmony. They're all described in Chapter 2.

GRANDPARENTS

Your grandparents may be far away in some sunny retirement spot. Don't forget them! They have a special place in the wedding ceremony itself, and if you tell them your good news, let them know your plans, and tell them about their upcoming honor, you will gladden their hearts and lengthen their days.

Made in Heaven

THERE IS A LEGEND (*MIDRASH*) THAT TELLS US THAT FORTY DAYS BEFORE YOU WERE BORN, ANGELS ANNOUNCED THE NAME OF YOUR ORDAINED MATE (YOUR *ZIVUK*) IN HEAVEN.

HOWEVER ... ANOTHER COMMENTARY IN THE TALMUD REMARKS THAT THE PERFECT MARRIAGE OCCURS AS OFTEN AS THE PARTING OF THE RED SEA.

WHICHEVER WAY YOU REGARD MARRIAGE, STILL ANOTHER COMMENTARY HOLDS THAT THE VERY FIRST QUESTIONS YOU WILL BE ASKED ON JUDGMENT DAY WILL BE: "ARE YOU MARRIED?" AND "HAVE YOU CREATED A FAMILY?"

CHAPTER 2

ENGAGEMENT ETIQUETTE

You've finally found the one person with whom you want to spend the rest of your life, you're both aglow and everyone shares your happiness. You're living out the most ancient of Jewish traditions—preparing to get married—and you are making some of the most momentous decisions of your life.

TRADITIONAL *TENAIM*—A LEGAL COMMITMENT

In the traditional betrothal, once an engagement is entered into, the terms are spelled out in a binding contract (*tenaim*). It used to specify the bride's dowry, the support the parents would provide for the young couple, the date and time of the wedding and a penalty if either party backed out of the agreement. Traditionally, the signing was formalized by the exchange of an object of value, and then a plate or some other piece of crockery was smashed—as a symbol of the destruction of Jerusalem, some say, or of the breaking of childhood ties to parents. Amid cries of "*Mazel tov!*" the celebration began, inaugurating a year of formal courtship and gifts.

Nowadays, this custom (it is not required in Jewish law) has all but vanished; it has been reduced to the private signing, just before the actual ceremony, of an agreement to wed, and the "consideration of value" is often a handkerchief presented by the groom to the bride. Some rabbis take this moment to confirm that the bride is entering into this agreement of her own free will.

MEETING THE FAMILY

TELLING YOUR PARENTS

You're so happy you want to shout it from the rooftops—or at least call everyone you know to broadcast the good news. Before you do, the very first people you must tell about your intentions are—surprise, surprise!—your parents. No one today really expects a young man to ask a woman's father formally for his daughter's hand and you both may feel that you do not need your parents' permission to marry, but you will still want their approval and their blessing. The expected

---

A Heavenly Job

"WHAT HAS GOD BEEN DOING SINCE HE FINISHED THE CREATION OF THE WORLD?" A SKEPTIC ONCE ASKED HIS RABBI. THE RABBI REPLIED, "EVER SINCE THEN, HE HAS BEEN BUSY WITH MATCH-MAKING, A TASK AS DIFFICULT AS THE PARTING OF THE RED SEA."

MAYBE ALL THOSE FRIENDS AND RELATIVES WHO KNEW THEY HAD JUST THE "RIGHT" BOY (OR GIRL) FOR YOU WERE SO INSISTENT ON THE INTRODUCTION BECAUSE THEY SENSED THEY WERE DOING A "HEAVENLY" JOB. HOWEVER YOU MET, AREN'T YOU GLAD YOU DID?

מֵשַׂמֵּחַ

order is that first, the groom-to-be (sometimes accompanied by his fiancée) discusses his intentions with the bride's father (or her mother, if the father is not living) and as soon as possible after that he "announces" to his parents and brings his fiancée to meet them. If they live at a great distance, he should write or phone his parents at once to give them the good news and tell them some wonderful things about his bride-to-be.

EXPECTED FORMAL VISITS—PROTOCOL

You've told them—now what? To keep relations between the two families on an even keel, certain formalities should be observed. First, the groom's mother is expected to call or write the bride's parents, telling them of the family's pleasure in the engagement and welcoming the bride into their family.

If the two families live near enough to visit, it is customary for the bride's mother to invite her in-laws-to-be (*mehutonim*) for an informal visit, accompanied by the engaged couple. Usually, this is when you begin to discuss your preliminary plans for the wedding.

Mothers must keep their cool at this early stage of the blending of two families. Should the groom's mother fail to write or call with the conventional welcome, the bride's mother should not create a grievance by standing on ceremony. She should take the initiative herself and invite the groom's family to visit.

Next comes the return visit—to *his* family. Unless you have all known each other for years, these are stressful encounters, not only for you, but for your parents as well. They may feel as shy as you do about this first, rather formal, move. Informality, cordiality and sincere pleasure at the happiness in store for you will go a long way to smooth the meeting.

LONG-DISTANCE RELATIONSHIPS

Many families are separated by great distances these days, which can make family visits a problem in logistics. Sometimes this formal meeting of the parents can take place when they come to visit you. After meeting at the bride-to-be's apartment, you might all have

A Modern Couple's Contract

CELEBRATING YOUR UPCOMING MARRIAGE DOESN'T "REQUIRE" A FORMAL WRITTEN AGREEMENT, BUT MANY COUPLES DO USE THIS TIME, WHEN THEY ARE CONSIDERING HOW THEIR LIVES WILL CHANGE AND BLEND, TO PUT DOWN ON PAPER THE DECISIONS THEY HAVE REACHED ABOUT THEIR LIFE TOGETHER. SOME SPELL OUT EXACTLY WHAT ASPECTS OF HOUSEHOLD MANAGEMENT WILL BE UNDERTAKEN BY EACH, HOW JOB DECISIONS ARE TO BE MADE IN A TWO-CAREER FAMILY, HOW THEIR MONEY WILL BE MANAGED, HOW MANY CHILDREN THEY PLAN TO HAVE AND HOW THEY WILL BE RAISED, WHAT STEPS THEY WILL TAKE IN CASE OF MARITAL DIFFICULTIES. LIKE THE LISTING OF THE BRIDE'S DOWRY IN THE OLD *TENAIM*, SOME COUPLES LIST THE SPECIAL OBJECTS OF VALUE (HIS STEREO HI-FI, HER ANTIQUE CHINA) THEY ARE BRINGING TO THEIR COMBINED HOUSEHOLD. YOU CAN GO FOR FORMAL CALLIGRAPHY OF YOUR PLEDGES, OR KEEP IT AS SIMPLE AS A LETTER YOU EACH WRITE TO THE OTHER.

dinner at a restaurant as guests of her parents. His parents could then return the hospitality at a brunch.

It is really not important to match invitation for invitation. What truly matters is to keep an open line of communications for the wedding plans, by phone and mail if need be, and to develop a cordial, meaningful relationship between two families.

TRADITIONAL COURTSHIP GIFTS

As your relationship becomes serious, you will want to give each other more important gifts on special occasions, such as birthdays or Hanukkah. A gold bracelet or neck chain or a fine gold watch, in ascending order, are the expected gifts in traditional circles. Cufflinks or a fine briefcase are popular choices for a man. In Orthodox communities, where people do not carry keys in their pockets on the Sabbath, a gold tie-clip made to hold a gold-plated key-blank is appropriate for a man.

When the engagement is announced, the parents or grandparents may follow a centuries-old custom of giving gifts as a way of welcoming a new son or daughter into the family. Usually ceremonial objects (especially family heirlooms) as given, such as a *Kiddush* cup, a lace Sabbath scarf, a *Seder* plate or a silver cover for a prayer book or Bible. If the engagement is a short one, these gifts may be given just before the wedding.

ANNOUNCING THE NEWS

TELLING THE WORLD

You can tell everyone you know or do business with, from your closest colleague to the paper boy, but if you have children from a previous marriage, you really must tell them of your upcoming marriage as soon as you become engaged. Take the stress out of the situation for the youngsters by addressing their anxieties and reassuring them. Be sure they meet your fiancé and spend time with him. And do give them a place in your wedding plans.

Could You Meet This Test?

IN DAYS GONE BY, PROSPECTIVE BRIDES AND GROOMS WERE PUT TO "PERFORMANCE" TESTS BY THEIR IN-LAWS-TO-BE TO CHECK THEIR EDUCATION AND TRAINING. YOU CAN BE THANKFUL THAT A YOUNG MAN TODAY WILL PROBABLY NOT BE MADE TO DEMONSTRATE HIS TALMUDIC SCHOLARSHIP BY HIS FUTURE FATHER-IN-LAW, NOR WILL A YOUNG WOMAN BE ASKED TO SHOW HER SKILL AT NEEDLEWORK BY THREADING A FINE NEEDLE WITH THE MOST GOSSAMER OF THREADS.

THE TALMUD ALSO TELLS YOUR PARENTS HOW TO JUDGE THE *MEHUTONIM*, THE FAMILY ABOUT TO JOIN YOURS. THEY SHOULD BE PEOPLE WITH WHOM "ONE CAN SIT DOWN AT THE TABLE," MEANING, ONE SUPPOSES, SOCIAL EQUALS.

Others who should be told early on of your wedding plans are an ex-spouse or the parents of a deceased spouse (your former in-laws). There are many delicate issues involved here. For a full discussion, see the section on second weddings in Chapter 6.

Now that you've met these obligations of courtesy—go ahead, shout it from the rooftops, if you want to—or go for the whole formal announcement.

FORMAL ANNOUNCEMENTS

Your decision to marry can be announced via the newspapers, at a big formal party, or at a Sabbath reception (a *Kiddush*) in the synagogue following services.

Some families send out formal announcement cards, though it is not generally considered proper etiquette, as it does seem to be asking for gifts. However, if the members of a large family live all over the world, sending out a card is much less of a chore than writing individual notes to all.

The card should be smaller than a wedding invitation and should be very simple.

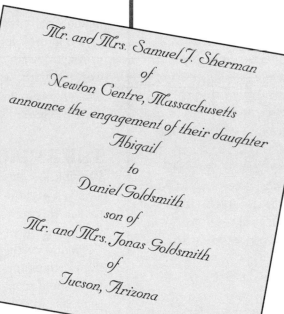

> Abigail Sherman
> Daniel Goldsmith
>
> Engaged   October 1996

or

> Mr. and Mrs. Samuel J. Sherman
> of
> Newton Centre, Massachusetts
> announce the engagement of their daughter
> Abigail
> to
> Daniel Goldsmith
> son of
> Mr. and Mrs. Jonas Goldsmith
> of
> Tucson, Arizona

NEWSPAPER RELEASES

Perhaps the simplest and most far-reaching announcement is one you publish in the local papers. Some newspapers will carry your personally written press release; others have forms they follow, making the

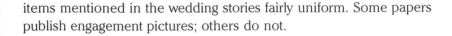
items mentioned in the wedding stories fairly uniform. Some papers publish engagement pictures; others do not.

MECHANICS OF A PRESS RELEASE

Call the newspaper office, ask for the society editor and find out what the engagement announcement policy is. Is there a form to follow? Do they print pictures? How many weeks' notice do they require? Usually it is three weeks. And is there a fee for publication? Some papers charge for social announcements. If the wedding date is more than a year away, most papers will not publish the announcement.

If the paper will accept your press release, study ones they have already published and model yours after them. Be sure you give a release date and a reference telephone number at the top of the page. Your article should not be more than a page long, unless you or your fiancé have a huge list of accomplishments and credits.

Send a copy of the announcement and the photo to your fiancé's parents if they live out of town, so that they can have it published in their local papers. You can also have your news published in Anglo-Jewish dailies or weeklies, Yiddish papers and any local weeklies that carry social news. Yiddish language papers will translate your announcement. So will papers in Israel, if you decide to send a release abroad.

THE ENGAGEMENT RING

We all know the classic TV or movie proposal scene, when the girl says yes and the boy pulls from his pocket the velvet box with the perfect ring in it. But what if she didn't really like his choice—and had to go on wearing it forever?

Many young men still do pick out a ring for their fiancée on their own, sometimes after taking her window-shopping to find out what she'd really like. Other couples shop together for this major purchase and sometimes even share the cost, especially when the ring is part of a matched set of wedding rings. Although the engagement ring, a token of love and hope for the future, should be as

Wedding Announcement Issues

THE REAL QUESTION HERE IS HOW PRIVATE YOU WANT TO BE ABOUT YOUR PLANS FOR THE FUTURE. DO YOU WANT TO BE THE STAR IN A SCENE FROM A HOLLYWOOD MOVIE, COMPLETE WITH FORMAL GOWNS, DRUM ROLLS FOR CHAMPAGNE TOASTS AND A CROWD OF ELEGANT GUESTS? OR WOULD YOU RATHER JUST SHARE YOUR HAPPINESS WITH THE PEOPLE WHO COUNT MOST TO YOU, IN A MUCH SIMPLER FAMILY PARTY? AND OF COURSE, THOUGH WE ALL HOPE TO BE PERFECTLY HAPPY, SOMETIMES ENGAGEMENTS ARE BROKEN OFF. WHEN THERE HAS BEEN NO BIG PUBLIC FANFARE, THE BREAKUP IS MUCH LESS EMBARRASSING.

NEWSPAPER FORM FOR AN ENGAGEMENT ANNOUNCEMENT

Prospective Groom's Last Name _____

Bride-Elect's Last Name _____

(Bride-Elect's Full Name) _____, daughter of

(Bride-Elect Mother's Full Name) _____
❏ Living ❏ Deceased ❏ Divorced

of (City, State) _____
(Leave blank if parents are together.)

and (Bride-Elect Father's Full Name) _____
❏ Living ❏ Deceased ❏ Divorced

of (City, State) _____

has become engaged to (Prospective Groom's Full Name) _____, son of

(Prospective Groom's Mother's Full Name) _____
❏ Living ❏ Deceased ❏ Divorced

of (City, State) _____
(Leave blank if parents are together.)

and (Prospective Groom's Father's Full Name) _____
❏ Living ❏ Deceased ❏ Divorced

of (City, State) _____

A _____ ❏ wedding is planned ❏ No wedding date has been set.
　　　　(date)

Signature _____
(If Bride-elect is younger than 18, this form must be singed by her parents.)

Home Number _____ Work Number_____

Suggested Engagement Copy: Names of schools, career titles, names of businesses, honeymoon destination, and any other copy requested.

fine as your means permit, there is no reason to go deep into debt and find the payments going on, like the diamond, "forever!"

Some people (especially jewelers) consider a diamond an investment, or, as stated in one buying guide, "an investment in beauty for a special person—an investment in individuality, for no two diamonds are alike."

GUIDELINES ON BUYING A DIAMOND

Choose a jeweler who is recommended as reputable by friends or family, preferably one who is a member of the American Gem Society, which sets high standards for its members. He or she should talk frankly and freely to you about the gem you want to buy and the price you want to pay. Bear in mind that the better stores are not necessarily the most expensive. Quality, integrity of the dealer and service are also components of value.

Ask to see the ring away from the spotlights under which the gems are usually displayed. How does it look in plain daylight?

Be sure the final sale is contingent upon your getting an independent appraisal of the value. Your purchase agreement should include clauses covering sizing, possible return within a specified period of time, and any tightening or cleaning required during the first six months.

This agreement should also describe the ring in full, including its value, for insurance purposes. Have your picture taken, wearing the ring prominently displayed, for the same purpose, and put it with your insurance papers.

A solitaire, or single-stone ring, is your best buy for any given sum because almost all the value is in the one diamond. If you choose side stones or baguettes, the total weight figure (T.W.) given will include these, and thus the principal diamond in such a design may be smaller and of lesser value.

THE DIAMOND: FOUR C'S

All diamonds are rare, and certain types are very rare. They are judged by the four C's—carat weight, color, clarity and cut—and these account for the difference in value among diamonds that seem to be almost identical.

Carat weight. The carat is a unit of weight—a word derived from the carob seeds used to balance scales in ancient times. There are 100 points in a carat, so a diamond of 27 points weighs a little more than a quarter-carat. The average rough diamond weighs less than a carat. Because larger stones are rare, they have a greater value per carat.

Color. Diamonds may be any color of the spectrum, but most are "white" with a tinge of color that gives them warmth. The "fire" in a diamond is created by the prism action of the stone, which breaks light into every color of the rainbow. A completely colorless diamond is very rare, therefore more valuable (and to some eyes, very cold).

Clarity. There are some natural imperfections in most stones—spots, bubbles or lines that formed when it was crystallized from carbon millions of years ago. The fewer imperfections, the more valuable the stone. A "flawless" diamond is one that, viewed under 10 power magnification, shows no imperfections to a trained eye.

Cut. This is what gives a stone the "twinkle" or fire—the first thing you notice in a diamond. It depends on the precise placement of the facets to handle the light passing through the stone for maximum beauty. Cut also means the shape of the finished diamond. Marquise, pear-shaped and oval stones tend to look larger than round (brilliant) or emerald cut diamonds of the same weight, but the round has more brilliance.

EMERALD	MARQUISE	PEAR	OVAL	ROUND

Inscriptions

IF YOU CHOOSE A SET OF RINGS, THE WEDDING BANDS CAN BE ENGRAVED ON THE INNER SURFACE. USUALLY THE INSCRIPTION READS "GROOM'S INITIALS / TO / BRIDE'S INITIALS / DATE" (FOR EXAMPLE, J. G. / TO /A. S. / 6/22/96); YOU MAY ADD OTHER APPROPRIATE WORDS, SUCH AS "WITH LOVE." FOR A MAN'S RING, THE ORDER OF THE INITIALS IS REVERSED. BE SURE THE RINGS FIT PROPERLY BEFORE YOU HAVE THEM ENGRAVED. THE BAND OF AN ENGAGEMENT RING IS USUALLY TOO NARROW FOR ENGRAVING.

TAKE CARE OF YOUR RING!

It's a sizable investment, so, even though you expect to wear your diamond engagement ring twenty-four hours a day, you should give it proper care.

- Don't wear it when you're doing rough work. Even though a diamond is durable, it can be chipped by a hard blow.
- Don't let your diamond come in contact with chlorine bleach when you're doing household chores. It can pit and discolor the setting.
- Do see your jeweler at least once a year to have your ring checked for loose prongs and the general wear of the setting. The jeweler will usually give the ring a professional "shine-up" too.
- Don't leave your ring on the rim of a sink when you remove it to wash your hands. It can easily slip down the drain.
- Keep your ring (and other diamond-set pieces) in a fabric-lined jewel case, or a box with compartments or dividers. If you prefer to use ordinary boxes, wrap each piece individually in tissue paper. Don't jumble your diamond pieces in a drawer or jewelry case, because diamonds can scratch other jewelry and can even scratch each other.

NOT NECESSARILY A DIAMOND

A diamond solitaire is not necessarily the only suitable engagement ring. A family heirloom ring or a birthstone (perhaps surrounded by tiny diamonds) may be used, or even a "dearest" ring—one set with tiny precious or semiprecious stones that spell "dear" or "dearest."

ENGAGEMENT PARTIES

ANNOUNCEMENT PARTIES

A formal wingding with a long guest list is usually given only if the engagement will be a long one or the wedding itself will be very small. Consider that, apart from the expense of a large party in a restaurant or private club, if the affair comes only a few months

משמח

before the "main event" it imposes on your guests the burden of giving two gifts at close intervals.

More often, the good news is spread at a family gathering, perhaps on a holiday, at which the grandparents, aunts and uncles and close friends will meet the couple. If you have synagogue or temple affiliations, a *Kiddush* following Sabbath morning services is a festive way to share the news and introduce the couple to the community and all the family members.

SHOWERS

Showers are very popular, but are often carried to an extreme, almost abuse, when the same guests are invited to many of them, since they will be expected to bring a gift to each shower. In fact, the name comes from the idea of "showers of gifts" that make up a kind of supplementary dowry for the bride.

Who May Give a Shower?

A shower should not be given by the bride or her immediate family, or the groom's, since it is obviously asking for a gift. It is supposed to be a spontaneous surprise arranged by friends or coworkers. In actual practice, the hostess of a shower often works out all the details with the bride's mother or sister, who may contribute to the cost. The shower is usually held about six weeks to a month before the wedding.

Whom to Invite

People invited should be close friends, relatives and colleagues of the bride and groom, all of whom are being invited to the wedding. Since people receiving a shower invitation feel obligated to give a gift, even if they cannot attend, it is really not considerate to invite people living at a great distance, to send invitations at the last moment, or to make up a list, especially in your office, that includes everyone in a department or on the floor without regard to whether they know the bride or the groom well.

~

**A Shower
Thank-you Note**

*Dear Aunt Julia,
I'm sorry you weren't able
to make the trip to the
engagement shower Cousin
Anne held for me. We
missed you. Thanks so much
for the tablecloth and
napkins you sent. They are
lovely and just the right
color. I do appreciate your
thoughtfulness. Daniel and
I hope you will be able to
come to our wedding in June.*

*Affectionately,
Abigail*

~

A Lo-o-ong Engagement

IN THE BIBLE WE FIND THAT ALTHOUGH ISAAC'S BRIDE, REBEKAH, WAS CHOSEN FOR HIM BY HIS PARENTS, THEIR SON JACOB CHOSE HIS OWN BRIDE. HE FELL IN LOVE WITH RACHEL, THE DAUGHTER OF HIS UNCLE LABAN, AND PROMISED TO WORK AS A SHEPHERD FOR SEVEN YEARS FOR HER HAND. ON THE WEDDING NIGHT, HIS UNCLE GAVE HIM LEAH, HIS OLDEST DAUGHTER, INSTEAD. JACOB STILL WANTED RACHEL FOR HIS WIFE (MEN WERE ALLOWED FOUR WIVES IN THOSE DAYS!) AND SO HE WORKED FOR SEVEN YEARS MORE TO GAIN THE WOMAN HE LOVED. JACOB HAD A LONG WAIT, BUT THINK HOW RACHEL MUST HAVE FELT—TO SEE HER SISTER MARRIED WHILE SHE SAT AT HOME, A FRUSTRATED SINGLE!

At showers given by coworkers, the guest list is sometimes restricted to people who will *not* be invited to the wedding, so that they, too, can take part in the rejoicing.

The bride's mother and the bridal attendants also go to every shower given for her.

It makes good sense for people planning showers to consult each other to avoid a conflict in dates or perhaps even to join forces in giving a party.

Invitations

Since a shower is an informal affair, invitations can be as simple as a round of phone calls if the guest list is not too long. Short, handwritten notes may also be used, or you can choose from a wide assortment of "store-bought" invitations. As a plus, this choice also allows you a colorful selection of coordinated paper goods to carry out whatever decorative scheme you decide on.

Themes

Most showers are arranged around a gift theme. The hostess should have a list of items the bride needs or wants, with colors or sizes. If the shower is to be a surprise for the bride, sit down with her mother to make up the list. If there is to be more than one shower, the hostesses should coordinate with each other, so that a different theme is set for each one. This avoids duplication of gifts.

Some popular themes are kitchen, trousseau or linen showers, with invitations and decorations chosen to match the theme. If the bride is planning to keep a kosher kitchen, she will need two of almost everything. Usually, two different colors are used to differentiate the meat things from the dairy. The hostess should check out the colors the bride has chosen so she can be specific in her gift suggestions.

The occasion can be a brunch, a luncheon or a tea/coffee/cocktail hour.

Bride and Groom Showers

The groom and other men of the wedding party are usually completely uninvolved in the typical shower, except possibly when the groom arrives to pick up his fiancée and escort her home after the event.

Becoming more and more popular, however, is the egalitarian event known as a "Mr. and Mrs." or "Jack and Jill" shower, to which the men are invited. Often the theme is a household, hardware, or lawn and garden one. Tools, gadgets and equipment that both will use are the customary gifts. Hardware chains like Home Depot have even started a gift registry for such items. A power drill or a hedge clipper may delight the couple more than a sterling silver spoon!

A backyard barbecue is especially appropriate for a coed party. And for a change, let the men cook the meal!

The "Money Tree"

In some communities a "greenback shower" or "money tree" party may be given. Guests attach envelopes containing cash or checks to a small tree (a silk tree, a real one or a wall poster drawing), which is then presented to the bride and groom. Such an affair makes sense on the theory that the couple can then use the lump sum to buy one large item they really need for their new home, or that they will be moving to another city to live and would be burdened by transporting many small gifts. However, many people still regard such showers as being in poor taste.

The "Catalog Shower"

One way your hostess can be sure your friends will shower you with gifts you really would like is to have a "catalog shower." In the invitation, guests are asked to bring their favorite catalogs so that the bride and groom can order from them. Men friends, as well as women, are invited.

A Fortune-Telling Cake

YOU CAN HAVE FUN WITH YOUR SHOWER CAKE AND EAT IT, TOO, IF SOMEONE BAKES A BRIDE'S FORTUNE CAKE. THE BAKER PICKS UP A BATCH OF NOVELTY STORE FAVORS (VERY SMALL ONES) AND PUTS THEM INTO THE PREPARED BATTER AT STRATEGIC INTERVALS. THE ONE YOUR GUEST FINDS IN HER SLICE OF CAKE PREDICTS HER FORTUNE. SOME OF THE CHOICES ARE: A COIN (RICHES); A RING (THE NEXT PERSON TO BE MARRIED); A THIMBLE (OLD MAID—YOU MAY WANT TO SKIP THIS ONE!); A FOUR-LEAF CLOVER (GOOD LUCK); A TINY BOAT, CAR OR PLANE (TRAVEL); A HEART (ROMANCE); A DAGGER (INTRIGUE) AND SO ON AS YOUR FANCY AND THE CHOICE OF LITTLE NOVELTIES PERMITS. EXCEPT FOR THE RING, YOU CAN HAVE MORE THAN ONE OF EACH. AND DO WARN YOUR GUESTS THAT THERE ARE FAVORS IN THE CAKE—YOU WANT TO AVOID DENTAL MISHAPS!

Using catalogs saves everyone, including the happy couple, any number of shopping trips and can even eliminate using a bridal registry, if that's distasteful to you. You can agree on a price limit—for instance, fifty dollars per gift. Of course, this need not stop a group of your friends or relatives from joining together to give you something more costly. You can add to the pool of catalogs any that you particularly favor, providing for guests who do not bring one and ensuring that certain types of gifts, such as tools, camping supplies, or garden equipment, will not be overlooked.

At an informal lunch, a picnic or a barbecue, the host and hostess set out the catalogs and everyone enjoys browsing through them. The bride and groom are given markers which they use to circle items they would like to receive as gifts. After everyone has had a pleasant time eating and "window-shopping," the hostess collects the catalogs and makes up a master list for the guests to use as a shopping guide. Think of the time, energy and shoe leather saved by using the phone and the almighty credit card to complete an order and have the gifts delivered. And the bride does not have to wear a hat made of the ribbon bows from all the gifts she's unwrapped!

Just so the bride and groom will go home with some gifts under their arms, the centerpiece can be a set of decorated baskets—one containing small kitchen appliances, another garden tools, and a third bath accessories—with cards naming them as the first installment of the gift shower.

Keeping Track of Gifts

The principal fun at a shower is, naturally, opening the gifts. When the affair is supposed to be a surprise, the gifts may be hidden about the room. After all have arrived, the bride settles down to the serious business of the day. Someone who is well organized should be appointed to the task of recording each gift and the name of the giver, and keeping the gift cards in order as the pile of discarded wrappings rises on the floor.

The ribbon bows are sometimes used to fashion a fancy bonnet for the bride to wear for the duration of the party, or until her hairdo falls down and her head aches, whichever comes first!

Jewish brides do not use the traditional "bouquet" made of the ribbons as there is no wedding rehearsal prior to the ceremony.

The Office Gift

In many offices a collection is taken up from all the bride's (or groom's) coworkers toward a gift certificate or a large single gift, which is presented at an informal lunch gathering or at coffee or cocktails after work. Of course, you thank all those present for their generosity, but it is also an extra-nice gesture to post a note on the bulletin board thanking one and all. That makes it certain that you have expressed your thanks to any well-wishers who could not make it to the formal presentation.

Thank You So Much!

Be a super-thoughtful guest of honor and write your hostess a note thanking her for all the trouble she has taken to arrange this delightful party for you.

Although you have, of course, personally thanked each guest for hcr (or his) shower gift, a wise bride will lose no time in writing thank-you notes after the party to acknowledge the gifts, especially those that may have been sent by out-of-town folks who could not attend. They've gone to so much trouble for you—don't leave them wondering whether the store or the post office delivered their gifts.

ATTENDANTS' PARTIES

Drunken reveling is quickly becoming a thing of the past, and with it raucous bachelor parties and slightly less wild spinster or "bachelorette" affairs. You will want to give a party to honor your attendants—be smart and schedule it for the next-to-last week before the wedding. That will give everyone a chance to unwind a bit before the big day—and possibly prevent your having a group of badly hung-over people in your procession. Talk it over with your fiancé. You might want to make it a coed affair and have one party for both ushers and bridesmaids. This is the time to give

"Sage" Advice (continued)

THOUGH SOME OF THIS ADVICE SEEMS QUAINT TODAY, THERE IS SOME GOOD SENSE IN IT AS WELL. AND THESE BEARDED MALE CHAUVINISTS STILL RESPONDED TO A WOMAN'S BEAUTY, FOR AT THE END OF THE LIST THEY ADDED THIS THOUGHT: "A WOMAN WHO HAS BEAUTIFUL EYES NEEDS NO FURTHER RECOMMENDATION."

WHAT WOULD TODAY'S JEWISH WOMEN PUT ON THEIR LIST FOR AN IDEAL MATCH?

"Red-Handed"— A Women's Party

THOUGH BRIDAL SHOWERS ARE ABOUT THE ONLY WOMEN'S PRE-WEDDING FESTIVITIES LEFT OF EUROPEAN WAYS, A DIFFERENT CUSTOM STILL PREVAILS IN SEPHARDIC COMMUNITIES. THE FEMALE RELATIVES AND FRIENDS OF THE BRIDE (AND IN SOME COMMUNITIES, THE GROOM'S MOTHER AND FEMALE RELATIVES) GATHER SOME TIME DURING THE WEEK BEFORE THE WEDDING FOR A CONGRATULATORY FEAST. THERE IS SINGING AND PRAISE OF THE BRIDE, AND THEN HER HANDS AND FEET ARE PAINTED WITH HENNA (A REDDISH DYE) AS A PROTECTION AGAINST THE EVIL EYE. THE BRIDE-TO-BE MAY BE RITUALLY FED BY HER MOTHER SEVEN TIMES, AS A SIGN OF STRENGTH AND A WISH FOR ABUNDANCE. IN SOME COMMUNITIES, THE WOMEN ALSO GATHER TO ESCORT THE BRIDE TO THE MIKVEH AND, JUST BEFORE THE WEDDING, TO DRESS HER.

MANY BEAUTIFUL WEDDING SONGS IN LADINO, THE SEPHARDIC HOME LANGUAGE, CAN BE FOUND IN RECORDINGS. IF THERE IS SOME SEPHARDIC ANCESTRY IN YOUR HERITAGE OR YOUR FIANCÉ'S, YOU MAY WANT TO INCLUDE SOME OF THESE IN YOUR WEDDING MUSIC.

your attendants keepsake gifts as a token of thanks. See Chapter 3 for gift suggestions.

HOW TO SURVIVE THE FESTIVE ROUND

Party till you drop? Not if you want to walk down the aisle with a bright-eyed look and a genuine smile on your face! Everyone wants to honor an engaged couple and all the family wants to meet the new member about to join them. Much of this is agreeable fun; some of it is a polite duty. Since you will have the groom's Torah honor (*oyfruf*—see Chapter 4) and possibly a prenuptial dinner on the calendar in the last week before the wedding, it's a good idea to avoid any other big parties that week. Both mothers should tactfully spread the word so that you will not offend any relatives by declining a well-meant invitation. It also helps to have your mother or a close friend try to persuade would-be hostesses to pool their entertaining so that the number of parties you have to attend is cut down.

MODEST BEHAVIOR—THE JEWISH CONCEPT

Everyone has been embarrassed at least once by the behavior of an engaged couple who can't keep their hands off each other and are constantly "kissy-kissy" in public. By the mere fact of becoming engaged a couple have announced a romantic and exclusive interest in each other. Of course, you want to be together and be loving toward each other, but an open display of physical affection is in very poor taste.

In strict Orthodox circles men and women avoid all public physical contact with each other; indeed, they lead largely segregated social lives. Our notions of modesty and proper behavior between the sexes stem from this tradition. Public kissing, embracing and the like are offensive to these basic ideas. You're wearing his ring—that tells the world your intentions.

CHAPTER 3

INITIAL PLANS FOR THE WEDDING

As soon as people learn that you're engaged they ask when the wedding will be. So settle on a date as soon as you can, not merely to answer that question, but to be able to start planning in a concrete way.

STARTING TO PLAN

You must have a date in mind in order to reserve the synagogue or temple, rabbi and caterer of your choice. The most popular places and dates are often booked a year in advance. You need time to order a dress, order and send out invitations and arrange for your wedding attendants, not to mention shopping for your musicians and florist. There are so many factors involved that it's best to start planning early and keep flexible.

SETTING THE DATE

Before you set a date, you must take into account certain times when Jewish marriages may not be performed.

Religious Restrictions

Weddings are *not* permitted (in all denominations) on:

> The Sabbath (Friday evening to Saturday one half-hour after sundown)
> The Major Holidays—Rosh Hashanah, Yom Kippur, Passover, Shavuot and Sukkot—sundown to sundown

Orthodox and Conservative congregations also do *not* permit weddings during:

> The "Three Weeks" (the period on the Jewish calendar between the 17th of Tammuz and the 9th of Av—usually these fall in July and August)
> The *Sefirah* period (the seven weeks between Passover and Shavuot, except for the holiday of *Lag b'Omer*—usually in April and May)

These times are considered periods of national mourning because of historical tragedies—the destruction of the Temple, and a plague that ravaged the greatest scholars of the time.

Sephardic and Reform practice is as follows:

Sephardim allow marriages during *Sefirah* from *Lag b'Omer* on. Reform congregations allow marriages during both of these periods, except for the 9th of Av (the actual date of the destruction of the Temple).

Now you can see why June is such a popular month for Jewish weddings! If you have your heart set on a spring wedding, it's a very tight fit unless you follow Reform practice.

Mourning Periods

If you or your fiancé are in mourning, you cannot, in traditional practice, plan a wedding date during the thirty days of mourning observed for a brother or sister or the eleven months observed for a parent. Reform congregations keep the thirty-day rule for all mourning periods.

Once the date has been set, however, a wedding may not be postponed even if there is a death in the family, since not even mourning is allowed to interfere with a wedding, the highest of *mitzvot*. The wedding is held as scheduled, but usually the dance music is eliminated and the whole scale of the reception reduced.

Personal Considerations

Now you can begin to think about what season of the year you would prefer—do you want to be a June bride in a bower of roses, an autumn bride surrounded by chrysanthemums and harvest symbols, or a snowflake bride like something out of the "Nutcracker" ballet? Is there a date that's special to you—your birthday, your parents' anniversary? Do you have to wait for graduation day, vacation days or military leaves? Are there other weddings or graduations in

~ The Luach—A Lunar Calendar

THE HEBREW CALENDAR IS BASED ON LUNAR CYCLES OF THIRTEEN MONTHS; WHAT WE CALL THE "ENGLISH" (OR GREGORIAN) CALENDAR IS BASED ON A SOLAR CYCLE OF TWELVE MONTHS. AS A RESULT, THE DATES WHEN HOLIDAYS FALL, THOUGH THEY ARE ALWAYS THE SAME IN THE HEBREW CALENDAR, ARE WHAT WE COULD CALL "MOVEABLE FEASTS" IN THE ENGLISH CALENDAR.

HOW CAN YOU CHECK THE ENGLISH DATES OF THESE DAYS? GET YOURSELF A HEBREW CALENDAR (CALLED A LUACH). IT SETS FORTH ALL THE MAJOR AND MINOR JEWISH HOLIDAYS AND GIVES SABBATH CANDLE-LIGHTING TIMES AND MUCH OTHER USEFUL INFORMATION. YOU CAN GET ONE IN THE FORM OF AN APPOINTMENT DIARY OR A WALL CALENDAR FROM ANY OF THE MAJOR JEWISH ORGANIZATIONS OR YOUR SYNAGOGUE. THE YEAR STARTS AT ROSH HASHANAH (USUALLY SEPTEMBER) IN THESE CALENDARS. YOU WILL FIND A LUACH HELPFUL ALSO IN SELECTING OTHER PARTY DATES THAT WILL NOT POSE PROBLEMS FOR OBSERVANT GUESTS.

the family that will conflict with yours? Balance all the pertinent factors with the Jewish calendar requirements to come up with a date that suits you and your fiancé.

Should you pick a holiday weekend? Many couples like having the extra day off and some guests enjoy having more time to travel to and from the festivities. But others are upset because they have other holiday plans, so that they have to choose between a vacation and attending your wedding.

Bearing in mind that you can never please everybody, settle on an agreeable date and a fallback date, and go forth to find the perfect place. If it's a June Sunday you have in mind, start early! And be forewarned—Saturday nights are sometimes available during peak periods because you cannot start the ceremony until after dark, and on Daylight Saving Time that may mean as late as nine or nine-thirty in June or July, with dinner coming after ten P.M. and the party running on till after midnight. This results in overtime fees for wait staff and musicians. Saturdays on Standard Time in late fall, winter and early spring, on the other hand, are ideal, because you can start as early as five or six o'clock on these shorter days of the year.

Peak Season vs. Off-Season

The most popular months for Jewish weddings are April (before Passover), June, October and December.

A Saturday evening wedding is the most formal, but Sunday afternoon, starting at four or four-thirty, is the most fashionable hour, formal but less pretentious. Sunday noon is also very popular. Weddings are sometimes held on weekday evenings, beginning at about six and ending at a reasonable hour; among the Orthodox, Tuesday evening is a preferred time because on that day of Creation God twice said, "It is good." At one time, Jewish communities mandated Wednesdays (*Yom reve'ee*—the fourth day) for the wedding of a first-time bride.

Like any other commodities, wedding dates fluctuate in price. Because Saturday nights are so much in demand, caterers charge more for this date and favor larger, more elaborate affairs over modest functions. Florists, photographers and musicians do the same.

Sundays follow the same higher price structure during the period when the days are very long and Saturday nights are impractical. You may find it hard to secure the date and services you favor if you opt for the most popular times and the most in-demand venues and service providers.

What to do if your choice is simplicity and a small wedding? Go against the tide—by choosing a smaller room for your ceremony (sometimes the huge, fashionable places have small chapels that are available), a smaller caterer or restaurant for your reception, or an unconventional setting (see Chapter 6). Or decide on the exact date after you've checked the availability of the places you like.

One plus for "off-season" dates is that there probably won't be other functions going on at the same time at your chosen place. Being one of four or five Sunday afternoon brides at the same hotel or club can take away from the special feeling you are seeking.

How Much "Lead Time" Do You Need?

For the most fashionable places and the most popular times you may have to book reservations six months to a year in advance.

The minimum time, if you intend to observe any formality at all, is three months. Caterers, florists, musicians and photographers all require advance notice. Aside from the shopping time involved, delivery of custom-fitted dresses, engraved wedding rings, engraved invitations, personalized favors and the like takes at least four weeks.

Yes, you *can* arrange a small, informal wedding in a short time, but trying to do it in less than a month is not only no fun—it's a guaranteed pressure-cooker that leads to frazzled nerves, neglected details and family friction. Try to allow yourself enough time to set a sensible pace.

משמח

How Your Computer Can Help

YOU USE YOUR COMPUTER ALL THE TIME AT WORK. DON'T OVERLOOK HOW IT CAN HELP YOU IN PLANNING YOUR WEDDING. CONSIDER THESE POSSIBILITIES:

- THE DESKTOP CALENDAR. KEEP TRACK OF APPOINTMENTS, DEADLINES AND "PAY BY" DATES.
- THE SPREADSHEET. SET UP A COST CONTROL SYSTEM FOR YOUR WEDDING EXPENSES.
- THE DATABASE. KEEP ALL YOUR ADDRESSES—BOTH THOSE OF GUESTS AND THE PROVIDERS—UP TO DATE. ALSO RECORD YOUR GIFTS RECEIVED AND NOTES SENT.
- THE WORD PROCESSOR. MAKE UP YOUR TEXTS FOR ANNOUNCEMENTS, INVITATIONS, PRESS RELEASES AND BUSINESS LETTERS. *NOTE: NEVER SEND WORD-PROCESSED THANK-YOU NOTES!*
- DESKTOP PUBLISHING. PREPARE TRAVEL MAPS FOR YOUR GUESTS, WEDDING PROGRAMS AND BOOKLETS FOR GRACE AFTER THE MEAL.
- LASER PRINTING AND FANCY FONTS. ADD CALLIGRAPHY AND GRAPHICS TO YOUR BOOKLETS AND TO ADDRESS ENVELOPES.

"SHOPPING" FOR A WEDDING VENUE

When you are visiting a synagogue or a catering hall to consider the place for your wedding, take nothing for granted. Ask exactly what the ceremony ritual will be if you are unfamiliar with the procedures of the synagogue, temple, or club. Especially when the caterer provides the officiant, assure yourself that the ritual meets with your approval and is traditionally correct. You may properly ask to observe a wedding there before you finalize your agreement.

When you meet with the rabbi or the ritual director, you will want to discuss with him any original ideas you have for your ceremony, such as inserting readings, the bride's response to the marriage vow, the egalitarian *ketubah* and also any traditional elements you want to add, if the usual synagogue procedure does not include them. Two potential problems should be brought up early on: the question of a previous divorce, and that of a difference in religion. The answers to these questions will influence your choice of locale.

WHEN THERE IS A DIFFERENCE OF RELIGION

If one of you is not Jewish, your plan to marry may create a family storm. Jewish parents often regard intermarriage as a personal defeat and a threat to the survival of the Jewish people. You may hear the anguished cry that you are finishing Hitler's work for him. This is a problem you have to resolve by convincing your parents that your intended spouse is a truly wonderful person and by having them meet him or her and the other family so that the strangeness wears off.

Under Jewish religious law, all children born of a Jewish mother are regarded as Jewish. Sometimes you can calm the atmosphere by pointing this out to your parents and sincerely promising to keep a Jewish home and raise the children as Jews.

This is not the end of your problem, however. You may be disagreeably surprised to find that no Orthodox or Conservative rabbi and only a very few Reform rabbis will officiate at an interfaith wedding. Families can be very offended by this when they do not understand the reason. In the Jewish marriage vow, the groom agrees to marry the

bride "according to the laws of Moses and of Israel." This pledge obviously cannot be binding on a non-Jew and so the rabbis have ruled that such a marriage is not valid, no matter how sincere and trustworthy you know your fiancé to be.

What choices do you have, in such a situation?

You may be able to find a Reform rabbi who will perform your marriage ceremony on the pledge of both to keep a Jewish home and raise the children as Jews. To find such a rabbi, call the local office of the Union of American Hebrew Congregations. You may be able to find those whom some rabbis dub "mercenaries"—rabbis who will officiate, for a considerable fee, without concerning themselves much about a couple's beliefs, and some who will officiate together with a Christian clergyman in an interfaith or ecumenical ceremony. While these "dual" ceremonies sometimes appease the parents and satisfy a couple's desire to feel that their union has the blessing of both faiths, it is a compromise that is often uncomfortable to members of both religions.

The non-Jewish bride or groom may want to consider conversion. While conversion for the sake of marriage is discouraged by Jewish law, a sincere person can accomplish it. Be aware that it takes time—anywhere from six months to several years, depending on the rabbi's requirements. It is largely a matter of study, directed by a rabbi, immersion in the *mikveh*, and for a man, circumcision or ritual circumcision (the drawing of a drop of blood from one already circumcised). If conversion is in your plans, allow for the time it takes.

Perhaps the simplest decision, even if conversion is a possibility, is to have a civil, or secular wedding on "neutral" ground—the hotel, club or home where the reception will be held. You can have an Ethical Culture minister, a judge, or a justice of the peace officiate and add to the service whatever Jewish symbols and content you wish, as well as ideas desired by your non-Jewish partner, who may still feel committed to his or her faith. If you both feel you want a nonsectarian wedding, you can write your own ceremony, expressing the beliefs you both value and share.

You can have any reception you desire after such ceremonies.

WHAT STYLE FOR YOU?

You have many choices of style for your wedding—ranging from the picture-book, glamorous wedding you may have always dreamed of to the intensely practical one dictated by the time and money at your disposal. Your parents may have goals that differ from yours. And then there are your fiancé's (and his family's) wishes to consider.

Discuss with your fiancé the wedding style you two would really prefer. Be prepared to disagree, then make a loving compromise.

DON'T BREAK THE BANK—BUDGET!

A thoughtful bride will carefully consider her family's finances, or her own, before anything else in her plans. This is where the budget begins. How many people will your family invite? How many will his family want to invite? How much can you really afford to spend? Your parents may want to make a big splash or you both may feel that inviting all your colleagues and business acquaintances will give your careers a push, but stop and consider the figures after you have gotten a few estimates.

There is a fine line here: no bride or groom should demand, nor should any family consider, going deeply into debt to arrange a wedding that is far beyond their means. Also, no family should have the most extravagant wedding they can design just because they can afford it.

You can devise a budget that suits your means by not opting for all the unnecessary frills that will be offered you and by sensibly limiting your guest list. *Beware of the "might-as-wells"!* That's the provider's sales pitch that goes: "You are spending X thousands on the ceremony and dinner, so you might as well have . . ." all the showy extras he or she can think of to up the total cost. These may even include a waterfall with floating orchids in the lobby and white doves released when the bride enters!

You can prune some of your guest costs by inviting some guests to a buffet reception only, before a smaller dinner for family and close friends. Some collation must be offered to all who attend.

DON'T START A FEUD—COMPROMISE!

No social function can breed more discord than a wedding, paradoxical as this may seem. There are the ideas and standards of two families to consider, the feelings of relatives and close friends who may be offended if not invited or given an honor, and sometimes old family enmities still smoldering.

Tact and concern for each other's feelings and self-esteem are the clues to peaceful planning. It's true that you, the bride, should have the last word about your wedding plans, but you have to bear in mind that your parents—and your fiancé's—have been looking forward to this day of rejoicing with all their relatives and friends.

Above all, try not to deliver ultimatums to his family—about dress, number of guests, place, time and style of the wedding. Keep his family informed of your plans, ask for their input and try to work together to create a happy day.

STYLE CHECKLIST

You have many choices of style available, regardless of what you plan to spend on the wedding. The range is:

> **Traditional service.** Follows all the Jewish traditions; this wedding can be as elaborate or simple as you wish.
> **Contemporary service.** Combines traditional elements with "standard modern" ones, including original readings and songs. Again, this can range from elaborate to simple.
> **Formal.** the whole nine yards!—Involves full decorations, many attendants, evening dress (white or black tie), formal dinner service, elegant venue, many guests.
> **Informal.** Service is held in the home, a garden, or a small chapel; divided ceremony and reception, dressy but not evening attire, smaller guest list.

When There Has Been a Divorce

IF EITHER OF YOU (AND IN SOME ORTHODOX GROUPS, YOUR PARENTS) WERE DIVORCED, ORTHODOX AND CONSERVATIVE RABBIS REQUIRE PROOF THAT A RELIGIOUS DIVORCE DECREE (A GET) WAS GRANTED. REFORM RABBIS ACCEPT A CIVIL DIVORCE DECREE.

WILL THIS CREATE PROBLEMS FOR YOU? THEY CAN BE RESOLVED, BUT IT TAKES TIME. IF YOU ARE IN THIS SITUATION, SEE THE OFFICIATING RABBI AS SOON AS YOU SET THE DATE; DO NOT WAIT UNTIL A WEEK OR TWO BEFORE THE WEDDING.

WHERE TO HOLD THE WEDDING

You don't have to hold your wedding in a synagogue or temple, but the sanctuary is the most dignified and impressive place, if the size of your wedding party permits. In some ways, this is the least stressful choice, because most large synagogues have an official caterer who can supervise all the reception details for you and a ritual director who will watch over the correctness of the religious procedure.

Even if there is no caterer, or your party is too small for the reception space available, it might be possible to have the ceremony in the sanctuary or the small chapel and hold the reception elsewhere.

THE RANGE OF POSSIBILITIES

In order of decreasing formality and cost, wedding locales rank approximately as listed below.

1. fashionable synagogue, temple, club or hotel on Saturday night, Sunday or the eve of a legal holiday
2. same venue—weeknights
3. catering halls (Saturday nights and Sundays are more expensive than weeknights)
4. restaurants or clubs
5. home—yours or a friend's, with reception fully catered
6. a private ceremony in the rabbi's study (or judge's chambers, or City Hall) and a champagne or cocktail reception at home or in a restaurant
7. home or an unusual locale (see Chapter 6), with you or your friends acting as caterer.

A deciding factor, when you consider these possibilities, is the size of your party. If the number of guests is small (under forty), most institutional caterers will not be willing to consider it at all, because their basic cost is so high. They also reserve the most sought-after dates for the largest weddings. A small wedding reception is best accommodated at a private room in a hotel or club, in a restaurant or at home.

Save yourself time and energy wasted in looking at unsuitable places by doing a preliminary head count. About one-fourth of the people invited will probably not attend—more, if many are from out of town. When you have an estimate of the number of guests you expect, you will know better what size of reception hall you need.

USING A PROFESSIONAL PLANNER

To some harried people juggling high-pressure careers and a busy social life, hiring a professional to take over all the details of the wedding is the ultimate luxury. A good wedding consultant has expertise gained from arranging many social events, has good contacts among suppliers and knows which are the best and which the ones to avoid. But such help from an independent consultant can carry a hefty price tag, as much as 15 to 20 percent of the total cost of the wedding. Some consultants will work on an hourly basis, but the hours have a way of adding up. Theoretically, at least, they are supposed to pass along to you any discounts they work out on the services you choose. Their help should save you enough time and money to make up for their fee.

You can also get much free practical advice and assistance from "in-house" consultants provided by bridal shops, fine stores and catering establishments. You are already a client, so they stand ready to help you find your way among the bewildering choices they offer.

You will get the greatest benefit from these professionals if you are frank about your budget from the very beginning, so they know what your "ballpark" cost structure is. Be careful to make your dreams and wishes, and your final choices, perfectly clear, so that there are no misunderstandings. If you feel that consultants are overwhelming you, or not allowing you to express your own desires, don't retain their services. You should ask for references and check with the last few couples who used the consultant. And as with any other business arrangement, put everything agreed upon, including fees and commissions, in writing.

To find consultants and providers, you can try the Internet. Searching Web sites with the keyword "wedding" will bring you a host of pages. Even if you're not directly connected to the Internet,

online services will yield many names and phone numbers when searched with the same keyword.

ELEGANT SIMPLICITY

If you were given the choice between spending a small fortune on an opulent wedding or using a generous monetary gift for furnishing your first home, which would you and your fiancé choose? The "do-it-yourself" wedding held at home, in the hospitality suite of a hotel, or in a club room that does not have a resident caterer, is becoming more and more popular, especially in the face of soaring caterers' and florists' charges.

You can cut costs in such a setting, without sacrificing true elegance, by limiting the guest list to people who really know and care about the bride and groom, hiring a party cook or using a combination of purchased prepared foods and homemade delicacies. The goodies are served from a beautifully set buffet table, dispensing with the need for wait staff (and their tips). Guests seat themselves at tables set up around the room, as space permits.

Flowers and greenery can be gifts from your friends' gardens if it's the right time of the year. Or you can go for one perfect florist's centerpiece for the buffet table and dispense with flower arrangements at the tables. Your music can be provided by records and a good sound system, also rentable. Friends can be asked to bring their instruments and play.

Everyone who helps out will be participating in the *mitzvah* of increasing the rejoicing of the bride and groom. With some effort on everyone's part you will have a warm and original wedding that will not break the bank.

A WEDDING AT HOME

"The bride was married from her parents' home" is a sentence that conjures up a classic picture of a highly personal, informal, yet memorable occasion. *But*—it can also be a very stressful effort unless family and friends really give substantial help or a reliable caterer takes over.

Using outside help and rented equipment can make your "simple" wedding at home almost as expensive as one catered at a hotel or synagogue, especially as the number of guests rises and luxurious details are added.

The atmosphere you want to create and the balance of cost against convenience and sentiment will be factors in your decision. If you have always wanted to be married on a June day in your family's garden, or in front of the fireplace in the living room, or you have a friend who will lend you her mansion, give careful consideration to all the matters in the checklist on page 36 before you make up your mind.

Add at least half again to your total approximated cost to allow for unforeseen contingencies (for example, sales taxes, price increases). Then compare the bottom line to the cost of at least one outside caterer before you reach a decision.

SUPPOSE YOU'VE ELOPED!

Have you and your fiancé, overcome by all the intricacies of planning, run off impulsively to be married in a civil ceremony and cut short all the rigmarole? If you are both Jewish, you may find that your parents will nevertheless insist on a traditional *huppah*.

They are not being unreasonably conventional or stuffy. According to Jewish law, a marriage between two Jewish partners is not valid, in the religious sense, until it has been sanctified by the religious vows and blessings. This conviction can be very strong even among people who are not especially observant in their daily practice.

Be gracious and loving toward your parents. Grant them this gratification of their good wishes for you (and your future children) by going through the religious ceremony with a good heart and by giving them the opportunity to rejoice at a reception. Even though you have already gone through the civil ceremony, the religious ceremony may appropriately be performed afterward. In fact, in some foreign countries it is customary to separate the civil and religious ceremonies in just this way.

CHECKLIST FOR A HOME WEDDING

1. What ambiance are you seeking? _____
2. Will your house and garden need extensive refurbishing? _____
    Approximate cost $_____
3. If the party will be held outdoors, is there adequate indoor space in case of
    rain? _____
4. Is there room (and budget) for music and dancing? _____
    Approximate cost $_____
5. Is there sufficient space for
    ❑ buffet tables
    ❑ food preparation and serving
    ❑ seating guests
    ❑ coats
    ❑ bathroom needs
    ❑ privacy for the bride before the ceremony
    ❑ parking for guest cars
6. Who will supply the food and drink? _____
    Approximate cost $_____
7. How much help will you need to serve and clean up? _____
    Approximate cost $_____
8. Will you have to rent chairs, tables, tableware? _____
    Approximate cost $_____
9. Who will be assigned to the house on the wedding day, while you are at the
    ceremony or out in the garden, to answer the phone, the doorbell, receive and
    store gifts, tidy up the bathrooms and oversee the coat storage? Will you have to
    pay this person? _____
    Approximate cost $_____
10. Can you hire a professional "host" or "hostess" to move the events of the wed-
    ding along as planned and see to the comfort of the guests? _____
    Approximate cost $_____
11. Will you need special police or parking attendants to control traffic at the
    house?_____
    Approximate cost $_____

שמח

If getting married is good, reaffirming that vow under the *huppah* must be even better!

A FEW FORMALITIES . . .

Hurrah! You've found the place, it's available on the date you want and it's within your budget. You've studied wedding traditions and you've decided on the exact way you want your ceremony to be held. So now you come to the next possible roadblock on the way to the wedding of your dreams. You have a conference with the rabbi, then with the caterer. They have their own ideas.

CONFERRING WITH THE RABBI AND THE RITUAL DIRECTOR

The rabbi who officiates will want to meet with you and your fiancé to determine that the wedding may properly take place under Jewish law and to obtain the information he needs to prepare your *ketubah*. You will both need to know your Hebrew names and those of your parents.

The rabbi or officiant will also, if he does not know you, seek some information so that he can make appropriate personal remarks in his sermon.

At your very first conference with the sexton (*shammash*) or ritual director, be sure to ask about these observances (if you want them):

Can we have   a *b'deken*?
               a candlelit procession?
               circuits of the groom?
               a double-ring ceremony?
               an egalitarian *ketubah*?
               special readings?
               special music?
               floral decorations?
               a *huppah* we have made?

The Vocabulary of Rejoicing

THESE WORDS ARE SO COMMONLY USED IN JEWISH CIRCLES THAT THEY ARE PRACTICALLY ENGLISH:

SIMHA—ANY OCCASION FOR REJOICING—ESPECIALLY YOUR WEDDING.

KVELL—TO BE FILLED WITH JOY AND PRIDE.

NAKHES—THE SELFLESS PLEASURE THAT PARENTS GET FROM THE LIFE EVENTS AND SUCCESSES OF THEIR CHILDREN AND GRANDCHILDREN.

SO—YOUR WEDDING *SIMHA* WILL ENABLE YOUR PARENTS TO *KVELL* AND GLOW WITH *NAKHES*.

THAT USES ALL THREE WORDS IN ONE SENTENCE. GOT IT?

Candles in Your Ceremony

SOME RABBIS WORK THE SOFT GLOW OF CANDLES INTO THE CER-EMONY BY ASKING THE COUPLE TO PROVIDE A PAIR OF CANDLESTICKS UNDER THE *HUPPAH,* TO STAND FOR THE BEGINNING OF THEIR NEW HOME. WHEN YOU ARRIVE UNDER THE CANOPY, YOU CAN HAVE TWO ATTENDANTS LIGHT ONE CANDLE EACH, WHILE ANOTHER READS THIS THOUGHT FROM THE BAAL SHEM TOV (A GREAT HASIDIC MASTER): "FROM EVERY HUMAN BEING THERE RISES A LIGHT THAT REACHES STRAIGHT TO HEAVEN. AND WHEN TWO SOULS THAT ARE DESTINED FOR EACH OTHER FIND ONE ANOTHER, THEIR STREAMS OF LIGHT FLOW TOGETHER AND A SINGLE BRIGHTER LIGHT GOES FORTH FROM THEIR UNITED BEING."

If you've chosen to hold the ceremony in a synagogue, you will have to be bound by its rules, but there are always some changes possible. If you want to be accompanied by your mother and father, and the groom wants his parents to walk with him in the procession, don't let yourself be talked out of it by some well-meaning but authoritarian "director" who has so-called modern ideas in mind. Everything on the list above, except for the egalitarian *ketubah,* is correct within the Jewish ritual, though not required. Be polite but firm about your desires.

You may have problems with the egalitarian wedding contract, and this will take careful discussion with the rabbi. If you want this synagogue and this one only, you may have to compromise. If the rules won't permit a floral *huppah,* the rabbi is actually doing you a favor and saving you money—don't fight it! But he should certainly let you use the canopy you have made specially for this occasion.

Candles may be a problem as well. If you can't have them for the procession, work with the florist to have candles in the centerpieces on all the tables at the reception, to shed the "light of rejoicing" then.

CEREMONY DETAILS AT AN INFORMAL WEDDING

If you're having a small wedding at home or in some unconventional setting, you will discover how easily you can dispense with the services of a ritual director. Just decide on the order of the procession (if you will have one), write the list out on a card and give it to a responsible friend or relative. That person will act as the "starter" for your procession, lining the participants up and sending them down the aisle in the order you have chosen. Here's where your sister-in-law or your aunt can be of real help to you while you honor her by giving her a part in the ceremony.

WEDDING BOOKLETS

Many couples make up a booklet that is a combination program and explanation of the ceremony for their guests. Some also include the

concluding Grace after Meals and use the booklet as a combination *bentsher* (text used for saying Grace) and memento of the wedding. You can be as elaborate or simple as you wish, providing anything from a typeset, illustrated little book to a single photocopied sheet. You can include a welcome to your guests, explain the rituals, or give the English text of the Seven Wedding Blessings or your *ketubah*. You can have a cover that reproduces your wedding invitation or your *ketubah*. The contents are entirely up to you. Whatever you choose to include will make this a souvenir of the day that is far more meaningful than the usual monogrammed matchbooks and other printer-invented ways of spending money.

PICTURE-TAKING

Will the synagogue permit picture-taking in the sanctuary? Don't fight the rabbis who don't allow it. In fact, don't allow it yourself. For the sake of "candid" shots, you are sacrificing the quiet sanctity of your ceremony and will be allowing the photographer's flash bulbs to dominate the proceedings.

You can make a special keepsake of the wedding party group photo by planning to order an enlargement to 12"×14" and buying a mat for a photo this size. At the picture-taking session, have all the people who will be going down the aisle with you sign the mat. When the finished photo is delivered, you mat it, frame it and hang it. Presto! Instant souvenir.

THE WEDDING PARTY

Who is going to walk down the aisle with you? You have choices ranging from the traditional to a theatrical entourage in a "modern" ceremony, which is really a medley of borrowings from other cultures. Consider these options:

PARENTS AND GRANDPARENTS

Mothers, in the non-Jewish tradition, are relegated to the front pews. The groom has no escort. He simply comes in through a side door and waits for the bride to come in on the arm of her father. But

~

Candles in Your Ceremony (continued)

IF YOU USE THE CANDLE-LIT CENTERPIECES INSTEAD OF CANDLES IN THE CEREMONY, YOU CAN ARRANGE TO LEAVE THEM UNLIT UNTIL EVERYONE IS SEATED AND THE BRIDE AND GROOM HAVE ENTERED (BE SURE THE CATERER INFORMS THE WAIT STAFF, SO THAT THEY DON'T RUN AROUND LIGHTING THE CANDLES BEFORE YOU ARE READY). THEN GIVE A FRIEND THE HONOR OF ASKING THE OLDEST PERSON (OR THE YOUNGEST) AT EACH TABLE TO LIGHT THE CANDLES SIMULTANEOUSLY WHILE HE OR SHE READS THE PASSAGE FROM THE BAAL SHEM.

~

 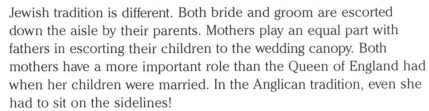
Jewish tradition is different. Both bride and groom are escorted down the aisle by their parents. Mothers play an equal part with fathers in escorting their children to the wedding canopy. Both mothers have a more important role than the Queen of England had when her children were married. In the Anglican tradition, even she had to sit on the sidelines!

No matter how "modern" your ideas may be, don't cheat your parents of this very special moment in their lives. Give them this chance to glow.

Grandparents are even more to be honored. Some ceremonies disregard this traditional honor, but it is a special mark of respect and always very touching. If your "grands" are frail or walk with difficulty, assign another grandchild or a niece or nephew to escort them, and provide seats by the *huppah* so that they do not have to stand during the ceremony. More glow will be your reward.

ARE OTHER ATTENDANTS NECESSARY?

Apart from your parents and the witnesses, no attendants are necessary in a Jewish wedding. The maid or matron of honor and the best man, who are supposed to assist the bride and groom, have become customary additions.

All the other attendants—pairs of bridesmaids, flower girls, ring bearers and even ushers—are borrowings from other ceremonies, not Jewish traditions, as many people think. You may have them or not, depending on whether you opt for simplicity or pageantry. To help you decide, consider the size of the place you have chosen for the ceremony, the degree of formality you want and the number of close friends and relatives you want to honor.

THE BRIDE'S ATTENDANTS

Whom to Choose

The maid or matron of honor should be your sister or your best friend.

What's an Unterfirer?

NO, IT'S NOT YOUR INTERFERING SISTER-IN-LAW! IT'S A TRADITIONAL HONORARY DESIGNATION YOU AND YOUR FIANCÉ CAN GIVE TO TWO MARRIED COUPLES (PEOPLE WHO HAVE BEEN MARRIED ONLY ONCE—THESE DAYS, THEY MAY BE HARD TO FIND!) WHO WILL ESCORT YOU TO THE *HUPPAH*. THEY COME BEFORE THE BRIDE AND HER PARENTS, BUT AFTER THE MAID OF HONOR; SIMILARLY, AFTER THE BEST MAN AND BEFORE THE GROOM AND HIS PARENTS. WHEN IT IS PERMITTED, THEY ALSO CARRY CANDLES AND MAY, RESPECTIVELY, HOLD THE RING AND THE *KETUBAH*. YOU MAY ALSO DECIDE NOT TO HAVE A MAID OF HONOR OR BEST MAN AND GIVE THEIR DUTIES TO AN *UNTERFIRER* COUPLE, IF YOU PREFER. IT'S A NICE WAY TO INCLUDE THE SPOUSE OF A PERSON YOU WOULD HAVE CHOSEN TO BE MATRON OF HONOR OR BEST MAN.

If you decide to have bridesmaids, they should be chosen from among your relatives and close friends. Include your fiancé's sisters, if you can. Remember, they'll be part of your family after the wedding.

You are really not under any obligation to "return the honor" and choose as bridesmaids women at whose weddings you may have been an attendant.

Remember also that it is customary for bridesmaids to pay for their own outfits, including all the special accessories. You may be doing your friends a favor by not "honoring" them with another financial burden.

Non-Jewish friends may serve as attendants in most congregations, since they will not be part of the service, but are simply honoring the bride.

Duties of the Maid/Matron of Honor

The maid or matron of honor, who precedes you down the aisle, has a few real duties. Before the wedding day, she may help you compile your guest list, address invitations or run some errands for you. On the big day, she helps you finish dressing, holds your bouquet during the ceremony, and, if you have a double-ring ceremony, holds the groom's ring till it is needed. You may have her hold the *ketubah* during the ceremony.

If your veil and gown have a long train, she will straighten it out behind you as you turn to go back down the aisle on the arm of your husband.

When there is a large wedding party, the maid of honor is a kind of "camp mother," responsible for checking that all the members of the party have arrived, have the proper accessories and flowers, and assemble promptly for picture-taking and the ceremony.

Since she presumably is less emotionally involved than you or your mother, the maid of honor should expect to be the cool head and supporting presence during those inevitable last-minute jitters. Have her tuck in with her accessories a little "first-aid kit" of needles, thread, pins, tissues, Band-Aids (for new-shoe blisters), comb and

hairspray, some aspirin, and change for emergency phone calls. Though a good caterer will have some of these on hand, it's a lot better not to have to go frantically looking for them when you need them on the spot.

Duties of the Bridesmaids

Bridesmaids are purely ornamental. The idea is to have their youthful beauty, warmth and charm add to the festivity and rejoicing with the bride. Their main duty is to be on time—for fittings, picture-taking and above all, the ceremony. And, of course, to be pleasant and tactful to all the guests.

Bridesmaids often plan showers for the bride.

WEDDING PARTY GIFTS

It is customary to give each of your attendants (bride to bridesmaids, groom to ushers) a small personal gift. The gifts should all be alike. If they are silver or gold they can be engraved with the date and initials and be a significant memento of the day. Among the gift possibilities for the bridesmaids are: silver key chains; bangle bracelets, a monogrammed leather earring box, silver hair ornaments or a pendant on a chain. For the ushers, your fiancé might choose silver key chains, cuff links, a monogrammed leather stud box, or a silver jigger. A silver picture frame with a picture of the wedding party is also a popular gift, but, of course, you won't have the picture itself till after the wedding.

THE GROOM'S ATTENDANTS

Whom to Choose

In choosing the ushers, follow the same criteria as those the bride uses for her attendants. Try to include her brothers in the party.

The best man should be your brother or your closest friend.

משמח

Duties of the Best Man

The best man will precede the groom in the procession.

He is responsible for the details of outfit rental, for assembling the ushers (if any) for fittings, checking to see that all have picked up the complete outfit and accessories, and after the wedding, that the rented things have been returned. He is also the one who will "ride herd" on the ushers to make sure they are on time for picture-taking and the ceremony. They should be asked to come an hour early, to be available to assist the best man.

The best man will also help the groom finish dressing and run any last-minute errands. He is the cool head and right hand for him. He should hold the ring until it is needed, check to make sure the groom has the marriage license and, if he wishes, hold it until it is time to turn it over to the rabbi. He should also help in the leave-taking arrangements and see that the luggage is ready—he may even drive you to the airport for the start of your honeymoon. Your fiancé may ask the best man to check to see that your honeymoon reservations are in order. In short, he is your "panic-stopper" on your wedding day.

At the reception, the best man usually gives the first toast to the bride or the couple and may act as your MC for any entertainments your guests want to offer you.

Duties of the Ushers

Guests may sit wherever they wish during the wedding ceremony, except for the first row, which is reserved for family members who will not be under the *huppah*, so ushers are not really necessary. Their main function is to serve as an honor guard during the ceremony and to assist with transportation and hospitality. If they are unmarried, they are expected to help the bridesmaids get to the reception when it is held in a different place from the ceremony. When there is mixed dancing, they are expected to dance with unescorted women guests so that everyone has a good time.

~

Touched by Angels

THERE IS ONE TRADITION, GOING BACK TO THAT VERY FIRST WEDDING IN THE GARDEN OF EDEN, THAT SEEMS TO BE THE PRECEDENT FOR THE BEST MAN AND MAID OF HONOR. AT THAT WEDDING, THE ANGELS GABRIEL AND MICHAEL ATTENDED THE BRIDE AND GROOM AS A ROYAL ESCORT—OR *SHUSHVINIM*. TRADITIONALLY, THE BRIDE AND THE GROOM HAVE TWO *SHUSHVINIM* EACH, WHO CARRY LIGHTED CANDLES AND SERVE AT THEIR RIGHT AND LEFT HANDS.

~

Children at the Reception

THE QUESTION OF ALLOWING GUESTS TO BRING THEIR CHILDREN TO THE RECEPTION CAN BECOME AN ACRIMONIOUS ISSUE, IF YOU DECIDE THAT THERE ARE TO BE NO CHILDREN AND THEN MAKE EXCEPTIONS FOR TWO OR THREE. BE PREPARED TO EXPLAIN SWEETLY THAT ONLY THESE FEW, BECAUSE OF THEIR CLOSENESS TO YOU, CAN BE INVITED, OR ELSE REVISE YOUR PLANS TO MAKE NO EXCEPTIONS, EVEN FOR THE PROCESSION.

ONE POSSIBLE COMPROMISE IS TO ALLOW THE KIDDIES TO COME TO THE CEREMONY AND THEN HUSTLE THEM ALL OFF HOME AFTER SOME HORS D'OEUVRES AND A THANK-YOU. THIS DOES RATHER SHORTCHANGE THEIR MOTHERS, UNLESS THEY HIRE A SITTER, BUT IT DOES PERMIT THEM ALL TO PARTICIPATE IN THE MITZVAH OF REJOICING.

FOR A DAYTIME WEDDING, YOU MIGHT CONSIDER HIRING A SITTER OR TWO TO KEEP THE KIDDIES AMUSED WHILE THEIR PARENTS ENJOY THE RECEPTION.

THE BACHELOR DINNER

When there is a bachelor dinner, it is arranged by the best man and the ushers, who join together to give the bride and groom a gift. In many communities this has been replaced by the prewedding dinner.

CHILDREN IN THE WEDDING PARTY

When there are adorable little brothers and sisters or nieces and nephews, you may be inclined to include them in the procession as flower girls, ring bearers or train bearers. Little flower girls, with their frilly dresses and dainty baskets, make a charming picture, as does a little boy bearing the ring on a pillow.

But do think twice about including children in your wedding party. They are notorious scene-stealers, to begin with. They should be very close relatives and old enough (at least a mature four) to understand what they have to do and do it without tears or other embarrassments. If the reception will be in the evening, the party may run to very late hours for such youngsters. Try to provide a place for the mothers to retire with a cranky or sleepy child.

CHAPTER 4

NOW IT'S THE GROOM'S TURN!

Breathes there a groom with soul so dead,
Who never to himself has said:

> "Enough of all this female fussing! Let's just go off by
> ourselves and get married!"

That's not the way it works in a Jewish family.

YOUR STARRING MOMENTS

You and your parents have fewer hospitality obligations than the
bride and her family, but as a Jewish bridegroom, you have a special
role to play in the ceremony and the surrounding festivities.

YOUR TORAH HONOR—THE *OYFRUF*

Since the whole community rejoices with the bride and groom, you
will be publicly congratulated at an *oyfruf*—a Yiddish word that
means "calling up." On the Sabbath before the wedding, it is traditional for the groom to be given the honor of an *aliyah*—the blessings before and after the reading of the Torah portion (the
parasha)—and a *Kiddush*, a reception after the services. You and
your parents make all the arrangements for this party.

Most of the time, the Torah reading will actually be done by the
lay reader of the congregation. You need only refresh your memory
of the blessings before and after the readings—the same ones you
said at your bar mitzvah. If you would like to do more, you can
arrange to read the portion yourself, or even lead the entire additional service (*musaf*).

Your father, the bride's father and other male members of the
family (and women, in egalitarian services) may also be assigned to
read portions (*aliyot*). Participation in the service is an honor.

When you have finished your *aliyah,* the congregation will
shower you with raisins, almonds and sweets, for a sweet life to
come. If you have prankster friends, duck fast!

משמח

In congregations where women may be given *aliyot*, the bride is called up together with the groom and they share the blessings—and the shower of candies and nuts afterward. There will be hearty cries of *mazel tov* and *siman tov*, applause, singing, and even dancing.

Together with your parents, discuss all the details of the service with the rabbi. He will tell you how many *aliyot* you may have (there may be other celebrations in the congregation) and how much participation in the service he will allow. Prepare a list of the Hebrew names of all those who will be called up, and give it to the rabbi during the week before the service.

Don't forget to tell those who will be honored, so that they may be prepared for the reading.

FOR THE PARENTS OF THE GROOM

Mazel tov! Rejoice in your son's happiness. Though you do not have the main responsibility for the wedding hospitality itself, you do have a large role to play in the wedding ceremony and the prewedding celebrations.

It may seem hard not to be in full control, but do recognize that your daughter-in-law-to-be properly has the deciding vote when there is a question about any of the arrangements. If she and her mother decide to make all the plans themselves (especially if they live at a distance from you), do not feel offended or forgotten. The young couple may even decide to make the arrangements on their own, without consulting either set of parents. But try not to be too upset. Your splendid moment, unique to the Jewish wedding ceremony, will come as you escort your son down the aisle and stand beside him under the wedding canopy.

And, if you also have daughters whose weddings you will be arranging some day, seize this opportunity to relax and enjoy being highly honored guests instead of a harried host and hostess.

King Solomon and You

THE SYNAGOGUE CELEBRATION FOR THE GROOM IS A CUSTOM THAT GOES BACK TO THE DAYS OF KING SOLOMON. HE BUILT A GATE IN JERUSALEM WHERE JEWS WOULD SIT ON THE SABBATH AND HONOR NEW GROOMS. WHEN THE TEMPLE WAS DESTROYED IN 70 C.E. AND THE SYNAGOGUE GRADUALLY TOOK ITS PLACE, THIS ANCIENT PRACTICE WAS MOVED INSIDE, AND CENTURIES LATER BECAME KNOWN AS THE *OYFRUF*.

When a Ring Becomes a Coin

IN YEMENITE HOMES, EVEN IN MODERN TIMES, MANY GROOMS CEREMONIOUSLY ASK THEIR MOTHERS, ON THEIR WEDDING DAY, FOR FORGIVENESS FOR HURTING HER IN THE PAST. THE SON KNEELS AND KISSES HIS MOTHER'S KNEES. HIS MOTHER, OF COURSE, FORGIVES HIM (WHAT'S A MOTHER FOR?) AND GIVES HIM A COIN TO USE AS THE "CONSIDERATION OF VALUE" IN THE WEDDING SERVICE, ALONG WITH THE RING. IF YOU'RE A COIN COLLECTOR, YOU CAN SEEK OUT AN ANCIENT P'RUTAH (THE COIN MENTIONED IN THE HEBREW WEDDING CONTRACT) TO USE IN ADDITION TO THE USUAL RING. THIS IS A SYMBOLIC LINK TO OUR ANCESTORS AND OUR HISTORY.

SHALL YOU SHARE EXPENSES?

Talk expenses over frankly with your son. You may feel that a substantial wedding gift, the cost of fitting out the couple's new home, and perhaps paying for the wedding trip, are a sufficient contribution from you.

On the other hand, you may want to play a larger part in the wedding hospitality, especially if your guest list is much longer than the bride's. Although you can offer a gift of the champagne, the flowers, the music or the photos, it is usual for the bride's family to make the final decision as to how much they will spend on the wedding and what type of reception is planned. Be tactful when you offer your gift, so that you do not seem to be demanding a more elaborate wedding—or implying that her family is ungenerous or cannot afford your standard of living or the kind of wedding you expect. The conventional division of the wedding expenses and some suggested ways of sharing are discussed in Chapter 7.

PEACEFUL PLANNING

Wedding planning generates tension and friction. The way to avoid turning every detail into the subject of a pitched battle is simply—COOPERATION. As the parents of the groom, you may make suggestions, but you should accept the bride's—and your son's—decisions graciously. Some of the ways to avoid a quarrel are:

- Stay within the number of invitations the bride's parents have allotted you. Don't strain the budget—or the space.
- Have your guest list organized and ready on time for the bride's use. Check it for correct spelling of full names and titles, complete addresses and zip codes and phone numbers.
- Offer to help address the invitations, but don't be offended if the bride decides to control the process by doing it herself.
- Help in the follow-up on the guests on your list who do not respond.
- Give the bride's mother your seating plan for the dinner, but be flexible about it.

- Remember: different generations, different tastes. Respect the choices of the young couple in china, silver and furnishings for their own home. After all, they, not you, will have to live with whatever "look" they've decided on.
- Do they want a simple, perhaps unconventional wedding? Consider their ideas seriously, instead of demanding that they do it your way. A neo-Orthodox ceremony they have written themselves, or a wedding in an arboretum or on a secluded beach, can be very lovely—and very different!
- For your own happiness, don't put your son in the middle, between his fiancée and you, when a problem must be resolved. It's *his* day, and your joy must grow from his.

WHERE TO HOLD THE *OYFRUF*

If you are synagogue members, your choice is obvious. Unless your son is a member of another congregation which he prefers, your own congregation is the best choice, since it is almost an extended family.

Students can sometimes arrange a pleasant, informal *oyfruf* through their college Hillel.

All synagogues and *havurah* groups will be happy to arrange for this Torah honor, even if you are not a member. A generous contribution should be made in the bridegroom's name.

WHOM TO INVITE

It is customary to invite members of both families, friends and business associates, and in some congregations, all those present at the services, to the *Kiddush* afterward. Friends of other faiths may also be invited.

Invitations are informal, either by telephone or by simple note; sometimes the *Kiddush* may be announced from the pulpit as well. For Orthodox guests, who may not travel on the Sabbath, it is best not to make an invitation but simply to announce that the *oyfruf* will take place, so that they do not feel obliged to attend if it would necessitate travel.

ARRANGING FOR SABBATH OBSERVANCE

An *oyfruf* almost always takes place on the Sabbath, but you can consult with your rabbi for other possible times that are not Sabbaths, when travel is permitted. You may wish to make weekend arrangements for some very close relatives—grandparents or married siblings, for example—so that they can attend and rejoice with you and your son. The bride and her family may need the same courtesy if they do not live nearby.

Accommodations

Put your overnight guests up at a nearby hotel or motel, or with your friends and neighbors (this is often done in Orthodox communities). Your guests pay for their accommodations, though, as a gracious gesture, you may want to pay the bill for your closest relatives.

As the hosts, you provide their weekend meals and *Shabbat* afternoon activities, since they will not be able to travel home till after dark. You can prepay your guests' breakfasts at most motels and hotels, and the Friday evening and Sabbath dinner are family affairs.

Hats, Bags, Umbrellas, and the Like

Check the synagogue practice if you are not familiar with it. In Orthodox congregations, both men and married women may need head coverings. In such settings, they also may not carry handbags, briefcases, umbrellas, books and other impedimenta. Inform your guests, if they are not Orthodox. Such "baggage" is really not appropriate in any synagogue on the Sabbath. Some synagogues provide a checkroom where such items may be left, but this is rare.

THE *KIDDUSH*

And now it's time to eat! The word *Kiddush* refers to the blessing said over wine and has come to mean the buffet that is served after that on the Sabbath or a festive occasion. You can arrange for this

משמח

with the synagogue-approved caterer or, if you would prefer, prepare the spread yourself. Check carefully with the sexton about whether you will be permitted to bring in refreshments of your own and precisely which foods will be allowed. You may be asked to use approved kosher bakeries for cake and bread and to serve only certified kosher takeout foods.

Your spread can range from the simplicity of nuts, fruits, sweets, cake and wine to an elaborate buffet luncheon. Some families provide a sweet table and wine for all, so that the entire congregation may join in rejoicing with them, and then serve a luncheon for their invited guests, either in the synagogue's reception room or at home.

Only the wine and cake are essential, so that the appropriate blessings may be said. Your decision as to the other dishes to be served will depend on how many guests you have, whether they come from a distance and whether you plan to entertain them for the rest of the day. If the *Kiddush* will take place on the day before the wedding and you are hosting the prewedding dinner that evening, it is probably wisest to keep the *Kiddush* simple.

REHEARSAL DINNERS

A wedding rehearsal before the ceremony, and the dinner for the wedding party that usually follows it, is not really a Jewish custom, though there are communities in which it is done. Many rabbis frown on the practice and counsel against it. Not only does it burn up time when you could be resting and thinking about your future, it is also stressful and quite unnecessary. Entering under the wedding canopy is a private moment for the bride and groom, these rabbis hold, and should not be rehearsed. The ceremony itself is simple and is guided, step by step, by the rabbi.

If there is a rehearsal, the bride does not take part.

A family dinner on the night before the wedding usually takes the place of a rehearsal dinner. Whichever you choose, this hospitality also comes from the groom's family. If you have not been able to meet

For a Sweet Life!

HOW TO HAVE FUN IN *SHUL*: WHEN YOUR SON, WHO IS NOW OFFICIALLY A *HATAN* (A BRIDEGROOM) FINISHES HIS *ALIYAH*, HE IS SHOWERED WITH SWEETS, ALMONDS AND RAISINS BY FAMILY AND FRIENDS TO THE ACCOMPANIMENT OF CLAPPING, SINGING AND SHOUTS OF "*MAZEL TOV AND SIMAN TOV.*" THE NUTS AND RAISINS ARE SYMBOLS OF FERTILITY AND RICHNESS, WHILE THE SWEETS ARE JUST THAT—FOR A SWEET LIFE.

TO PREVENT CARPET CATASTROPHES, YOU SHOULD FILL LITTLE WHITE BAGS, SECURELY TIED, WITH A SMALL HANDFUL OF THESE TREATS AND PASS THEM OUT TO YOUR GUESTS BEFORE THE TORAH READING BEGINS. THE CHILDREN PRESENT WILL HAVE A GRAND TIME SCRAMBLING ABOUT TO PICK UP THE BAGS OF GOODIES. IT'S MUCH MORE FUN THAN GRAINS OF RICE!

IN SOME VERY FORMAL VENUES, YOU MAY COME ACROSS A *SHAMMASH* (SEXTON) WHO WON'T ALLOW YOU TO DO THIS. BUT MOST WILL, IF YOU PROMISE TO USE BAGS FOR "STICKY CONTROL."

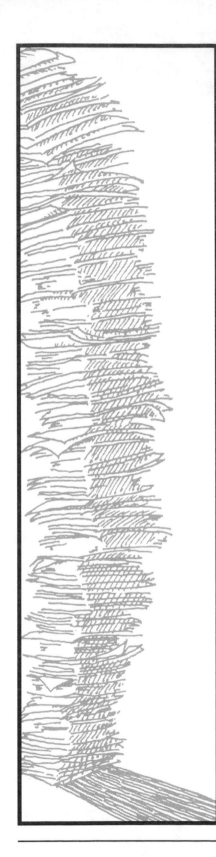

before, this dinner enables your two families to get to know each other and develop a relationship before the wedding-day formalities. Guests may include spouses and fiancés of family members and also any relatives who have come from a distance to attend the wedding.

You may have a simple buffet, a dinner at home, or an elaborate meal in a restaurant with dancing, or anything in between. You will all be going to the wedding soon after, so it is good to keep the party small, informal, relaxed and fun for all.

Invitations are informal, but it is wise to send a written note to people out of town to be sure there will be no confusion as to time and place.

PLANNING FROM A DISTANCE

When the prewedding dinner and the *oyfruf* take place in a town far away, where the bride's family lives, you will have to work with the bride's mother or, if your son lives in the wedding area, entrust the arrangements to him.

The bride's family can suggest a caterer for the *Kiddush*, or suitable restaurants for the prewedding dinner. However, you deal with the caterer yourself by phone or mail.

CHECKLIST FOR A KIDDUSH

1. Flowers:
   for the synagogue? _____
   for the buffet table? _____
   ordered through the synagogue_____
   my florist_____
   cost $_____

2. Table settings:
   provided by_____
   tablecloths (number) _____
   tableware (amount) _____
   platters and serving pieces _____
   paper goods _____

3. Food:
   menu (write it all out!) _____
   refrigeration? _____
   time when food can be brought in _____
   containers for leftovers _____
      (food will have to be kept till after the Sabbath)

4. Help:
   for setup and serving? _____
   for cleanup—before and after? _____
   cost (including tips) $ _____
      (arrange to pay before or after the Sabbath)

5. Do-it-yourself questions:
   What is the timetable for the day? _____
   Can we set up the day before?_____
   Who will help on the day? _____
   How much time is there after the Torah reading? _____
      (You will have to leave the preparations and come up smiling for the congratulations at the end of the services.)
      If you want to take your table flowers home after the Sabbath, or give them to a hospital or senior home, make clear arrangements with the sexton. Flowers for the *bimah* (platform) remain there as your gift to the synagogue.

CHECKLIST FOR A PREWEDDING DINNER

Ask the restaurant or caterer for:

- several menus from which to choose _____
- the wine list or details of an open bar arrangement _____
- complete prices for food, drink and services you will require _____
- What table arrangements will there be?
  round_____ T shape____ or U shape_____ or several smaller tables _____
  _____

- Is there a private dining room or separate section? _____
- Is there music? Or can you provide your own? _____
- What will the table settings and other decorations be? _____
  _____
  _____
  _____

NOTES: _____
_____
_____
_____
_____
_____
_____
_____
_____

CHECKLIST FOR AN OYFRUF

Have your son or the bride's family find out whether there is a synagogue caterer. Then go over the *oyfruf* checklist with him or her.

If there is no caterer, have them find out for you:

where you can order the food and wine you want to serve _____

_____

_____

_____

_____

where you can hire paid help for the day _____

_____

_____

_____

_____

_____

Deal with these sources yourself by mail or phone.

If you will have to bring the food and disposable dishes with you, simplify! Make a list and a menu and check and doublecheck before you leave home. Consider leaving a day earlier so you can do the shopping on the spot yourself instead of shlepping.

Remember—you're supposed to ENJOY—not worry!

NOTES: _____

_____

_____

_____

_____

_____

CHAPTER 5

TRADITIONS TO HONOR AND CHERISH

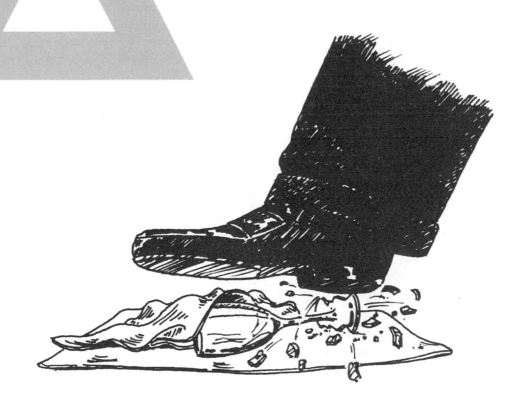

משמח

~
Increasing the Rejoicing

AT ORTHODOX WEDDINGS, THE
INCREASE OF REJOICING IS A
MITZVAH. GUESTS APPEAR IN WILD
COSTUMES, CLOWNING AND PER-
FORMING FUNNY SKITS AND ACRO-
BATIC DANCING BEFORE THE BRIDE
AND GROOM, WHO ARE SEATED IN
THRONE-LIKE CHAIRS IN THE
CENTER OF THE ROOM. DANCING
WITH A BROOM AND DANCING
WHILE BALANCING A BOTTLE ON
ONE'S HEAD ARE POPULAR
STUNTS. POEMS AND SONGS
WRITTEN FOR THE OCCASION ARE
OFTEN RECITED.

~

Jewish weddings follow a tradition that goes back to the first betrothal and wedding mentioned in the Bible, that of Isaac and Rebekah. Over the centuries, many local customs have been added, but the basic elements of the ceremony remain unchanged. The ritual you will go through under the wedding canopy (*huppah*) incorporates, actually or symbolically, the three ancient Jewish methods of establishing a marriage: the groom gives the bride a contract, which she accepts (*ketubah*), he presents her with an article of known value (the ring) which she accepts (*kinyan*), and they spend ten or fifteen minutes together in seclusion or union (*yihud*)—all in the presence of witnesses. This is the origin of the Jewish wedding party, which can be as large as you and your fiancé desire, or strictly limited to your parents, with the assembled guests making up a body of witnesses.

A Jewish wedding is a religious ceremony and it is necessary to have a quorum, a *minyan*, so even the smallest wedding should include ten men among the family and guests. If circumstances make it impossible to assemble a *minyan*, consult your rabbi for permissible exceptions and any necessary changes in the ceremony. Conservative and Reform ceremonies will include women in counting a *minyan*.

Among the Orthodox, the traditions discussed in this chapter are the norm; other religious groups may have some variants. In the search for "modernized" or "creative" wedding styles, most of these time-honored rituals are often dropped in favor of a Jewish version of a High Church Anglican ceremony, or the finale of a fashion show; however, many brides are now returning to ancient custom to arrange an authentic Jewish wedding, perhaps the most "original" because it is based on its own roots. One symbol that has survived every innovation is the breaking of the glass at the end of the ceremony. Everyone recognizes that as the hallmark of a Jewish wedding.

If you are not following strict Orthodox ways, you may choose among those elements of the ceremony that appeal to you as a direct connection to the long chain of brides and grooms that stretches back through four thousand years of history.

משמח

THE WEEK BEFORE THE WEDDING

TORAH HONOR TO THE GROOM (THE *OYFRUF)*

As discussed in Chapter 4, it is customary to honor the bridegroom in synagogue by calling him up to the Torah on the Sabbath before the wedding. The rejoicing over the coming marriage formally begins then, with a reception (*Kiddush*) after services, hosted by his family. In some congregations the bridegroom is showered with nuts, raisins and sweets as he finishes his reading, to symbolize the wish for a sweet, fruitful life.

BRIDE'S TORAH HONOR

In a few modern Orthodox women's study groups, a custom of honoring the bride with a Torah reading is slowly gaining acceptance. In some, a serious Torah study hour is spent, focused on passages about marriage. This is followed by a women-only party for the bride.

The bride may also be honored at a Sabbath afternoon women's gathering, following the *oyfruf*, which is known as *Shabbos Kallah* (the bride's Sabbath). The guests honor her with Torah discussions, personal anecdotes about their friendship, and thoughts about her upcoming marriage.

THE BRIDE'S VISIT TO THE *MIKVEH* (RITUAL BATH)

Traditionally observant brides and all converts go to the ritual bath (the *mikveh)* for the first time just before the wedding, for ceremonial immersion and purification. It is a joyful occasion, followed by a small party for the women in the family. Among Sephardim the bride is accompanied to the bath by her friends, who also attend the party afterward to celebrate the approaching nuptials.

THE GROOM'S VISIT TO THE *MIKVEH*

Some men also go to the *mikveh* just before the wedding day to prepare themselves for this important moment in their lives. Often they are accompanied by a group of friends and have a men-only party

The First Couple

THERE IS AN ANCIENT TALE ABOUT THE WEDDING OF THE VERY FIRST BRIDE AND GROOM— ADAM AND EVE. GOD, IT IS SAID, BRAIDED EVE'S HAIR TO PREPARE HER FOR THE CEREMONY AND ACTED AS ADAM'S WITNESS. THEN GOD PRONOUNCED THE WEDDING BLESSINGS AND THE ANGELS SHOUTED "MAZEL TOV!" WHEN YOU LOOK INTO THE EYES OF YOUR BELOVED UNDER THE *HUPPAH,* MAY YOU, TOO, HEAR THE ANGELS SING.

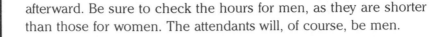

The Mikveh

YOU CAN LOCATE A *MIKVEH* NEAR YOU BY ASKING YOUR RABBI OR CALLING AN ORTHODOX SYNAGOGUE. THERE IS ALSO A WEALTH OF JEWISH COMMUNITY INFORMATION ON AMERICA ONLINE AND THE INTERNET.

BEFORE YOU GO, CALL TO CHECK THE HOURS (MANY ARE EVENINGS ONLY), AND ASK WHAT THE FEES ARE (YOU WILL NEED CASH FOR THIS AND TIPS FOR THE CLEANERS AND THE *MIKVERIN*— THE *MIKVEH* LADY). ALSO ASK WHAT YOU SHOULD BRING WITH YOU BESIDES A FRESH CHANGE OF CLOTHES. YOU MAY NEED YOUR OWN HAIRDRYER, SHAMPOO, SOAP, LOTIONS AND SO ON, OR THEY MAY BE SUPPLIED.

PROCEDURE: YOU WILL BE SHOWN TO A PRIVATE BATHROOM, WHERE YOU WILL CLEAN AND TRIM YOUR FINGERNAILS AND TOENAILS, CLEAN YOUR EARS AND FLOSS AND BRUSH YOUR TEETH. NEXT COMES A TUB BATH, WHERE, IF THE *MIKVEH* IS NOT TOO CROWDED, YOU CAN SOAK AND RELAX AWHILE.

afterward. Be sure to check the hours for men, as they are shorter than those for women. The attendants will, of course, be men.

SECLUSION OF THE BRIDE

After she has been to the *mikveh*, a traditional bride will not see or speak to her fiancé until the wedding ceremony, a period that can vary from a day or two to a week. At a time when anxieties are high and your nerves are frazzled, observing this custom may save you from many moments of friction and tears. This sensible custom is followed by practically all Jewish brides, whether they go to the *mikveh* or not.

THE TRADITIONAL CEREMONY

In the old Eastern European villages (the *shtetls*) the bridegroom and his party would arrive at the bride's home on the wedding day accompanied by music, dancing and merry-making. In Orthodox communities today, there are separate receptions for the women guests greeting the bride and the men accompanying and welcoming the groom. Traditionally, the groom would attempt to display his learning in Talmudic discourse at the signing of the marriage contract, but, all in fun; the teasing, joking and interruptions of his friends would rarely let him finish his speech. Meanwhile, the bride, enthroned in a chair at the center of the women's party, is greeted with good wishes, song and dance.

GREETING THE BRIDE

You and your attendants may choose to finish dressing at the place where the wedding will be held. After you've put on your headdress and your veil, you will have time for formal portraits. You may or may not receive guests at this time. Since this is usually the high point of prewedding nerves, you may want to limit the group to your family and the bridesmaids, then make a dramatic first appearance in the procession.

משמח

On the other hand, you may follow the old tradition and have a full-scale women's reception, surrounded by your attendants and the floral beauty of all the bouquets banked around your bridal throne. Some brides actually find that the happy presence of many guests, all vibrating on the same note of anticipation, is a soothing distraction while they wait for the groom's reception to end. In either case, you do not see the groom until the ceremony begins.

SIGNING THE *KETUBAH*

The climax of the men's reception comes when the teasing stops and the rabbi formally asks the groom whether he is ready to accept the obligations set forth in the marriage contract. He indicates his consent by receiving a handkerchief or some other small object handed to him from the rabbi and returning it to him (*kinyan*). In the presence of both fathers and the witnesses he signs the contract, and then the marriage ceremony can begin.

In Conservative and Reform congregations, the rabbi will go through a similar action with the bride to indicate that she is entering into this marriage of her own free will. In Orthodox practice this assent is contained in the public reading of the marriage contract.

VEILING THE BRIDE—*B'DEKEN DI KALLE*

Now comes an emotional high point in the Orthodox wedding. Escorted by the two fathers and surrounded by his fervently singing friends and jubilant musicians, the groom comes to claim his bride. He approaches her where she sits flanked by the two mothers. Then he looks directly into her eyes and lowers her face veil. This shows that he accepts this woman as the one who was promised him. By "covering" her with the veil, he sets her apart from all others.

The fathers bless their children and the marriage that is about to take place. There is a great burst of congratulatory music and the party moves on to where the wedding canopy has been set up.

The Mikveh (continued)

THEN YOU SHAMPOO YOUR HAIR AND FINISH WITH A THOROUGH RINSING IN THE SHOWER. YOU COMB ALL THE HAIR ON YOUR HEAD AND BODY IN THE SAME DIRECTION. THERE WILL BE A SHEET OR A TOWEL TO WRAP UP IN BEFORE YOU RING FOR THE MIKVEH LADY. SHE WILL LEAD YOU TO THE MIKVEH AND INSPECT YOU TO MAKE SURE YOU'RE READY TO IMMERSE. SHE WILL LEAD YOU THROUGH THE RITUAL PROCEDURE AND THE PRAYERS. THE MIKVEH ITSELF IS MUCH LIKE A SMALL TILED SWIMMING POOL. THE DIFFERENCE IS THAT IT MUST BE FED FROM A SPRING OF "LIVING WATERS"— FRESH RUNNING WATER.

THINK ABOUT THE RITUAL AS A WAY TO ENTER INTO A NEW STAGE OF YOUR LIFE. MANY WOMEN FIND THIS IMMERSION AN EMOTIONAL, MYSTICAL PREPARATION FOR THE UNCHARTED FUTURE.

~

From Tree to Pole

IT'S A PLEASANT TRADITION TO
PLANT A TREE WHEN A CHILD IS
BORN—A CEDAR FOR A BOY AND
A CYPRESS OR A PINE FOR A GIRL.
THEN, WHEN THE PARENTS
REALIZE THEIR DREAM OF MAR-
RIAGE FOR THEIR CHILDREN, THEY
USE LIMBS FROM THESE TREES TO
FASHION POLES FOR THE *HUPPAH*.

HOW LONG SHOULD THE POLES
BE? THREE OR FOUR FEET IS A
COMFORTABLE CHOICE—TALL
ENOUGH TO REACH WELL OVER
THE HEADS OF THE PARTICIPANTS
WHEN THE BEARERS RAISE THEM
ALOFT, BUT NOT SO LONG AS TO
BE HEAVY AND UNWIELDY. YOU
MAY ALSO USE POLES ABOUT SIX
FEET LONG AND PLAN TO REST
THEM ON THE FLOOR.

THE POLES OF SUCH TEMPO-
RARY CANOPIES ARE USUALLY
HELD BY MALE FRIENDS OR RELA-
TIVES. YOU HONOR THEM BY
ASKING THEM TO PARTICIPATE.
JUST BE SURE YOU CHOOSE TALL
MEN WITH STRONG ARMS!

~

At this point some Hasidic women add yet another veil over the bride's face before she enters, so that it is completely hidden during the procession and most of the ceremony.

You can add the fervent emotional moment of the *b'deken* to your wedding, if you would prefer it to being hidden away from the guests till your first theatrical appearance as you walk down the aisle. Check with your rabbi (some do not allow pre-ceremony receptions) and with the caterer to be sure there is an adequate space for this festivity. Some couples have worked out an egalitarian "covering" ceremony in which the bride places a skullcap (*kippah* or *yarmulke*) on the groom's head before he lowers her veil and they recite blessings to each other. Allow at least half an hour before the ceremony begins.

THE WEDDING CANOPY (*HUPPAH*)

The wedding ceremony takes place under the wedding canopy. As a reminder of the promise to Abraham that his descendants would be as numerous as the stars in the heavens, it became a custom to hold the ceremony out of doors, under the open sky, preferably at night, when the stars could be seen.

In Eastern Europe, the procession of wedding guests carrying candles as a sign of rejoicing would make their way to the *shtetl* square where the *huppah* would be set up. The whole village was a witness to the event.

The *huppah* also symbolizes the new home that will be created by the couple. In ancient times it was a specially decorated tent that had been set up in the courtyard of the bride's family. The newly-weds actually lived there for seven days of feasting after the wed-ding. Over the years, the *huppah* evolved into a velvet canopy, elabo-rately embroidered and fringed, supported by four poles, which were often decorated with garlands of flowers and greenery.

Among Sephardic Jews and in Israel, a large prayer shawl (*tallit*) is held over the couple as a *huppah*. Many couples prefer the

משמח

classic simplicity of the *tallit* or the traditional velvet canopy to the elaborate arbors devised by florists, or the plastic greens and blooms in use in some caterers' halls.

Some brides have taken up the idea of making their own *huppah*, embroidered, appliquéd or painted, which after the wedding will become an heirloom wall hanging. Friends can share in the rejoicing by working on the embroidery with you. (See the next page.)

In modern Israel, at an army wedding, the *huppah* is formed by a *tallit* supported by four rifles, one at each corner, held by friends of the couple.

A Tale of Two Veils

WHY DOES THE BRIDE WEAR A VEIL? ACCORDING TO THE BIBLE (GEN. 24:65), WHEN REBEKAH SAW ISAAC APPROACHING HER ACROSS THE FIELDS WHERE SHE WAS GUARDING HER FATHER'S SHEEP, SHE ASKED, "WHAT MAN IS THAT?" WHEN SHE WAS TOLD HE WAS HER PROMISED BRIDEGROOM, SHE DREW HER VEIL OVER HER HEAD AND COVERED HER FACE OUT OF MODESTY. THIS MIDDLE EASTERN CUSTOM HAS GIVEN US THE BRIDAL VEIL.

PERHAPS THE MOST DECEPTIVE WEDDING VEIL WAS THE ONE USED BY LABAN TO COMPLETELY SWATHE HIS OLDEST DAUGHTER, LEAH, SO THAT HE COULD PASS HER OFF TO JACOB AS RACHEL, THE WOMAN HE REALLY WISHED TO MARRY. THE B'DEKEN CUSTOM IS THE DIRECT OUTGROWTH OF THIS ANCIENT "BAIT AND SWITCH" WEDDING.

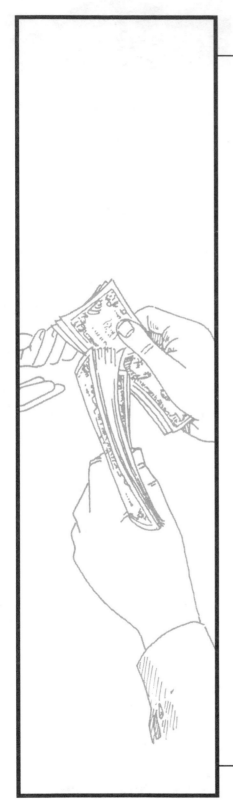

Check your original ideas with the rabbi to be sure they will be acceptable. Some synagogues do not allow a floral canopy and may have elaborately draped canopies that you are required to use.

Orthodox *huppahs* are often held outdoors, outside the hall, on a street that has been briefly closed to traffic, or in catering halls equipped with special skylights that open over the canopy so that the stars can be seen during the ceremony. Hotel rooftop terraces are also popular. You can have your ceremony outdoors in your own garden, on the grounds of a synagogue, temple or country club, in a public garden, greenhouse or park, or, if you're really adventurous, on the deck of a yacht chartered for the evening.

If you think you might like one of the public areas or a boat, start looking into permits and reservations well ahead of time. See Chapter 6 for a checklist covering these special sites.

Making Your Own Huppah

Some rabbis do not allow floral *huppot*, nor can trees alone count as a canopy, because the *huppah* must be a temporary, handmade structure. Other than that rule, there are no restrictions as to the size or ornamentation of a *huppah* you make yourself. Many synagogues, temples and catering establishments have traditional embroidered velvet canopies they use in the wedding ceremony. For a floral touch you can decorate the poles and the edge of the *huppah* with garlands.

You also have the option of making your own *huppah*. It can be as simple as a three- by five-foot length of a fabric, in a color or pattern you like, that you hem and possibly trim with fringe. If you're more ambitious, you can embroider or appliqué the traditional symbols on the underside: sun, moon and stars, doves, verses from the Song of Songs, the outstretched hands of the Priestly Blessing, or icons that are personally meaningful. You can find patterns for these designs in needlework shops.

If you don't have quite so much time to spend on this project, you can paint the designs on fabric, or use many colors of broad-tip felt pens to draw them on, or you can give squares of fabric to close friends and relatives and ask each one to make a square for you. Then you sew them together like a quilt.

משמח

Whichever way you choose to make it, be sure your creation has grommets or secure curtain rings to fasten it to the poles so that it stays put during the ceremony. It should not be much larger than three by five or four by seven feet, to prevent drooping and billowing between the poles. This is especially important in an outdoor wedding where vagrant breezes may cause problems.

You will have created a family heirloom. Many couples use the *huppah* as a canopy over their bed, or mount it as a wall hanging. You can lend it to your siblings or dear friends for their weddings, or save it for your own children to use and hand down.

CANTOR AND/OR RABBI

BEST MAN

FATHER GROOM, MOTHER

THE TRADITIONAL PROCESSION

A Jewish wedding is, above all, a family affair. To lead their children to the *huppah* is considered a parent's highest joy. Both bride and groom are escorted by their fathers and mothers. If there are grandparents, they are given a special place in the procession. A very frail grandparent may be escorted by a grandchild, niece or nephew. All stand under the canopy, if space allows, as witnesses and participants.

MAID OR ATRON OF HONOR

OWER RL

You may have as many or as few attendants as you like. Ideally, all the brothers and sisters should be part of the wedding party, but you need not have any attendants other than your parents if a simple wedding is your wish. Ushers are really not necessary at a Jewish wedding, as guests may sit where they wish during the ceremony.

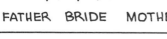

FATHER   BRIDE   MOTHER

Charity—Tsedakah

IN A TIME OF REJOICING, THE JEWISH TRADITION IS TO REMEMBER THE POOR, THE LONELY AND THE SICK. BOTH THE BRIDE'S AND GROOM'S FAMILIES MAY MAKE A CHARITABLE DONATION IN THEIR CHILDREN'S HONOR; AND SOME GUESTS OFTEN MAKE A GIFT IN THE COUPLE'S NAME TO THE SYNAGOGUE, TEMPLE OR ORGANIZATION THEY FAVOR.

IN THE SAME SPIRIT, SOME FAMILIES MAKE A DONATION OF A PERCENTAGE OF THE BANQUET COST (SOME RABBIS SUGGEST THREE PERCENT) TO MAZON, A JEWISH CHARITY THAT FEEDS THE POOR AND HOMELESS. SOME FAMILIES GIVE THE FLORAL CENTERPIECES AND OTHER DECORATIONS TO HOSPITALS OR SENIOR CITIZENS' HOMES AFTER THE RECEPTION. YOU MAY HAVE THE MASTER OF CEREMONIES ANNOUNCE YOUR FLORAL GIFTS BEFORE THE GUESTS START TAKING THE FLOWERS APART, AND PLACE A CARD ON THE TABLES TELLING OF YOUR GIFT TO MAZON AS WELL.

משמח

The traditional order up the aisle is:

Rabbi and/or Cantor
Grandparents of the Groom
Ushers (if any)
Best Man
Father, Groom, Mother (to the right of the Groom)
Grandparents of the Bride
Bridesmaids (if any)
Maid/Matron of Honor
Flower Girls (if any)
Father, Bride, Mother (to the right of the Bride)

Under the canopy, the groom's parents take places at the right side of the rabbi, and the bride's parents face them at the left. The bride stands at the groom's right. Best man and maid of honor stand behind the groom and bride. Ushers line the aisle on one side, bridesmaids on the other. Grandparents may stand or sit on the platform beside the canopy, or if there are no chairs there, they may sit in the first row on the aisle.

~

Candle-Lit Processions

YOU MAY WANT TO BRING BACK THE OLD VILLAGE CUSTOM OF CARRYING LIGHTED CANDLES AS A SYMBOL OF REJOICING, BUT BE WARNED—MOST CATERERS WILL NOT ALLOW IT BECAUSE OF THE FEAR OF FIRE. WHEN YOU CAN HAVE THEM, THE BRIDESMAIDS CARRY FLOWER-TRIMMED CANDLES INSTEAD OF CONVENTIONAL BOUQUETS. SOMETIMES THE USHERS CARRY BRAIDED *HAVDALAH* CANDLES. THIS IS MOST EFFECTIVE IN A DARKENED INTERIOR OR AT DUSK OUTDOORS.

~

At strictly segregated Orthodox weddings, the two fathers may escort the groom; the mothers then escort the bride. At the recessional in such arrangements, the two fathers follow the bride and groom (who are always first up the aisle), then the two mothers, then paired ushers, then paired bridesmaids. The best man leads the ushers, the maid or matron of honor leads the bridesmaids.

A widowed mother or father may alone escort the bride or groom. When a widowed parent has remarried, the stepmother or stepfather may or may not join in the procession, as your feelings dictate.

Divorced parents should see Chapter 8 for a discussion of this rather involved situation.

CIRCLING THE GROOM—SEVEN REALMS OF JOY

Arrived at the *huppah*, the Orthodox bride now enters into the mystical again, in the very ancient custom of "circling." Escorted by the two mothers carrying candles, she circles the groom seven times before taking her place at his side. Some people do only three circuits, but seven is the preferred number.

Why seven? By the parallel to the idea of the seven heavens, the seven wedding blessings and the seven days of Creation. Symbolically, the bride is thought to be entering the seven spheres of her beloved's soul.

The circle can also be seen as an act that defines a new family circle—the bride has created the space the couple will now share, separate from parents.

Hasidic Jews chant a solemn, wordless melody for the circling. Many less traditional brides are now adding this impressive and moving ritual to their ceremonies. Most rabbis will allow it if you ask. Instead of a Hasidic choir, you can have the traditional melodies played by a violin or solo flute. Give your music people time to find the sheet music and prepare it.

משמח

Ring Fingers

YOU MAY WONDER WHY THE RING IS PLACED ON YOUR RIGHT INDEX FINGER DURING THE CEREMONY. THIS PRACTICE, NEARLY A THOU-SAND YEARS OLD, HAS SEVERAL EXPLANATIONS. AN ANCIENT BELIEF WAS THAT THE INDEX FINGER WAS CONNECTED BY A SPE-CIAL ARTERY TO THE HEART, AND SO THE RING THERE JOINS YOUR HEART TO HIS. ANOTHER IS THAT THE INDEX FINGER, THE ONE WE USE TO POINT WITH WHEN WE READ FROM THE TORAH, IS THE SEAT OF INTELLIGENCE. PLACING THE RING THERE INDICATES INFORMED CONSENT.

AFTER THE CEREMONY YOU MAY TRANSFER YOUR RING TO THE LEFT RING FINGER, WHERE IT IS CUSTOMARILY WORN.

MEMORIAL PRAYERS

At some traditional weddings, a memorial prayer for a deceased parent may be offered just before the ceremony begins. If you feel this is too disturbing emotionally for a happy occasion, you may have the prayer said privately for the family just before the cere-mony. Less loaded with emotion, and more appropriate to some, is the inclusion of the memorial prayers in the services when the groom is called up to the Torah (the *oyfruf*).

THE WEDDING SERVICE

The service begins with blessings of welcome chanted by the rabbi or cantor. The ceremony falls into two parts that once were separate in time: the betrothal (*erusin*) and the marriage vows (*nisuin*). In the first portion two blessings are recited, one over the wine and one proclaiming the sanctity of marriage. The rabbi hands the first cup of wine to the groom, who takes a sip from it. The bride's mother or the maid of honor raises the bride's veil so that the groom may look at her once more; then he hands the cup to the bride so that she may sip from it.

THE WEDDING VOWS AND THE RING

At this point, the bride may pass her bouquet to the maid of honor to free her hands for the wedding ring. Now the best man hands the ring to the rabbi. The groom takes the ring from the rabbi and places it on the bride's right index finger as he recites the ancient Aramaic wedding formula:

Harey at mekuddeshet li b'taba'at zo k'dat Moshe v'Yisrael

הֲרֵי אַתְּ מְקֻדֶּשֶׁת לִי. בְּטַבַּעַת זוֹ. כְּדַת מֹשֶׁה וְיִשְׂרָאֵל:

and the English:

Behold, thou art consecrated unto me with this ring according to the law of Moses and of Israel.

משמח

This declaration from the groom, and the bride's acceptance of the ring, make your marriage legal under Jewish law. This is the one essential part of the whole ceremony.

Why a Plain Gold Band?

The wedding ring is the "object of value" (worth at least one ancient *p'rutah* or in modern coinage, a dime) that the groom presents to the bride to seal the agreement, in the action called *kinyan.* Jewish law requires that the ring must be an unpierced band of a single pure metal, with no precious stones, so that there is no mistaking its value.

Many brides, seeking to create equal status with their grooms in the ceremony, decide to use double rings, giving the groom his ring with the same Aramaic formula, cast in the feminine form and translated as "In accepting this ring, I consecrate myself to you as your wife, in accordance with the law of Moses and of Israel." However, there is no specified response from the bride at this point. Instead of the Aramaic formula, she may choose a verse from the Song of Songs, such as *"Ani l'dodi, v'dodi li—*I am my beloved's and my beloved is mine," or "Set me as a seal upon thy heart, as a seal upon thine arm." You should talk this over with your rabbi..

This is a relatively new custom; in fact, some traditional rabbis do not permit it on the ground that it invalidates the act of *kinyan,*or acquisition. There's no need to fight this. You will simply give your new husband his ring after the ceremony and he can wear it during the reception and ever after, just as you do.

THE MARRIAGE CONTRACT (*KETUBAH*)

The marriage contract, a legal document spelling out the rights and obligations of both parties, is central to the wedding service, which is designed to sanctify and bless the contract. Traditionally, it is read aloud in the original Aramaic and then in English and given to the bride for her safekeeping. Properly signed and witnessed, it is the

~

Stepping Out Correctly

TRADITION-MINDED GRAND-MOTHERS AND AUNTS WILL REMIND THE BRIDE TO START OUT DOWN THE AISLE AND ON HER CIRCUITS WITH HER RIGHT FOOT. THAT ASSURES A GOOD START IN YOUR NEW LIFE. NEVER MIND THE BLUE GARTER—IT'S THE RIGHT FOOT THAT COUNTS!

~

משמח

A Paper Peacemaker

THE BAAL SHEM TOV, EIGH-
TEENTH-CENTURY MYSTIC AND
FOUNDER OF HASIDISM, ONCE
SAID THAT IF A COUPLE BECAME
INVOLVED IN A QUARREL, THEY
SHOULD READ THE KETUBAH
ALOUD TO EACH OTHER. THIS
SHOULD HELP THEM RECALL THEIR
WEDDING DAY, WHEN THEY MADE
THESE PLEDGES TO EACH OTHER,
WHEN THEY WERE SURROUNDED
WITH LOVE AND GOOD WISHES
AND HOLINESS ENTERED THEIR
RELATIONSHIP. TEARS, APOLOGIES
AND RESOLVES TO DO BETTER
SHOULD FOLLOW.

Jewish equivalent of a marriage certificate and should never leave your possession.

The traditional *ketubah* outlines the duties of the husband to his wife, specifies the dowry she brings to the marriage, and safeguards her rights in this dowry and its increase, should he die or divorce her. In many liberal services the reading is abbreviated to an English summary, often accompanied by background music. There are some who consider this practice disrespectful. The text is a meaningful and moving description of the mutual devotion involved in marriage.

In one translation, the groom declares: "I faithfully promise that I will be a true husband unto thee. I will honor and cherish thee, I will work for thee and will provide all that is necessary for thy due sustenance, even as it becomes a Jewish husband to do."

The bride, in this version, says, "I plight my troth unto you in affection and sincerity and take upon myself all the duties incumbent upon a Jewish wife."

You may want to use a modern egalitarian contract, one that gives you both an equal voice and equal responsibility. If this is your wish, consult your rabbi, who will tell you which of the many available versions he will accept.

You can order a decorated *ketubah* from an artist-calligrapher, frame it and hang it in your new home as a cherished heirloom-to-be. After it has been signed, it is often displayed on an easel during the wedding reception.

All About the Ketubah

The *ketubah* is a document that, since the Babylonian Exile (586–536 B.C.E.) has spelled out the husband's obligations to his wife and protected her property rights. There are papyrus records dating back to 440 B.C.E., written in Aramaic, that indicate the bride price and the dowry contributed by both bride and groom, and in addition, name the wife as the heir to the estate, should the husband die.

By the first century C.E., this "bill of sale" became a contract that gave women legal status in the event of a divorce or the death of the husband and defined his basic obligations to his wife: to provide

her with food, clothing and conjugal rights. No romance, no love-birds cooing in the moonlight, just the rock-bottom essentials of a household and a shared life.

The properly signed and witnessed document was given to the bride, who was instructed to keep it in her possession at all times, since there could be no marital relations if it was lost or destroyed. And so the contract became a cherished and respected accessory to the *mitzvah* of marriage. Over the centuries it has been lovingly illuminated and ornamented in keeping with the concept of *hiddur mitzvah*—the beautification of a ritual object. Richly decorated *ketuboth* can be found in the great museums of the world, and are a miniature social history of their time and place. Some copy the glowing decorations of Persian carpets; others are embellished with symbols ranging from flags and crowns to the whole range of Jewish symbols, from the lions of Judah to tiny pictures of holiday observances. The ornate calligraphy is itself an art form worthy of study.

Joanne Fink

There has been a revival of *ketubah* art in our day. There are calligraphers and artists who specialize in custom-designed documents that are original works of art. Having your *ketubah* individually created for you can take several months—and cost thousands of dollars. There are also prints available from some artists who will letter in the names and places for you, preprinted forms with blanks to fill in available from Hebrew bookstores, and at the utilitarian end of the scale, a simple certificate given by the rabbi to the bride. As you might expect, the costs vary tremendously.

The traditional document is, for the most part, still the same as marriage contracts of the second century C.E. So what does it say? The text is written in Aramaic, and since it is required that the couple understand it, many versions also show the English text.

The Orthodox Text

On the _____ day of the week, the _____ day of the month _____ in the year five thousand seven hundred and _____ since the creation of the world, the era according to which we reckon here in the city of _____ that _____ son of _____ said to this virgin _____ daughter of _____ **"Be my wife according to the practice of Moses and Israel, and I will cherish, honor, support and maintain you in accordance with the custom of Jewish husbands who cherish, honor, support and maintain their wives faithfully.** And I here present you with the marriage gift of virgins, two hundred silver zuzim, which belongs to you, according to the law of Moses and Israel; and I will also give you your food, clothing and necessities, and live with you as husband and wife according to universal custom." **And Miss _____ , this virgin consented and became his wife.** The trousseau that she brought to him from her father's house, in silver, gold, valuables, clothing, furniture and bedclothes, all this _____ , the said bridegroom accepted in the sum of one hundred silver pieces, and _____ the bridegroom, consented to increase this amount from his own property with the sum of one hundred silver pieces, making in all two hundred silver pieces. And thus said _____ , the bridegroom: "The responsibility of this marriage contract, of this trousseau, and of this additional sum, I take upon myself and my heirs after me, so that they shall be paid from the best part of my property and possession that I have beneath the whole heaven, that which I now possess or may hereafter acquire. All my property, real and personal, even the shirt from my back, shall be mortgaged to secure the payment of this marriage contract, of the trousseau, and the addition made to it, during my lifetime and after my death, from the present day and forever." _____ , the bridegroom, has taken upon himself the responsibility of this marriage contract, of the trousseau and of the addition made to it, according to the restrictive usages of all marriage contracts and the additions to them made for the daughters of Israel, according to the institution of our sages of blessed memory. It is not to be regarded as a mere forfeiture without consideration or as a mere formula of a document. We have followed the legal formality of symbolic delivery (kinyan) between _____ the son of _____ , the bridegroom, and _____ the daughter of _____ , this virgin, and we have used a garment legally fit for the purpose, to strengthen all that is stated above, and everything is valid and confirmed.

Attested to_____ Witness _____
Attested to_____ Witness _____

The entire Aramaic text is read at the ceremony. The rabbi reads in English at least the sentences of the translation that appear here in boldface and may read more, at his discretion. Ketubah information courtesy of Ted Labow.

The Orthodox Text

ב בשבת לחדש שנת חמשת אלפים ושבע מאות לבריאת עולם

למינין שאנו מונין כאן במידנת איך החתן בר

אמר לה להדא בתולתא בת הוי לי לאנתו כדת משה וישראל

ואנא אפלח ואוקיר ואיזון ואפרנס יתיכי ליכי כהלכות גוברין יהודאין דפלחין ומוקרין וזנין ומפרנסין

לנשיהון בקושטא ויהיבנא ליכי מוהר בתוליכי כסף זוזי מאתן דחזי ליכי מדאוריתא ומזוניכי

וכסותיכי וספוקיכי ומיעל לותיכי כאורח כל ארעא וצביאת מרת בתולתא דא והות

ליה לאנתו ודין נדוניא דהנעלת ליה מבי בין בכסף בין בזהב בין בתכשיטין במאני

דלבושא בשימושי דירה ובשימושי דערסא דעסא הכל קבל עליו חתן דנ במאה זקוקים כסף צרוף

וצבי חתן דנ והוסיף לה מן דיליה עוד מאה זקוקים כסף צרוף אחרים כנגדן סך

הכל מאתים זקוקים כסף צרוף וכך אמר חתן דנ אחריות שטר כתובתא דא נדוניא

דין ותוספתא דא קבלית עלי ועל ירתי בתראי להתפרע מן כל שפר ארג נבסין וקנינין

דאית לי תחות כל שמיא דקנאי ודעתיד אנא למקנא נבסין דאית להון אחריות ודלית להון

אחריות כלהון יהון אחראין וערבאין לפרוע מנהון שטר כתובתא דא נדוניא דין ותוספתא דא

מנאי ואפילו מן גלימא דעל כתפאי בחיי ובמותי מן יומא דנ ולעלם ואחריות וחומר שטר

כתובתא דא נדוניא דין ותוספתא דא קבל עליו חתן דנ כחומר כל שטרי כתובות

ותוספתות דנהגין בבנת ישראל העשויין כתקון חכמינו זכרונם לברכה דלא כאסמכתא

ודלא כטופסי דשטרי. וקנינא מן בר חתן דנ למרת ברת

בתולתא דא על כל מה דכתוב ומפורש לעיל במנא דכשר למקניא ביה והכל שריר וקים.

Ketubah Questions

How do we know which text we may use?

Rabbis are very particular about the text used, since the ketubah is actually a solemn, legal contract. They generally use the text officially approved by the central rabbinical authority of their denomination.

Aside from the Orthodox ketubah, there are several variants that exist. Depending on your religious affiliation within Judaism, you might want to create your own Ketubah, using the following worksheet. If you find a variant text or translation you especially like, ask your rabbi about it. You will need to know if he will accept it as a valid document and use it to officiate your marriage.

Conservative Ketubot: What is the Liberman clause?

This clause, added to Conservative Ketubot, specifies that both parties agree to a religious divorce (a *get*) as well as a civil one, in the event that the marriage fails. This most important clause makes it impossible for a husband to refuse his wife a *get* and prevents the unfortunate situation of the *agunah*—the chained wife—which may occur if a couple decides to get married using an Orthodox ketubah. While this information may not seem too pressing at the time of your wedding, it is actually very important protection for the bride. Without it, she might not be able to get married again by a rabbi, should such a situation arise.

The Reform choice: What is an Egalitarian text?

This is text that gives the bride and groom equal responsibilities in the marriage—including financial support. It also includes poetic material and remarks about the Jewish home and Jewish marriage. It is sometimes used in Reform ceremonies, although other Reform rabbis will use the traditional Orthodox text instead. While the text is certainly modern, it is not accepted by Orthodox, Israeli, and most Conservative rabbis as a binding marriage document.

A Few Ketubah Sources:

IF YOU HAVE ADMIRED A FRIEND'S KETUBAH, ASK WHERE SHE GOT IT AND HER EXPERIENCE WITH THE COMPANY'S SERVICE.

YOU CAN ALSO START SHOPPING FOR A KETUBAH FROM YOUR COMPUTER. AMONG POSSIBLE WEBSITES ARE:

AOL-Jewish Community Store.ketubot

AOL ALSO HAS AN EXTENSIVE WEDDING SHOPPING SITE IN LIFESTYLES

YAHOO—ketubah.com

judaicconnection.com

ketubah.net

THESE SITES SHOW YOU FULL COLOR PICTURES OF THE KETUBOT THEY SELL AND WILL SEND YOU CATALOGS AND ORDER FORMS. SOME WILL SEND YOU COPIES OF THE TEXTS THEY OFFER. ALL HAVE 800 NUMBERS SO YOU CAN CALL AND TALK TO A REAL PERSON.

Which texts are valid?

Be careful! Variant Hebrew texts are often not recognized outside the group in which they have been used. Only Conservative and Orthodox texts are recognized in the State of Israel. Of course, your state's marriage certificate is legal proof of a civil marriage; the ketubah is your proof of a Jewish marriage performed according to Jewish law, or *halakhah*.

What if one of us isn't Jewish?

The question of providing a ketubah for an interfaith marriage is involved with many aspects of halakhah and logic. Reform rabbis who are willing to officiate at an interfaith marriage (not many do) can provide a text if you want it. Or you can write your own, with his approval. Some Judaica publishers can provide you with the art form with a blank text space, which you can fill in yourself, many will set up your text for you and insert it in the space.

Caution: this is not a legal, binding religious document. It is simply a poetic statement of your devotion to each other's heritage and a beautiful memento of your wedding day. You still need that legal, civil marriage certificate.

If I have an artist create a ketubah after the wedding, what do I do with the legal paper our rabbi gave us at the ceremony?

You can have the certificate incorporated into the text design, if you wish. Or you can regard your art ketubah as a precious memento and safeguard your rabbi's certificate as your legal document. In other words, if you want your art ketubah to be used as a legal document, order it before the wedding and bring it to the ceremony!

Storm Warning

BE EXTRA CAREFUL ABOUT THE NAMES, SPELLINGS AND OTHER HARD DATA TO BE INSCRIBED. CHECK WITH YOUR RABBI ABOUT THE ACCEPTABILITY OF ANY TEXT YOU CHOOSE. ONCE YOU PLACE YOUR WRITTEN ORDER, THESE DEALERS WILL NOT BE RESPONSIBLE FOR YOUR ERRORS AND MAKE NO REFUNDS FOR CANCELLATION OF THE WEDDING, OR NON-USE OF THE KETUBAH. AND DON'T FORGET TO ALLOW TIME FOR DELIVERY BEFORE THE ACTUAL DATE OF THE WEDDING, ESPECIALLY IF IT WILL BE ON A SUNDAY.

OUR KETUBAH WORKSHEET

Companies and catalogs consulted _____

_____

Design Chosen _____

Size _____

Price _____

Plus personalization _____

Frame _____

Company or shop name _____

Address _____

Phone# _____

Salesperson _____

Text chosen _____

Rabbi approves _____

Time needed to complete after ordering _____

INFORMATION NEEDED FOR PERSONALIZATION OF ANY KETUBAH

You will need to know everyone's full Hebrew name. If you have problems with this, consult your rabbi. If you or your parents were never given a Hebrew name or have forgotten it, he will suggest an appropriate choice for you. Start early on this bit of information. Initials are not used for English names; only full names are valid.

Names of deceased parents are entered. You may add the letters לז (Zikhronim Livrakha) (of blessed memory) after their names. Mark these entries.

HIS FAMILY

Groom's Full Name

English: _____

Hebrew: _____

His Father's Full Name

English: _____

Hebrew: _____

His Mother's Full Name

English: _____

Hebrew: _____

HER FAMILY

Bride's Full Name

English: _____

Hebrew: _____

Her Father's Full Name

English: _____

Hebrew: _____

Her Mother's Full Name

English: _____

Hebrew: _____

For Orthodox ketubot, the bride's marital status will be added: Is this her first marriage or is she divorced, widowed?

PLACE AND TIME

Ask your rabbi to fill out the information in Hebrew, fully and exactly as it will appear in the ketubah. It must also appear in English in the English portion. This data is of legal importance.

WITNESSES

Traditionally, two Jewish males over the age of thirteen, not related to the bride or groom, must sign the ketubah. Often the rabbi and cantor will serve as the witnesses. Other less traditional texts may include other witnesses.

And of course the bride and groom sign the ketubah as well. This is done before the formal ceremony.

ADDING SPECIAL TEXTS

In non-traditional texts, you may add passages of poetry—texts taken from the Song of Songs, Psalms and the like. If you wish to exchange vows in this way, discuss with your rabbi the content and placement of these readings in the ceremony.

TEXTS WE WOULD LIKE TO ADD:

_____

_____

Egalitarian Texts

Do you seek a *ketubah* that gives the bride an equal role to that of her husband in the creation of a modern Jewish home? Several different forms of egalitarian texts are available. In the text below, the bride and groom each speak the second paragraph to the other.

ב

בשבת לחדש שנת חמשת אלפים ושבע מאות
לבריאת עולם למנין שאנו מונים כאן במדינת
אמריקא הצפונית

אמר החתן · אמרה הכלה ·

לכלה לחתן
הרני היה

לי לאשה כדת משה וישראל ואני לי לאיש כדת משה וישראל ואני
אוקיר ואכבד אותך באמונה ובמסירות אוקיר ואכבד אותך באמונה ובמסירות
כדרך בנות ישראל המוקירות ומכבדות כדרך בני ישראל המוקירים ומכבדים
את נשיהם פיניהם יפיפה. את אישיהן פיניהם יפיפה.

אנו מבטיחים מגזגת זה לזה לשאוף ולהשיג את היצרות הבאות במשך חיינו
המשותפים: להגיע לקירבה וגלוי לב הדדי שיאפשרו לנו להתחלק ברגשותינו
ומחשבותינו הכמוסים ביותר: להיות רגישים ומבינים ותמיד לצרכי השני: להיות
שותפים לשמחות ולעזר בשעות צער וצרה: לעודד אחד את השני להגשמה
עצמית ולשאוף יחד לשלוה נפשית. אנו גם מבטיחים זה לזה להקים ביחד
בית נאמן למסורת ישראל ולאהבת עם ישראל, בית שופע הערכה לכל האדם;
באשר והוא משכן אהבה, חכלה, לפידה וצדק.

On the   day of the week, the   day of the month of   in the year 57 ,corresponding
to the   day of the month of   in the year   , the holy covenant of marriage
was entered into in   between
the groom,   and
the bride,   .

The bride said to the groom: The groom said to the bride:
"Be thou consecrated to me as my husband   "Be thou consecrated to me as my wife
according to the tradition of Moses and Israel. according to the tradition of Moses and Israel.
I shall treasure you and respect you with honor I shall treasure you and respect you with honor
and devotion as is customary among Jewish   and devotion as is customary among Jewish
women who have loved and cherished their   men who have loved and cherished their
husbands through the ages."   wives through the ages."

As we share life's everyday experiences, we promise to strive for an intimacy that will enable
us to express our innermost thoughts and feelings; to be sensitive at all times to each
other's needs; to share life's joys and to comfort each other through life's sorrows; to
challenge each other to achieve intellectual and physical fulfillment as well as spiritual and
emotional tranquility

We also promise to establish a home committed to our Jewish heritage and linked
eternally to the community of Israel; a home filled with respect for all people;
a home filled with love, learning, compassion and integrity.

All this is valid and binding

Witness _____
Witness _____
Bride _____
Groom _____
Rabbi _____

Text for an Interfaith Marriage

There is a text for an interfaith marriage that is not a legal Judaic *ketubah* text, but is favored by some couples as validating their joint commitment in "the spirit of Moses and Israel." Discuss the use of this text with the officiant at your wedding.

This Ketubah witnesses before God, family and friends that on the _____ day of the week, the _____ day of the month of _____ in the year 57 _____ corresponding to the _____ day of the month of _____ in the year _____ here in _____ the bride _____ and the groom _____ made this mutual covenant as equal partners in marriage. "With these rings we unite our hearts in tenderness and devotion. We will honor each other's culture as we link customs to form a trusting relationship. We will protect, support and encourage each other as we create a loving future together. May our lives be intertwined forever and be as one in faith and hope.

As we share life's everyday experiences, we promise to strive for an intimacy that will enable us to share our innermost thoughts and feelings; to be sensitive at all times to each other's needs; to share life's joys and to comfort each other through life's sorrows; to challenge each other to achieve intellectual and physical fulfillment as well as spiritual and emotional tranquility.

We promise to establish a home for ourselves and our children shaped by our respective heritages; a loving environment dedicated to peace, hope and respect for all people; a family filled with love and learning, goodness and generosity, compassion and integrity."

This marriage has been authorized by the civil authorities of the state of _____ and is in the spirit of the traditions of Moses and Israel.

שנת חמשת אלפים ושבע מאות   לבריאת עולם למנין

באו בברית הנישואין   החתן   והכלה

מ ש מ ח

THE SERMON

When the rabbi preaches a wedding sermon, it is usually done at this point in the service. You may also add readings or vows you have made to each other, ask friends to sing special songs to you or add anything else that is meaningful to you, with the permission of the rabbi.

Many passages from the Song of Songs are especially appropriate. In one ceremony, for example, the bride and groom read responsively:

Groom: As a lily among the thorns, so is my love among the daughters.

Bride: As an apple tree among the trees of the wood, so is my beloved among the sons.

Groom: Come away my fair one, for lo, the winter is past
The rain is over and gone

Bride: The flowers appear on the earth
The time of the singing of birds is come
And the voice of the turtle is heard in the land

THE SEVEN WEDDING BLESSINGS

The liturgy of the wedding service ends with the chanting of the seven wedding blessings (*sheva berakhot*) over the second cup of wine. The bride's veil is drawn back, and first the groom and then the bride sip from this cup.

In addition to the blessing over wine, these benedictions include praise for God as the creator of the world, of man and of woman, a prayer for the restoration of Jerusalem, one for the happiness of the young couple and praise for the Creator of ten degrees of rejoicing: "joy and gladness, mirth and exultation, pleasure and delight, love, brotherhood, peace and fellowship."

At most ceremonies, the rabbi or cantor chants all the blessings in Hebrew and English, but there is also a tradition of honoring special guests by asking them to read or chant some verses of the blessings. If you have a relative who is a rabbi or cantor, he may be asked to participate in the wedding service together with the rabbi of the synagogue or temple. The more people who participate in your wedding service, the more honor is shown to you and your parents.

The Basics of a "Modern" Jewish Ceremony

MANY COUPLES PREFER A SO-CALLED MODERN CEREMONY TO THE PURELY TRADITIONAL. TO BE A LEGAL JEWISH WEDDING THE CEREMONY MUST INCLUDE:

- THE COMPLETE WEDDING SERVICE
- THE VOW BY THE GROOM
- A PLAIN GOLD WEDDING BAND GIVEN TO THE BRIDE
- A *KETUBAH* SIGNED BY BOTH, THOUGH IN SOME REFORM GROUPS THIS IS DONE IN PRIVATE AND NOT READ ALOUD
- THE DECLARATION BY THE RABBI THAT YOU ARE NOW HUSBAND AND WIFE.

YOU MAY ADD TO THIS WHATEVER TRADITIONAL ELEMENTS YOU CHOOSE AND ANY READINGS AND VOWS THAT THE RABBI APPROVES.

The Seven Wedding Blessings (Sheva Berakhot)

1 Blessed art Thou, O Lord our God, King of the universe, who has created the fruit of the vine.

2 Blessed art Thou, O Lord our God, King of the universe, who has created all things to thy glory.

3 Blessed art Thou, O Lord our God, King of the universe, Creator of humankind.

4 Blessed art Thou, O Lord our God, King of the universe, who made man in thine image and prepared for him, out of his very self, a woman, for human succession. Blessed art Thou, Creator of humankind.

5 May Zion, who was barren, be exceeding glad and exult when her children are gathered within her in joy. Blessed art Thou, who makest Zion joyful through her children.

6 O cause these loved companions to rejoice greatly, as of old thou didst gladden Adam and Eve in the Garden of Eden. Blessed art Thou, O Lord, who causes the bridegroom to rejoice with the bride.

7 Blessed art Thou, O Lord our God, King of the universe, who has created joy and gladness, bridegroom and bride, mirth and exultation, pleasure and delight, love, brotherhood, peace and fellowship. Soon may there be heard in the cities of Judah, and in the streets of Jerusalem, the voice of joy and gladness, the voice of bridegroom and bride, the jubilant voices of bridegrooms from their canopies and of youths from their feasts of song. Blessed art Thou, O Lord, who causes the bridegroom to rejoice with the bride.

Note: These blessings are also recited during Grace after Meals at the wedding banquet and "sheva brokhes" meals.

1

Baruch Ata Adonai,
Eloheinu melech ha-olam,
borei pri hagafen.

בָּרוּךְ אַתָּה יְיָ, אֱלֹהֵינוּ
מֶלֶךְ הָעוֹלָם, בּוֹרֵא פְּרִי הַגָּפֶן.

2

Baruch Ata Adonai,
Eloheinu melech ha-olam,
she-ha-kol bara lichvodo.

בָּרוּךְ אַתָּה יְיָ, אֱלֹהֵינוּ
מֶלֶךְ הָעוֹלָם, שֶׁהַכֹּל בָּרָא
לִכְבוֹדוֹ.

3

Baruch Ata Adonai,
Eloheinu melech ha-olam,
yotzer ha-adam.

בָּרוּךְ אַתָּה יְיָ, אֱלֹהֵינוּ
מֶלֶךְ הָעוֹלָם, יוֹצֵר הָאָדָם.

4

Baruch Ata Adonai,
Eloheinu melech ha-olam,
asher yatzar et ha-adam
b'tzalmo, b'tzelem d'mut
tavnito, v'hitkin lo mimenu
binyan adei ad. Baruch Ata
Adonai, yotzer ha-adam.

בָּרוּךְ אַתָּה יְיָ, אֱלֹהֵינוּ
מֶלֶךְ הָעוֹלָם, אֲשֶׁר יָצַר אֶת־
הָאָדָם בְּצַלְמוֹ, בְּצֶלֶם דְּמוּת
תַּבְנִיתוֹ, וְהִתְקִין לוֹ מִמֶּנּוּ בִּנְיַן
עֲדֵי עַד. בָּרוּךְ אַתָּה יְיָ, יוֹצֵר
הָאָדָם.

5

Sos tasis v'tagel ha-akara
b'kibutz baneha l'tocha
b'simcha. Baruch Ata
Adonai, m'samei-ach tziyon
b'vaneha.

שׂוֹשׂ תָּשִׂישׂ וְתָגֵל הָעֲקָרָה
בְּקִבּוּץ בָּנֶיהָ לְתוֹכָהּ בְּשִׂמְחָה.
בָּרוּךְ אַתָּה יְיָ, מְשַׂמֵּחַ צִיּוֹן
בְּבָנֶיהָ.

6

Samei-ach t'samach rei-
im ha-ahuvim k'sameichacha
y'tzircha b'gan eden
mikedem. Baruch Ata
Adonai, m'samei-ach chatan
v'kala.

שַׂמֵּחַ תְּשַׂמַּח רֵעִים
הָאֲהוּבִים כְּשַׂמֵּחֲךָ יְצִירְךָ בְּגַן
עֵדֶן מִקֶּדֶם. בָּרוּךְ אַתָּה יְיָ,
מְשַׂמֵּחַ חָתָן וְכַלָּה.

7

Baruch Ata Adonai,
Eloheinu melech ha-olam,
asher bara sason v'simcha,
chatan v'kala, gila rina ditza
v'chedva, ahava v'achava
v'shalom v'rei-ut. M'heira
yishama b'arei Yehuda uv-
chutzot Yerushalayim kol
sason v'kol simcha, kol
chatan v'kol kala, kol mitz-
halot chatanim meichupatam
u-n'arim mimishtei
n'ginatam. Baruch Ata
Adonai, m'samei-ach chatan
im hakala.

בָּרוּךְ אַתָּה יְיָ, אֱלֹהֵינוּ
מֶלֶךְ הָעוֹלָם, אֲשֶׁר בָּרָא שָׂשׂוֹן
וְשִׂמְחָה, חָתָן וְכַלָּה, גִּילָה
רִנָּה דִּיצָה וְחֶדְוָה, אַהֲבָה
וְאַחֲוָה וְשָׁלוֹם וְרֵעוּת. מְהֵרָה
יְיָ אֱלֹהֵינוּ יִשָּׁמַע בְּעָרֵי יְהוּדָה
וּבְחוּצוֹת יְרוּשָׁלַיִם קוֹל שָׂשׂוֹן
וְקוֹל שִׂמְחָה, קוֹל חָתָן וְקוֹל
כַּלָּה, קוֹל מִצְהֲלוֹת חֲתָנִים
מֵחֻפָּתָם וּנְעָרִים מִמִּשְׁתֵּה
נְגִינָתָם. בָּרוּךְ אַתָּה יְיָ, מְשַׂמֵּחַ
חָתָן עִם הַכַּלָּה.

משמח

A Note on Breaking the Glass

THERE IS NO RELIGIOUS REQUIRE-MENT FOR THIS ACT, BUT IT'S BECOME SUCH A WIDESPREAD CUSTOM THAT IT HAS PRACTI-CALLY THE FORCE OF LAW—IT'S NOT A JEWISH WEDDING WITHOUT THAT FOOT STAMP.

WHAT IS THE SIGNIFICANCE OF BREAKING THE GLASS? SOME RABBIS EXPLAIN IT AS A REMINDER THAT EVEN IN HAPPY MOMENTS WE MUST BE AWARE OF THE FRAGILITY OF LIFE AND OF ALL HUMAN RELATIONSHIPS. OTHERS HOLD IT TO BE A REMINDER OF THE DESTRUCTION OF THE TEMPLE IN JERUSALEM, SO THAT EVEN AT THE HEIGHT OF REJOICING, WE REMEMBER THIS SADNESS—IN FACT, ALL THE LOSSES SUFFERED BY THE JEWISH PEOPLE.

IN ADDITION TO THE QUASI-RELIGIOUS INTERPRETATIONS OFFERED FOR THE CUSTOM, SOME PEOPLE REGARD THE BREAKING OF THE GLASS AS A BREAK WITH CHILDHOOD, WITH THE PARENTAL HOME AND WITH ALL OTHER

BREAKING THE GLASS

The rabbi makes the formal pronouncement required of him by law: "By the power vested in me by the state of _____ and according to the laws of Moses and Israel, I now declare _____ (bride) and _____ (groom) to be husband and wife."

In some communities the Priestly Blessing (colloquially known as "Y'verekhekha" from the first Hebrew word) is now invoked:

"The Lord bless thee and keep thee.
The Lord make his countenance shine
    upon thee and be gracious unto thee.
The Lord lift up his countenance towards
    thee and give thee peace."

Now comes the moment the world recognizes as the symbol of a Jewish wedding, perhaps because it is so startling after the solemnity that has gone before. The rabbi places a glass under the right foot of the groom, who crushes it amid cries of "*mazel tov!*" and a burst of joyous music that signals the recessional.

The groom may or may not kiss the bride, depending on the custom of the community. Among the Orthodox, it is never done.

THE RECESSIONAL

The couple turns and faces the guests and leads the way back down the aisle in the reverse order of their entrance.

In Orthodox recessionals, the mothers walk together after the

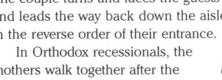

CANTOR AND/OR RABBI

FLOWER GIRL

MAID OR MATRON OF HONOR AND BEST MAN

GROOM'S PARENTS

BRIDE'S PARENTS

BRIDE AND GROOM

משמח

couple, followed by the fathers, the maid of honor, the paired bridesmaids and the best man and the paired ushers. Among Hasidic Jews the groom's young friends dance jubilantly, even turn cartwheels up the aisle in front of the newlyweds, to escort them to the room where the couple will retire for the *Yihud.*

UNION—*YIHUD*

The bride and groom traditionally start fasting at sundown the day before a morning or afternoon wedding. However, if a wedding ceremony is to be held *after* sundown, the fast begins on the wedding day and lasts only through the ceremony—perhaps only an hour or less.

After the ceremony, you and your new husband retire to a private room, where, in traditional practice, you break your fast together. This first light meal you take together is the symbolic consummation of the marriage. It is customary to serve a rich golden chicken broth—symbolic of the rich life to come for you.

These precious quiet minutes alone give you time to savor the events that have just taken place. During this brief retreat, you can remove your veil, keeping only the headdress. If your husband has worn a *tallit* (prayer shawl) and *kittel* (ceremonial gown) during the ceremony, as the Orthodox do, he now takes them off.

In Conservative practice this seclusion is also followed, though food may not be served to you. You may remove not only your veil, but the whole headdress if you wish. Your husband may put aside the hat he wore during the ceremony and simply wear a skullcap.

Apart from its traditional significance as the beginning of married life together, *yihud* does away with the tedious and time-consuming receiving line, with its repetitious greetings. For the guests, it also eliminates an awkward period of waiting about for the receiving line to end.

Instead, after you leave for your private moment together, your parents receive the congratulations of the guests and the reception begins immediately with champagne and hors d'oeuvres. There is enthusiastic singing and dancing to joyful traditional tunes. And then when you enter as a married couple, there is a triumphant fanfare, applause, and jubilant music from the orchestra. Singing and dancing

~

A Note on Breaking the Glass (continued)

PREVIOUS LIAISONS. THERE IS ALSO A SEXUAL CONNOTATION TO THE BREAKING OF THE GLASS, WHICH IS WHY PEOPLE THINK IT IS SO IMPORTANT THAT THE GROOM "ACCOMPLISH" THIS DEED.

A VERY THIN GLASS IS USED. TO PREVENT ACCIDENTS FROM FLYING SLIVERS, IT IS USUALLY PLACED IN A PAPER BAG OR A NAPKIN, READY FOR THE RABBI'S USE. SOME CATERERS USE A FLASHBULB BECAUSE IT MAKES AN EXPLOSIVE NOISE WHEN BROKEN, GIVING RISE TO MANY RIBALD REMARKS. TRY TO PREVENT THIS PRACTICE WHEN YOU MAKE YOUR PLANS.

IF YOU GO FOR EGALITARIAN IDEAS, YOU MAY WANT TO CRUSH THE GLASS TOGETHER. BE MINDFUL OF A SUPERSTITION THAT IF THE BRIDE'S FOOT OVERLAPS THE GROOM'S, HE WILL NOT BE THE MASTER OF HIS HOUSEHOLD. THEN AGAIN, THAT MAY BE WHAT YOU TRULY WANT!

~

What to Do with a Broken Glass

SWEEP IT UP AND THROW IT OUT? NOT WHEN IT'S THE GLASS YOU BROKE TO CLOSE YOUR WEDDING CEREMONY. YOU CAN TURN THE FRAGMENTS INTO A CHARMING KEEPSAKE BY MAKING A LITTLE WHITE SATIN BAG FOR THEM (MAYBE FROM THE REMNANTS OF YOUR WEDDING GOWN FABRIC), DECORATING IT WITH RIBBON FLOWERS OR EMBROIDERY AND FRAMING IT IN A SHADOW BOX TO HANG ON THE WALL. IF YOU MAKE THE BAG AHEAD OF TIME, YOU CAN WRAP THE GLASS IN IT FOR THE CEREMONY AND NOT WORRY ABOUT WHETHER THE PIECES WILL BE KEPT FOR YOU.

ANOTHER POSSIBILITY IS TO HAVE THE GLASS BITS ENCASED IN THE MEZUZAH YOU PUT UP ON YOUR DOORPOST. YOU WILL HAVE TO FIND A MEZUZAH ARTIST TO MAKE THIS FOR YOU. ASK YOUR RABBI OR SOMEONE AT YOUR HEBREW BOOKSTORE, OR POST YOUR REQUEST ONLINE ON A JEWISH COMMUNITY BULLETIN BOARD. THE PIECES CAN ALSO BE ENCASED IN LUCITE AS A PAPER-WEIGHT ON A PLAQUE. THIS IS A BEAUTIFUL WEDDING PRESENT TO SUGGEST TO SOMEONE WHO IS VERY CLOSE TO YOU BOTH.

friends may accompany you to your seats at the bridal table and shower you with sweets on the way. Let the feasting begin!

While the meal is served, you will take the opportunity to circulate among your guests and greet them all.

TRADITIONAL DANCING

Circle dancing to lively Hasidic and Israeli music is an essential part of the rejoicing. Even the most staid of wedding receptions comes alive when the first notes of these popular melodies are heard. Klezmer music is making a comeback, and most bands know many of the tunes. The sheet music has been published in several collections available at Jewish bookstores.

The climax of the dancing comes when both of you, the queen and king of the day, are raised aloft in chairs in the center of the whirling circle.

Orthodox men and women do not dance together. But you may dance with your father or new father-in-law or grandfather by holding the end of a kerchief stretched between you. Even at affairs where mixed dancing is permitted, this happy custom (the *mitzvah-tants*) is often followed.

Another tradition that is spreading from Orthodox to more liberal circles is the *mazinkeh-tants*, a special dance for the parents when either the bride or the groom is the last child of the family to be married. The parents are seated in the center of a circle, sometimes presented with wreaths to wear by the bridal couple, and all sing and dance in their honor. This is a unique recognition of the "empty nest" and the accomplishment of the classic Jewish goal—marrying off all one's children. Your parents will cherish this honor even as they shed a few tears of joy. The music is usually the Yiddish song *"Di mazinkeh oysgegeben"* (Our youngest child is given in marriage).

משמח

APPROPRIATE MUSIC FOR A JEWISH WEDDING

Brides of every faith have begun to avoid using the march from *Lohengrin* (you may know it as "Here Comes the Bride") and the Mendelssohn recessional as too clichéd. For a Jewish wedding, this music is particularly inappropriate. The *Lohengrin*, written by Wagner, a notorious anti-Semite, celebrates a mystical Christian union that was never consummated; the march from *A Midsummer Night's Dream* is part of a pagan wedding and the work of an apostate Jew. Not really the right flavor, when you think about it, no matter how conventional.

You have a choice of many beautiful Hasidic and Israeli melodies that are less trite and more suitable. The procession music should be stately, but joyful. Israeli settings from the Song of Songs are among the most popular, for example: *"Dodi li"* (I am my beloved's), *"Erev shel shoshanim"* (Evening of roses), *"Hanava babanot"* (Lovely one). Hasidic music has many lyrical meditative pieces that are used for processions and the *b'deken*. There is a trove of Jewish sheet music in Jewish bookstores and synagogue and temple libraries, among which you can find melodies for processions and dancing. It's not just *"Hava nagileh"* and songs from "Fiddler on the Roof" any more.

~

Increasing the Rejoicing

AT ORTHODOX WEDDINGS, THE INCREASE OF REJOICING IS A *MITZVAH*. GUEST APPEAR IN WILD COSTUMES, CLOWNING AND PERFORMING FUNNY SKITS AND ACROBATIC DANCING BEFORE THE BRIDE AND GROOM, WHO ARE SEATED IN THRONE-LIKE CHAIRS IN THE CENTER OF THE ROOM. DANCING WITH A BROOM AND DANCING WHILE BALANCING A BOTTLE ON ONE'S HEAD ARE POPULAR STUNTS. POEMS AND SONGS WRITTEN FOR THE OCCASION ARE OFTEN RECITED.

~

CHAPTER 6

UNCONVENTIONAL WEDDINGS

~

Fa-a-r Out!

YOU SAY YOU WANT AN ORIGINAL LOCALE? HOW ABOUT THE 50-YARD LINE OF A FOOTBALL STADIUM DURING HALFTIME? FIFTY COUPLES DID JUST THAT RECENTLY IN TALLAHASSEE, HOME OF THE FSU SEMINOLES. DRESS RANGED FROM SHORTS AND A VEIL TO FULL BRIDAL REGALIA. THE OFFICIANTS SURELY MUST HAVE BEEN FOOTBALL FANS!

YOU CAN HAVE A TRUE FAIRY-TALE SETTING (OR THE ULTIMATE IN KITSCH) BY CHOOSING DISNEY WORLD IN ORLANDO—SUNSET IN FRONT OF CINDERELLA'S CASTLE, A GLASS COACH DRAWN BY SIX WHITE HORSES, TINKERBELL FLYING ABOUT SPRINKLING PIXIE DUST, FIREWORKS EXPLODING FOR THE FIRST KISS, AND SO ON THROUGH THE LIST OF EXTRAS INCLUDING A ROYAL BANQUET. THE TAB AT THE DISNEY WEDDING PAVILION CAN RUN FROM $2,500 TO $20,000 FOR ONE HUNDRED GUESTS.

YOU CAN SAVE BY SPENDING YOUR HONEYMOON AT THE DISNEY COMPLEX! ONE TRIP COVERS ALL!

~

Some couples choose to rewrite the wedding service, to hold the ceremony at some unconventional hour (dawn, for instance) or to set up the *huppah* in some unusual place, such as a mountaintop or a deserted seashore. Your decision about the setting in which you will take one of the most important and meaningful steps in your life signifies your group affiliations and your attitudes.

CHANGING THE WEDDING RITUAL

Feminist-oriented brides often regard traditional rituals as "enslaving" or "male chauvinist." Many variants of the service and the *ketubah*, rewritten to be more egalitarian, exist today. The magazine *Lilith* (200 West 57th Street, Suite 2432, New York, NY 16107) and the Resource Center of the National Council of Jewish Women (9 East 69th Street, New York, NY 10021, phone 212–535–5900) have many versions you may want to copy or use as a springboard for your own ideas.

Be forewarned, though. Very rarely will a rabbi allow any changes in the ritual or the legal formula of the Jewish ceremony. These were developed over the centuries to make crystal clear the rights and obligations of both parties to a contract, to provide maximum security for both husband and wife, and to sanctify this legal relationship with blessings, making it a holy bond and an exchange of vows that is dignified, impressive and poetic.

CHOOSING THE SITE

You will probably not want to do as one couple did—they had their ceremony at the bus stop where they met—but if you depart from conventional places for parties, you must carefully plan every step so that your special day will not be marred by avoidable glitches.

BASIC QUESTIONS
1. Is the place reasonably accessible?
2. Is there sufficient off-road parking?
3. What cover is there in case of rain? Is there shade for a very hot day?
4. If your choice is a public park, do you need a permit? How far in advance must this be obtained?
5. Is there adequate privacy from wandering hikers, curious picnickers or uninvited onlookers?
6. Can you hold your reception in the same place?
7. Should you arrange a car pool to transport your guests from one central meeting place to the ceremony and then to the reception?
8. Sound carries poorly out of doors. Will you need a sound system to be sure the service will be heard? Can you rent this?

CHOOSING THE OFFICIANT
1. How much extra time will this excursion demand of him or her?
2. Will the officiant be agreeable to the demands of the site (climbing a hill, sailing on a yacht)?
3. Discuss your plans, including the refreshments, with your rabbi, to be sure he approves of your "original" ceremony. If the food is not kosher, some rabbis will not perform the ceremony; others will not officiate outside of their synagogues.
4. Who will provide the ritual accessories?

RITUAL CHECKLIST

❑ Tables and tablecloths (for *ketubah* signing and under the *huppah*)
❑ *Ketubah* and pen for signing
❑ *Huppah* and poles
❑ *Kiddush* cups (2) and wine
❑ Glass to break (in a bag or cloth napkin)
❑ Ring(s)

Et ceteras:
❑ Candles and matches
❑ Yarmulkes for guests
❑ Wedding booklets (See Chapter 3)

NOTES _____

_____

_____

_____

_____

_____

_____

_____

_____

_____

_____

_____

_____

_____

DRESS

Once you depart from conventional arrangements, you can decide on any style of informal dress you like. You can go rustic, ethnic/peasant, medieval, western, or whatever theme suits you. The bride usually wears white in the style she's chosen. The men will undoubtedly welcome the release from formal black and white and be happy to wear colorful, unusual clothes. Bridesmaids can be out-fitted in any simple, informal clothes you decide on. They, too, will probably be very happy not to have to buy an elaborate gown they will never wear again. Mothers may be unhappy about not wearing a gown, but when they see what beautiful options they have, they, too, may be pleased with the informality.

INVITATIONS

Informal invitations may be handwritten, or photocopied from a hand-lettered original on a colorful folder that carries out your theme.

Be sure you include:

1. Travel directions and a map. If it is a little-known or out-of-the-way place, note the travel time from some well-known point so guests can arrive on time.
2. Alternate arrangements in case of rain and a phone number for guests to call if the weather is uncertain.
3. Address and time of the reception, if it will be in a different location from the ceremony.
4. RSVP and information phone numbers.

Telephone invitations are neither proper nor practical, unless this is a last-minute arrangement. There's just too much information to convey.

REFRESHMENTS

If the location is not suitable for a reception buffet, plan to open a few bottles of champagne or wine to toast the couple after the *mazel tov*'s (you'll need disposable glasses) and have the other food and drink served elsewhere. Check to make sure, if it's a public park or greenhouse, that you will be allowed to serve alcoholic beverages.

Refrigeration of some kind for any food you are planning to serve is a must. If you are using a caterer, specify this. If you are doing it yourself, provide picnic coolers and plenty of ice.

Make the meal an elegant picnic. Have fancy salads, finger foods and little sandwiches. Remember, there may be no kitchen nearby, so don't plan on hot foods. Skip custards, cream sauces and whipped cream, as these do not keep well. Have a sugar frosting on your cake to avoid worries about spoiling.

You will need at least one table on which to spread your feast. Everything should be packed in advance. You will need:

- ❏ folding tables and chairs (if you have the transport)
- ❏ plastic sheets and cushions for seating
- ❏ plastic glasses, cutlery, dishes and paper goods
- ❏ serving pieces (don't forget the knife for the cake!)
- ❏ garbage bags for cleanup
- ❏ containers for leftovers

Do your planning ahead of time, but don't expect to do anything on the day. You and your mother should be honored guests, not servers. If family and friends are going to be your helpers, give each one specific functions for the day. One person should be in charge of the serving team; another *responsible* person should head the cleanup crew.

MUSIC

Shakespeare said it well: "If music be the food of love, play on!" Music will provide the mood you want.

Portable sound equipment will give you a wide choice of music. Check to make sure electricity is available. If it is not, use fresh batteries and bring spares.

If you have friends who play instruments, invite them to bring their flutes, guitars, accordions or whatever, and play for you. After the wedding, send them photos of their performance with your thank-you note.

PHOTOS

You will always regret it if you do not have pictures of the great day. If a professional photographer is unwilling to make the trip, or is too expensive, provide film for as many photographer friends as you can muster. You arrange for the developing and printing. Some of the pictures, if not all, will be superb candid records of the day. Your principal photographer will rate a thank-you note and copies of the best photos.

One caveat: Try to keep the photographers away from too much champagne. The plan does not include "tiny bubbles" in the photos.

INTERESTING SITES TO CHECK OUT

Besides beaches, mountaintops, and meadows, there are sure to be many interesting places in your area you may want to explore. You can choose from historic mansions or estates; museums or art galleries; college or university chapels, halls, or courtyards (especially if you or a member of the family is an alumnus); botanical gardens or greenhouses.

Some public venues are inexpensive and only involve getting permits, but some charge astronomical four- and five-figure rental fees—and that's before the caterers sharpen their pencils and start to write! The Metropolitan Museum of Art in New York, for instance, will cost you $35,000, and some historic places charge $3,000 for six hours. Fees elsewhere can range from $25 to $100 an hour.

Some institutions will let you use only their caterers or restaurant facilities. The rules about serving alcoholic beverages vary; so do the rules about amplified music outdoors.

The beauty and historical associations of a particular site more than compensate for the limitations the rules impose on you. But if you just want to spread a simple picnic on the green after the ceremony, you may have to search hard to find a site that is accessible and not regulated into stiff correctness.

~

Double Weddings?

IN TRADITIONAL PRACTICE, ONE *SIMHA* OR HAPPY OCCASION IS NOT TO BE MERGED WITH ANOTHER, AND SO DOUBLE WEDDINGS ARE USUALLY OUT. WE ARE SUPPOSED TO SAVOR THE REJOICING FOR EACH OCCASION SEPARATELY, TO MAKE THE MOST OF EACH HAPPY MOMENT IN LIFE. BESIDES, UNLESS SHE'S YOUR TWIN SISTER, WHY WOULD YOU WANT TO SHARE YOUR STARRING MOMENT WITH ANOTHER BRIDE?

BY THE SAME TOKEN, THEN, MANY PEOPLE REACT AGAINST THE IDEA OF SELECTING A BIRTHDAY OR A PARENT'S ANNIVERSARY AS THE DATE FOR THE WEDDING. LET EACH GREAT DAY REMAIN SEPARATE AND SPECIAL.

~

OPTIONS FOR THE WEEKEND WEDDING

After you recover from sticker shock when you see the estimates of some caterers, you may want to consider having your wedding at a country inn or hotel. Especially in off-season times, you can invite your guests to come on Friday or Saturday after lunch, join you at a prewedding dinner, stay overnight and enjoy a morning in the country before your noon wedding and luncheon, and still find the tab to be less than that for an elaborate, "main ballroom" affair in the city. You may have to trim your guest list down, or invite some people to come on Sunday just for the ceremony and luncheon, if the capacity of the inn or hotel is too small.

If you choose one of the kosher hotels that have services on the grounds, you could have the immediate family arrive on Friday afternoon, have a family dinner and hold the *oyfruf* at the services the next morning.

Your fiancé's family usually pays for the Saturday night meal and the *kiddush* at services; the parents may also decide on some equitable share of the Friday bill and other extras.

If you are observing traditional *sheva brokhes* (see Chapter 11), you can even stay on for a few days for that practice and for your honeymoon.

Did you first meet each other at a summer camp? Sometimes you can arrange to have your wedding there, pulling out all the sentimental stops and having a rollicking informal affair over a weekend.

WEDDINGS ON THE WATER

You can be married on a cruise ship, enjoy all the beauty and luxury of the public rooms and have your honeymoon right there— that is, if you don't mind having a thousand or so fellow passengers later teasing you as newlyweds. Of course, it's a kind of legend that the captain can perform a marriage—"'tain't necessarily so." Shipboard weddings are usually performed by one of the ship's staff.

Carnival, Dolphin and Norwegian Cruise Lines offer this service at any of their ports in the continental United States. It's especially appropriate if you're planning a civil wedding, since they provide a

משמח

notary to tie the knot. If you want to have your own rabbi do the full religious service, check with the cruise line and also make sure your rabbi is willing to come to the ship. If you number rabbinical students among your friends or family, they could officiate together with the notary and pronounce the blessings, while the notary makes it all legal.

The amenities offered range from a champagne toast (complimentary) to a full-blown reception with all the trimmings. You will enjoy all the elegance and beauty of the ship's public rooms at a very budget price. The cost starts at $500 for a basic ceremony and increases modestly with the number of guests and the refreshments you order. Some ships will even serve a sit-down luncheon at a really moderate cost for such an up-scale setting.

There are a few drawbacks, however. The available dates coincide with the ship's sailing schedule and are always in the morning, often on weekdays. You may have to reserve very far in advance. The number of nonsailing guests is limited unless you pay a surcharge.

A cruise ship offers a unique "two-fer" combining ceremony and honeymoon. And you don't have to take your rabbi along on the cruise. Or a hundred wedding guests!

Other boat possibilities are a chartered yacht, a party boat, or a harbor cruise line. The trip around the harbor at dusk as the lights go on all over the city can be almost magical, and you can have the whole ship to yourself, if you reserve far enough ahead, since most of these ships are not very large. Second best is to have a whole deck reserved exclusively for your party.

Don't try to combine sailing with your ceremony if you or your fiancé get seasick easily! In any case, have Dramamine on hand for motion sickness. (Remember that it's a bad combination with alcohol.)

SECOND WEDDINGS

Have you been divorced? Widowed? Your single state is considered undesirable in Jewish thought. There's no disgrace attached to divorce. Singles, whether divorced or widowed, are encouraged to remarry as soon as possible after a decent interval.

Legal Notes

NO MATTER WHAT PLACE YOU SELECT FOR YOUR WEDDING, YOU MUST HAVE A MARRIAGE LICENSE TO GIVE THE OFFICIANT BEFORE THE CEREMONY STARTS, SO HE OR SHE CAN CHECK THAT ALL THE FORMALITIES HAVE BEEN OBSERVED. USUALLY, THE BEST MAN IS ENTRUSTED WITH THE RESPONSIBILITY OF HOLDING THIS IMPORTANT PAPER UNTIL IT IS NEEDED.

ALTHOUGH YOU DO NOT HAVE TO HAVE A RABBI TO PERFORM YOUR CEREMONY, IF YOU ARE PLANNING SOME ALTERNATE STYLE OF WEDDING, BE SURE THAT THE PERSON YOU CHOOSE TO OFFICIATE IS LICENSED TO PERFORM WEDDINGS IN YOUR COUNTY AND STATE. JUDGES AND JUSTICES OF THE PEACE HAVE THIS POWER; OTHERS ALSO MAY BE SO LICENSED. DOUBLE-CHECK ON ANY "GURU" OR FRIEND YOU CHOOSE, TO BE SURE.

YOUR MARRIAGE WON'T BE LEGAL UNLESS YOU COMPLY WITH THESE REGULATIONS. THE INVALID MARRIAGE IS THE KEYSTONE OF MANY A VICTORIAN NOVEL AND ROMANCE PLOT. YOU DON'T WANT TO BE THE STAR IN ONE.

Your second (or subsequent) wedding should bring the same feelings of joy as the first. If you are part of an older couple, or if one of you has only recently been widowed, the celebration may be a bit more restrained, but as bride and groom you are honored in the same way as first-timers.

THE CEREMONY

The ceremony is the same as for a first wedding. Parents, if they are still alive, escort both bride and groom to the *huppah*. If you have no parents surviving, a close friend or relative may escort either one of you and also serve as best man or matron of honor. You can also choose a couple to escort you. They will stand under the *huppah* with you, as your parents would have.

A young bride may have as many bridesmaids as she wishes (especially if she is marrying again after an elopement and divorce), but a more mature bride usually dispenses with attendants except for the escort.

If you opt for a simple ceremony at home or in the rabbi's study and your parents are not present, you may simply take your places under the *huppah* before the officiant in the presence of your guests. You won't have a recessional then, but simply turn and face the company to receive their congratulations and lead the way to the reception you are hosting.

DRESS

No matter what your age, or how many times you have been married before, as a Jewish bride you may always properly wear white. It is a symbol of the solemnity of the day, not of virginity. A second-time bride wears a veil and a head covering (required in traditional practice, but optional in Conservative and Reform congregations). If you're a young second-time bride, you may choose a long veil and a formal wedding gown, even a train, if you wish.

If you're a more mature woman, you may be wise to go with off-white or ivory shades. They are softer and more becoming than

pure white. A shorter veil and a simple cap, or a becoming hat when a veil is not required, are also good choices. More sophisticated dress is also in order, ranging from a soft suit or a street-length cocktail dress to a full-length dinner dress. No matter how slender and petite you are, it may be best to leave the miniskirts, ruffles and flounces to the very young.

The groom and the other members of the bridal party dress according to the time of day and the formality of the occasion.

PAYING FOR THE SECOND WEDDING

A mature bride and groom may decide to share the costs of their wedding, or the groom, as host, may pay for everything. Parents of the bride do not usually pay for a second wedding unless the bride is a very young woman or the couple cannot assume all of the costs themselves.

Flowers, music, food and drink may be as elaborate as you wish. A joyful reception is in the best tradition.

YOUR CHILDREN AT YOUR SECOND WEDDING

Should your children be present when you marry again? Yes, no and maybe.

In some Sephardic communities, the children of a remarrying couple are excluded from the wedding. But in most communities, the children are happily present as guests, or even attendants, if they are old enough.

The "maybe" depends on sensitively perceived feelings. When there has been a divorce, the spouse who has custody may sometimes object to the child's attending the wedding of an "ex." When a parent has died, the child may feel renewed grief and a great deal of anxiety at the prospect of having a stepparent. In such situations, children often feel a deep conflict of loyalty. Try to understand how your child feels and be guided by that.

A teenager may serve as maid of honor or best man, but a reluctant or ambivalent adolescent should not be dragged into being

שמח

an attendant. A younger child may be capable of acting as a flower girl or ring boy, but ask a caring relative to stand by on the alert for emotional or behavioral problems that may surface as the party goes on. Even an older child may be glad to feel the caring arm of a loving aunt or uncle as feelings well up. There is always some sense of sorrow and loss underlying a parent's second marriage.

If you can, by all means include your children in your plans. It will help them feel that your new marriage does not mean yet another emotional loss to them. The emphasis should be on making them feel attractive, loved, and part of the special happiness of the day.

FORMER (OR EX) IN-LAWS
Should your former or ex in-laws be invited to a second wedding? No—unless, in the case of a widow or widower, the first marriage lasted a long time and you have maintained a close relationship with the family of your first spouse. Otherwise, it is most unlikely that you would invite them, and when there has been a divorce, most inappropriate.

Courtesy does require that the in-laws of the widowed or divorced should be notified that a second wedding is impending, either by an informal note or a telephone call. If there are children, the grandparents obviously have a real interest in meeting the step-parent of their grandchildren. The best way to handle this is to host an informal social gathering at which the new spouse may meet that branch of the family. It is a gracious gesture to give such a party, when the wedding has been small, for all the friends and relatives you could not invite to the ceremony and reception.

TIMING OF A SECOND MARRIAGE
The timing of a second marriage is a highly personal matter, and of course, you should let your own emotions and circumstances be your guide. You might want to note that, according to Jewish law, a divorcée or widow should not marry again for ninety-two days, to eliminate any question as to the paternity of children born after a second marriage.

~

The Sages Said . . .

In Proverbs (18:22) we read: "Whoso findeth a wife, findeth a great good." You can generalize that "wife" to "mate" and it will be even more true.

And this you may want to post on the fridge (or needlepoint it onto a cushion) in your new home: "He who has no wife lives without joy, without blessing and without goodness." (Babylonian Talmud)

~

Formal mourning for a spouse ends after thirty days, but most people find that it takes almost a year to adjust to a new social life. The "decent interval" has by custom been about a year, roughly corresponding to the time lapse between the funeral and the unveiling of the tombstone of the departed spouse, or among the Orthodox, the rule that three major festivals must elapse: Pesach (Passover), Shavuot and Sukkot.

Older persons certainly need not unduly delay a second marriage because of "appearances" or the possible objections of their children. Remember that God said, when he created Eve, that "it is not good for man to be alone." Nor woman, either!

INVITATIONS AND ANNOUNCEMENTS

The protocol for formal invitations is the same as for a first wedding. For a small, simple wedding, handwritten notes are fine.

Small Ceremony, Large Reception

For a young widow or divorcée, the parents may issue the invitation. When the ceremony will be a small, intimate one and the reception a large one, the card would read:

> *Dr. and Mrs. Edward Gold*
> *request the pleasure of your company*
> *at the wedding reception of their daughter*
> *Elizabeth Stone*
> *and*
> *Mr. David Bronner*
> *on . . . etc.*

The couple's own invitation:

Mrs. Jonathan Stone
and
Mr. David Bronner
request the pleasure of your company
at their wedding reception
on . . . etc.

In this text, the bride, who is a widow, may choose instead to use her given name, Mrs. Elizabeth Stone, if she wishes.

A divorcée may issue her invitation in whatever name she has used after her divorce: Mrs. Elizabeth Gold (her birth name), Mrs. Elizabeth Stone, or in the older form, Mrs. Gold Stone.

To be slightly less formal, you may dispense with the honorifics (Mrs. and Mr.).

If you decide to send out announcements, mail them a day or two after the wedding. Follow the name style of the invitations. You may also send a release to the newspapers, if you wish.

PART TWO

THE NITTY-GRITTY DETAILS

RECEPTION

USHERS GIFTS (PENS)

BAND or DJ

BOUTONNIERES

TUXEDO

BRIDAL BOUQUET

BOUQUETS

BRIDESMAIDS GIFTS (NECKLACES)

LIMO

USHERS

RING

BEST MAN

BRIDAL GOWN

MAID OF HONOR

BRIDESMAIDS

PHOTOGRAPHER

CHAPTER 7

PAYING FOR THE WEDDING

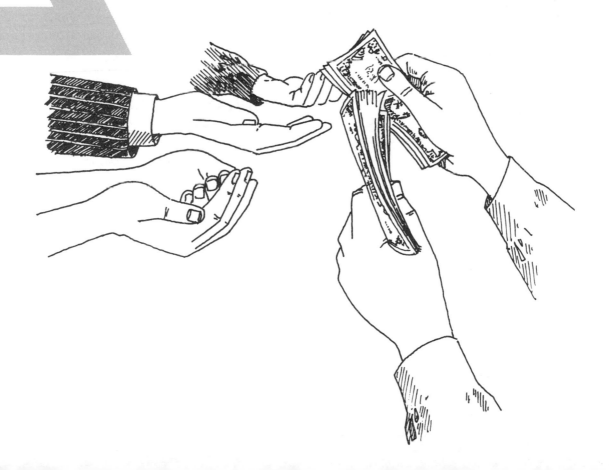

משמח

According to convention, the bride's family, as the hosts, pays most of the costs of the wedding. The two families sometimes decide to share costs, especially when the guest list is very large, or the groom's list is much longer than the bride's.

You and your family decide on the budget and type of wedding. Custom decrees that you may not demand that your fiancé's family contribute. They, in turn, may not ask for a more lavish reception style. They may offer to share expenses, but it must be done tactfully, so that there is no suggestion that your family is not generous enough or not able to live up to the hospitality standard of the other.

As a considerate bride, you will take your family's finances into account when you first make your plans, and also consult your fiancé as to his preferences. Your fiancé may insist on Spartan simplicity because he wants to escape all this female fussiness, or he may want an elaborate, full-scale formal affair because it will be helpful in his profession. There's a compromise possible in there, somewhere.

Your fiancé or his family should initiate any offer to share expenses at this very early stage, to eliminate friction later on.

WHO PAYS FOR WHAT (CONVENTIONAL ARRANGEMENTS)

The Bride or her Family Pay for:

the bridal gown and veil
the bride's shoes and other accessories
the bride's trousseau
the household trousseau (linens, kitchen equipment, etc.)
invitations and announcements, addressing and postage
rental fee for synagogue or hall and all incidental rentals
fees to sexton and to organist and any other musicians for the ceremony
floral decorations
bouquets and corsages for the bridal party (bride, her mother, bridesmaids, grandmother; her father's boutonniere)
gifts to bridesmaids

transportation of bridal party to synagogue and reception

tips for special-duty police, parking and cloakroom attendants,
    delivery people

all costs for the reception, including music

wedding pictures

wedding ring for the groom, if used

housing for out-of-town bridesmaids

charitable gift (*tsedakah*) in honor of the couple

bride's gift to the groom

parents' gift to the couple

The Groom or his Family Pay for:

the engagement and wedding rings

fees for the marriage license

oyfruf

Kiddush reception

fees for rabbi and cantor (if not included in the synagogue fee)

corsages for his mother and grandmother and boutonnieres
    for himself, his father and the ushers

the groom's wedding clothes

gifts to the ushers

housing for out-of-town ushers

rehearsal or prewedding family dinner

groom's gift to the bride

charitable gift (*tsedakah*) in honor of the couple

the honeymoon

the new home and most of its major furnishings

COSTS THAT ARE OFTEN SHARED
Flowers

Most grooms now consider the bride's bouquets and the flowers
for the bridal party a gift to the bride. They may pay for the bridesmaid's bouquets, or they may regard these as part of the floral decorations, and therefore the bride's responsibility.

Wines and Liquors

Many grooms offer to provide the champagne (traditional for weddings) and the other wines and liquors to be served at the reception as their contribution to the cost. Now that cigars are high-style, the groom may want to provide those for the male guests.

Wedding Pictures

The bride's family plans and pays for the photos, but it is gracious to ask the groom's family what photos they would like taken. They pay for any prints they order for themselves. Sometimes the cost of albums for both families and the couple is shared equally. If you decide to have the ceremony and reception videotaped, the cost is usually shared, since both families will want a copy of the tape.

You can cut your costs by having friends do the photography and videotaping, or by putting a disposable camera on each table and having your guests take pictures of each other and the reception action. You delegate someone to collect the cameras and develop the pictures, at your expense. You should get some wonderful candid shots (and some terrible ones).

Be warned, though, that unless your camera-bug friends are highly skilled (and sober), nothing takes the place of professional wedding portraits.

Sharing Per Invitation

When the caterer gives a per-person price for the reception, the groom's family may offer to pay for some or all of their guests. This is particularly equitable when the groom's guest list is much larger than the bride's, or exceeds the number of places the bride's family has allotted.

The groom's primary responsibility is for the costs listed above. His family may well decide to offer no additional contribution because of the expense of fitting out a new home and a professional office (if needed) and providing the wedding trip.

A mature and financially independent bride and groom making their own wedding arrangements often agree to share all the costs evenly between them.

WEDDING DAY GIFTS

Usually, bride and groom exchange gifts on the wedding day, often a piece of jewelry (perhaps a family heirloom) that will be a permanent keepsake of the occasion.

Traditional gifts of a *tallit* (prayer shawl) for the groom and Sabbath candlesticks for the bride are also often given by the parents on the wedding day. If you're handy with needle and thread, you might want to make an embroidered velvet or brocade case for the *tallit* that your husband will use every time he takes his prayer shawl to synagogue. And if you are a woman who also uses a *tallit* in prayer, you and your fiancé could give each other these meaningful gifts.

The wedding itself is a gift from the parents to their children.

JOYFUL *TSEDAKAH*—AN OFFERING OF THANKS

We are enjoined by tradition to give thanks in times of rejoicing by making charitable gifts. In the European *shtetl* it was the custom to invite all the *kaptsonim*, the poor folk, to the wedding and the feast after it. Nowadays, we make donations.

Many families give about three percent of the sum they've spent on the reception to Mazon, a Jewish organization that provides food for the hungry through food banks and meal centers. Many synagogues participate in this program, and your rabbi can help you contact this organization.

You can also make a donation to your synagogue or your favorite communal organization. Some couples, especially those marrying for the second time who have everything they need for their new home, even ask guests (via a card enclosed with the invitation) to make a donation in their name to the organizations they favor.

There are also a number of small, volunteer-run groups that practice *tsedakah* on a personal, highly individual basis. Called a

~

Responsibilities of a Divorced Father

HOW MUCH SHOULD A BRIDE'S DIVORCED FATHER CONTRIBUTE TO HER WEDDING EXPENSES? HE MAY COVER SOME, ALL, OR NONE. IT ALL DEPENDS ON HIS RELATIONSHIP WITH THE BRIDE'S MOTHER, WHETHER HE HAS BEEN PAYING CHILD SUPPORT AND ALIMONY, OR HAS MADE A GENEROUS SETTLEMENT AT THE TIME OF THE DIVORCE. THIS IS ALWAYS AN INDIVIDUAL MATTER, BEST SETTLED BY DISCUSSION BETWEEN THE PARENTS. FATHERS SOMETIMES PAY FOR THE ENTIRE RECEPTION OR THE HONEYMOON.

UNLESS YOU OR YOUR MOTHER HAVE HAD LITTLE OR NOTHING TO DO WITH YOUR FATHER, HE SHOULD BE TOLD ABOUT THE UPCOMING WEDDING, INVITED TO COME AND TAKE PART IN IT AND BE ALLOWED TO SHARE THE COST IF HE WISHES.

~

G'mach (the acronym stands for the Hebrew *Gemilut Hesed*—acts of loving kindness), the group collects money to help needy brides arrange a wedding and young families care for their children. One, Yad Batya l'Kallah, collects funds to buy all new household necessities for a bride and presents them to her at a shower they have arranged, so that a young woman on a tight budget is helped in setting up her first home. The recipients are carefully and confidentially screened, and the gifts at this "bridal shower" never seem like a charitable handout. As you contemplate your shower gifts, you may want to share your good fortune by sponsoring a shower for a young woman who really needs one. To reach Yad Batya, call Venezia Zackheim at 718–377–4349 or write to her at 1256 East 26th Street, Brooklyn, NY 11210.

Another unusual *G'mach* is Yad Eliezer, which runs a food bank, provides baby formula for the needy and arranges weddings for poor brides in Israel. Many couples, as they tally up the largesse in cash gifts they have received, decide to give a percentage of the money to Yad Eliezer. A thousand dollars will sponsor a wedding reception for a couple who could not otherwise afford one. The *G'mach* tells you the date of the wedding in Israel; thus, you can enjoy the feeling that through your marriage you have made another couple happy—and share in the joy of their anniversary and yours each year. Contact Mrs. Sori Tropper at 718–258–1580, 1102 East 26th Street, Brooklyn, NY 11210.

Your rabbi or local Jewish Family Services may know of other organizations of this nature. You may even want to start a *G'mach* as a project of your synagogue or social club.

CHAPTER 8

THE GUEST LIST

משמח

As all the decisions you make regarding the location and cost of
your wedding will hinge on the number of guests, your obvious first
step is to make up a preliminary guest list. Decide in conference
with your fiancé and his family on the estimated size of the list.
Start by counting in all the family members on both sides, close
friends of both families, business and professional associates and
perhaps even neighbors and family servants. The more the merrier,
at this point.

Sometimes people invite many more guests than they expect will
attend, letting the invitation serve as an announcement. Experience
shows that you can expect "regrets" from about 25 percent of those
invited from a large list.

It is customary to allow the groom's family half of the invitations.

What limits should you set when the list begins to balloon out
of sight?

LIMITING YOUR GUEST LIST
In determining your guest list, the basic rule to stick to is that no
one should be invited who is not related to, or does not know, the
bride, the groom or one of their parents well. Then consider these
specific limits:

NO CHILDREN
What age shall you make the cut-off point? Most people settle on six-
teen or eighteen as the age when a child rates a separate invitation.
Be sure you make this policy clear to both your mothers and to
anyone else who will be fielding inquiries about the wedding. If you
are making an exception for your little niece to be a flower girl, be
sure that they explain that she will be there only because she is a
member of the wedding party.

NO COUSINS OTHER THAN FIRSTS
Again, make no exceptions. If your third cousin on your mother's
side is a close friend, either have her serve as a bridesmaid or be

prepared to invite all the other "remotes." You will have to face a lot of music (of the chin variety) if you don't.

NO COLLEAGUES

This is a sticky one. Your parents may want to invite business partners or associates they have known for years. But can you really host your parents' associates along with all the people in your office or department—and your fiancé's associates as well? Most people will understand if you announce that you're having a small family affair and will not expect to be invited.

"AND GUEST"?

Should you invite your single guests to bring a date? Yes and no. Engaged couples are usually invited together. Your bridesmaids, who have gone to considerable expense and trouble to outfit themselves, deserve the reward of bringing a guest. If others ask to bring a "significant other," you may suggest that you can only give them a place if there should be a last-minute regret or cancellation.

RETURN COURTESY

You really are under no obligation to return invitations to people whose wedding you were invited to; neither are your parents. If you think some people may be expecting your invitation, you will have to explain to them, very early on, that you are having a small, family-only wedding.

EXES?

If you've been divorced, you certainly don't want your ex-spouse or ex in-laws at your wedding. At the very best, even if your relations with your ex-family are fairly amicable, their presence is bound to be embarrassing to your new husband.

   If your parents have been divorced, that's another ball game. The ex is a parent, and should be there to take part in the child's wedding. You will have to discuss this tactfully with the parent you

live with (or are closest to) and try to reconcile your wishes in this uncomfortable situation. If the ex has remarried, his or her spouse should be invited, but of course will have no part in the wedding ceremony itself.

DIVIDE AND CONQUER
If your budget permits, you can sometimes invite a larger group of guests to the ceremony and a reception afterwards and then a smaller group to a formal dinner after the reception. In Jewish tradition no one is invited only to the ceremony. All guests are served some refreshments and wine at the very least, to wish a long and happy life to the newlyweds (to "make a *lehayyim*").

GETTING ORGANIZED
Start on the chore of writing up your guest list as soon as you can after you've decided on a wedding date. You will need it not only for addressing invitations and announcements, but also for your seating arrangements, your gift records and your thank-you notes. It will become a useful family directory after the wedding.

You will be combining the guest lists of two families. Set a date, at least eight weeks ahead of the wedding date, for your fiancé to give you his family's completed list, with full names, addresses with zip codes, phone numbers, and some notation as to relationship. (Is Mr. Green an uncle or a business partner?)

At the same time, assemble your own list, making the same notations.

For a large list, a card file is the most flexible way to organize. You will need a file box, plenty of file cards and at least two sets of alphabetical dividers. Using different color cards for his family, your family, and your own business associates and friends is very helpful.

For a small list (under one hundred names), you might want to make up a "bride's book." It is more versatile and easier to use than a card file. After the wedding, there will be one slim notebook to keep, instead of a cumbersome file box full of loose cards.

∼

Invitation Checklist

ASK YOURSELVES,
SHALL YOU INVITE: NUMBER

PEOPLE WHO DO
NOT KNOW THE
BRIDE OR GROOM   _____

RELATIVES YOU
HAVEN'T SEEN
IN YEARS   _____

PARENTS' BUSINESS
CONNECTIONS   _____

PROFESSIONAL
COLLEAGUES   _____

CHILDREN   _____

NUMBER OF PEOPLE ×
COST PER PERSON = $_____

∼

Whichever system you choose, organize the list by first dividing the names into three categories:

Bride's list: family
                  parents' friends
                  your friends

Groom's list: family
                  parents' friends
                  his friends

Our mutual friends and associates

If you are going to send out announcements, each family should prepare a similar list for that purpose.

THE CARD FILE

Make out a card, as complete as possible, for each name on your list, using the appropriate color card. If you don't have different-colored cards, mark each card with colored pencil or with a code in the upper right corner. If you've decided to have a divided reception and dinner, add a note showing what group this guest is in. Your entry should look something like this:

KAPLAN, Mr. and Mrs. Philip
    350 Central Park West—Apartment 305
    New York, NY 10025
    Phone: 212-222-1000

R (for reception only) or R/D (reception and dinner)

_____ Accept or _____ Regret

Gift _____ Note sent _____

If you don't use separate color cards, use the space in the upper right-hand corner to note the guest's category—Bride, Groom, Friend, Relationship, Bride—Uncle Philip, Aunt Sarah, etc.

Note the indentation and capitalization of family name and the places to indicate the response, the gift and your thank-you note. Using these boxes will save you writing up another list to register gifts.

If you are planning to send out announcements, set up a separate section for this category and write up cards for your announcement list similarly.

Alphabetize each set of cards behind the appropriate divider. If the lists of the two families are not long, you may merge them at this point, if you wish.

You may also want to set up another category for the names, addresses and phone numbers of your suppliers as you decide on them.

THE BRIDE'S BOOK

To make a bride's book that you will cherish as the years go by, purchase a nicely bound notebook, alphabet tabs and dividers. Head each section and large divider with the desired category, then enter the names and addresses in a column down the left half of the page. Rule columns down the remaining width of the page for these notations: Reception only or Reception and Dinner (R or R/D), Accept or Regret (A/R), Gift, Thank-you Note (N).

Make separate sections for your announcement list and your supplier list.

If you prefer a smaller notebook, use the facing right-hand page for the notations next to each name.

You can even go for a looseleaf set-up, rule a page once, photocopy it as many times as you need pages, and go on from there. You can use different color paper for each category in the looseleaf, and you will also be able to photocopy the filled-out pages to give

your mother-in-law a set of names and addresses (so that she can help check the responses).

See the Bridal Record Book for suggested forms to copy for your own book.

As you write, think about each family. If they have children over eighteen who will be invited, you need a separate card for each young person. Invitations are never sent "and Family."

If some of the single people will be invited to bring a friend, note that on the card, so that you count that card for two guests when you make your head count later on.

In your bride's book you may want to keep a copy of your menu, with notes about the food. When you plan your next big party you'll recall that the baked Alaska was delicious or that the Chinese tidbits were a disaster.

A Typical Page in a Bride's Book

```
BRIDE'S FAMILY
                              R/D  A/R  Gift            Note Sent
GREEN, Mr. and Mrs. Charles    D    A   Cut Glass Bowl  11/17/97
201 West Chestnut Street
Chicago, IL 60610
(R—Uncle Charles, Aunt Sarah)
312–864–8084

SCHWARTZ, Mr. and Mrs. Edward  D    R   —               —
350 Central Park West
New York, NY 10025
(R—Cousin Ed, Miriam)
212–423–9087
```

Checklist for Addresses

AS YOU WRITE UP YOUR ENTRIES, CHECK FOR "MISSING PARTS." DO YOU HAVE:

FULL NAMES— FIRST, LAST, NO ABBREVIATIONS _____

TITLES (DR., SENATOR, RABBI, ETC.)_____

STREET NAMES AND APARTMENT NUMBERS _____

ZIP CODES _____ (MISSING ZIP CODES CAN BE CHECKED IN THE POST OFFICE)

PHONE NUMBERS _____

CHAPTER 9

INVITATIONS AND ANNOUNCEMENTS

Since it is an honor to be invited to a wedding, many families send invitations to everyone on their lists, even when they live at a great distance and will obviously not attend. The invitation then serves as an announcement. This practice is very common in Israel. (So that's why Cousin Esti from Haifa sent you an invitation!)

Formal wedding announcements, which are optional, can be ordered at the same time as the invitations, in the same type style. You may also want "At home" cards done in the same style.

Your invitations can run the gamut from handwritten, informal notes for a small wedding to formal engraved folders for a large function. As soon as you have an estimate of the number of guests, order your formal invitations—at least three months ahead of the wedding date. Why? Because the printing will take about four weeks and invitations should be mailed out at least four weeks before the wedding, and you will need time to address and mail them.

Informal invitations should also be mailed four weeks ahead, though if you are making arrangements on short notice, two weeks ahead will do. For June or holiday weekend weddings, six weeks' notice to your guests is prudent.

WORDING THE FORMAL INVITATION

Almost any large stationer or department store can show you catalogs of invitations and announcements to browse through. If you're not going for custom engraving, you will find the same group of catalogs in every large shop. They are put out by a small group of printing giants who dominate the field and show predesigned cards of many types. Often the text is pre-set and only the facts need to be filled in. There is also a selection of customizing features you can order.

A fine stationer has a trained staff that can help you with suggestions as to text problems, but very few of them are knowledgeable about Jewish traditions. Unfortunately, you might find that a few of the "better" firms have been known to refuse to do Hebrew texts, to refuse to use the names of both families, or to allow it but refuse to put their distinctive logos under the envelope flap. Arm yourself with the information that's in these pages and then go around the corner from the "clitc" printer and have your invitations done, as you want them, by an invitation printer who will use your text together with his catalog forms, some from companies that specialize in Jewish-style invitations and Hebrew texts. You may be surprised to find out how much money you can save!

The most favored choice in printing today is thermography, which you may recognize as "raised type." It is hardly distinguishable from real engraving, except for the bill.

Calligraphy, that elegant penmanship art, is now available on computer typefaces that actually look handwritten. It comes close to what used to be the most expensive form of invitation. Many invitation printers provide this service, or, if you have the software, you can do it yourself.

Flat or offset printing is the least expensive, but also the least impressive. You may have to find a private printer for this, since catalog printers may not do this on the ground that it lacks elegance. If you're good with computers, you could set your invitation up in one of the ornamental typefaces available in your word processing program, print out a specimen and have it photocopied onto suitable card stock at a copy shop. This allows you flexibility, but it is really suitable only for informal invitations. Be sure to check for matching envelopes before you embark on this project. There is still no vogue for postcard invitations!

JEWISH TRADITIONAL FORMAL STYLE

The traditional Jewish wedding invitation is written in Hebrew and English. The names of both families appear as hosts in the set form, which incorporates many blessings. Where can you find a Hebrew text? You can have it hand-lettered with the traditional embellishments by a Hebrew scribe (a *sofer*) or a calligrapher, order it from the one or two invitation houses that have stock Hebrew plates, or, if Hebrew type is available in your area, have it set up in type for the invitation house to use in your thermographed invitation.

You can take a stab at setting it up yourself if you have computer skills. Many software programs have a set of Hebrew characters in the character map. But this is tricky to use—unless you are familiar

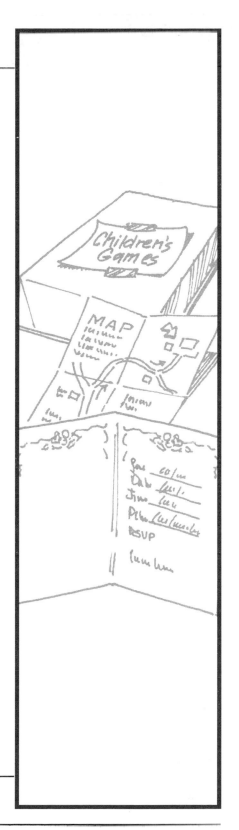

משמח

Panic-Stopper

AS SOON AS YOU ORDER YOUR INVITATIONS, ASK THE PRINTER TO GIVE YOU THE ENVELOPES, SO YOU CAN START ADDRESSING THEM WHILE THE CARDS ARE BEING MADE. YOU WILL NEED TWO SETS—THE OUTSIDE ENVELOPES (THE ONES WITH GLUE ON THE FLAPS) AND THE INSIDE ENVELOPES (WITHOUT GLUE ON THE FLAPS). ORDER SOME EXTRAS TO ALLOW FOR THE INEVITABLE MISTAKES. KEEP THE ADDRESSED ENVELOPES IN ALPHABETICAL ORDER AS YOU WORK, AND KEEP EACH SET IN ITS OWN BOX.

TAKE AN ENVELOPE COMPLETE WITH ALL THE INSERTIONS TO THE POST OFFICE AND CHECK TO SEE WHAT THE POSTAGE COST WILL BE. CHECK OUT THE OVERSEAS POSTAGE IF YOU'RE SENDING INVITATIONS ABROAD. THEN ORDER THE STAMPS YOU WILL NEED FOR THE MAILING AND FOR THE REPLY CARD, IF YOU ARE USING ONE.

YOU CAN SELECT A SPECIAL STAMP, SUCH AS THE "LOVE" DESIGN, WHEN YOU ORDER IN ADVANCE.

AN EXTRA-SPECIAL HINT: THE POST OFFICE WILL NOW DELIVER STAMPS TO YOUR HOME A FEW DAYS AFTER YOU ORDER THEM. USE THE ORDER FORM THEY GIVE YOU IN THE POST OFFICE.

with the Hebrew text and agile enough to set it up so that the text reads right to left!

With the Hebrew text in hand, you can proceed to the English text, which combines Hebrew tradition with a variant form of the usual formal invitation. You can use either of these forms:

> *Mr. and Mrs. Samuel Sherman*
> *and*
> *Mr. and Mrs. Jonas Goldsmith*
> *request the honour* of your presence*
> *at the marriage of their children*
> *Abigail*
> *and***
> *Daniel*
> *on Sunday, the eleventh of June*
> *at half after four o'clock*
> *Congregation Shearith Israel*
> *Two West Seventieth Street*
> *New York*

*The British spelling is preferred in formal invitations.
**(Note "and")

or:

> *Mr. and Mrs. Samuel Sherman*
> *request the honour of your presence*
> *at the marriage of their daughter*
> *Abigail*
> *to**
> *Mr. Daniel Goldsmith*
> *son of Mr. and Mrs. Jonas Goldsmith*
> *on, etc. . . .*

*(note "to")

Another possible, but less usual, arrangement of the English text parallels the Hebrew on the facing page this way:

> *Mr. and Mrs. Samuel Sherman and Mr. and Mrs. Jonas Goldsmith*
> *request the honour of your presence*
> *at the marriage of their children*
> *Abigail and Daniel*

If there will be a traditional pre-ceremony reception for the groom and the bride, the time of the ceremony is sometimes added after the announced assembly time, as *"Huppah at _____ o'clock."*

Note that the Hebrew and English texts have been given equal status by placing the two texts on facing inside pages of the folder. Or you may decide to put them on two consecutive pages, in which

Dr. and Mrs. Jack D. Morgenstern
Mr. and Mrs. Morris M. Goldberger
request the honour of your presence
at the marriage of their children
Rhoda Fran
and
Nathan
Tuesday evening, the eighteenth of December
nineteen hundred and seventy-nine
at seven o'clock
ZOA House
Daniel Frisch corner Ibn Gvirol
Tel-Aviv
chupah prompt at seven

בעזהשי"ת

ברוב פלא שמחה וברוב תודה לה'
מתכבדים אנו להזמין את כבודכם
להשתתף בשמחת כלולות בנינו היקרים

העלמה הכלה המהוללה   החתן המעולה
רבקה פרידא תחי'   נתן ני"ו

שיתקיים אי"ה לחיל טוב בשעה טובה ומוצלחת
אור ליום רביעי, כ"ט כסלו, תש"ם
נר חמישי של חנוכה
בשעה שבע בערב

בבית ציוני אמריקה
דניאל פריש 1 (פנת אבן גבירול)
תל-אביב

הורי החתן   הורי הכלה
משה ושרה   יעקב ודבורה
גולדברגר   מורגענשטירן
                   רהובות

case you will have to decide which is to come first. If you want the English first, have that printed on page one and the Hebrew on page three, so that the folder opens from right to left, in the usual book order. If the Hebrew is to come first, reverse the order, with the Hebrew on page four and the English on page two, so that the folder opens from left to right (Hebrew book order). If you find this altogether confusing, fold a sheet of paper and play with it. You will soon see how it works.

If you decide to go with the side-by-side arrangement, you can have an ornamental cover design on page one. The artwork usually incorporates the Hebrew letters of a line from the Wedding Blessings and the first names of the bride and groom. On a large invitation that will be folded in half again before insertion into the envelope, the artwork can be placed on the overleaf.

There is also a parallel-column style, with the Hebrew and English texts side by side on one page. You need a skilled hand for this, because the number of lines must be the same on each side.

Great, you say. I want all this. Now where do I find the people to do it? Ask at your Hebrew bookstore, look through the classified advertising pages of Jewish newspapers or look in the yellow pages of the phone book under "invitations" and "calligraphers." One printer-publisher who does excellent and tasteful work in this field is Art Scroll Printing Corporation, 27 West 24th Street, New York, NY 10010. Their catalog shows a wide choice of Hebrew typefaces and many unusual embellishments.

CONVENTIONAL FORMAL STYLE

In conventional formal style, only the names of the bride's parents appear as hosts; the names of the groom's parents do not appear. If your fiancé's parents want their names on the invitation even though a Hebrew page is not being used, you may follow tradition by using either of the first two English forms shown above.

The line "request the honour of your presence" is used for ceremonies held in a synagogue (formal religious occasions). When the wedding is held elsewhere—at home, in a hotel or club—this line should read "request the pleasure of your company" (a social occasion).

A conventional formal invitation would read:

> *Mr. and Mrs. Samuel Sherman*
> *request the honour of your presence*
> *at the marriage of their daughter*
> *Abigail*
> *to*
> *Mr. Daniel Goldsmith*
> *on Sunday, the eleventh of June*
> *at half after four o'clock*
> *Congregation Shearith Israel*
> *Two West Seventieth Street*
> *New York*

If all the people on your guest list will be invited to the dinner, you can eliminate one enclosure by adding the line "and afterward at the reception" or "and at the reception/following the ceremony" before the address where the wedding will take place. For example:

> *Congregation Shearith Israel*
> *and afterward at the reception*
> *Two West Seventieth Street*
> *New York*

VARIATIONS ON THE FORMAL STYLE

A less formal invitation using the names of both parents may have second and third lines reading

> *invite you to share in the joy*
> *of the wedding uniting their children*
> *Abigail*
> *and*
> *Daniel*
> *on, etc....*

or:

> *invite you to join in the celebration*
> *of the marriage of their children*
> *Abigail*
> *and*
> *Daniel*
> *on, etc....*

Note the use of "and" in these texts.

SOLVING NAME PROBLEMS

Special family situations may create problems in deciding how to style the names of the hosts and the bride. Check this table for solutions:

When	Use as Name of Host(s)	"At the Marriage of"
Divorced parents host together	Mrs. Martha Sherman Mr. Samuel Sherman (Separate lines, no "and")	their daughter Abigail
Divorcée hosts by herself	Mrs. Martha Sherman	her daughter Abigail
Divorcée has resumed her own name	Mrs. Martha Loewy	her daughter Abigail Sherman*
A widow is host	Mrs. Samuel Sherman	her daughter Abigail
A widower is host	Mr. Samuel Sherman	his daughter Abigail
A remarried mother hosts	Mr. and Mrs. David Rose or Martha and David Rose	her daughter Abigail Sherman*
A remarried father hosts	Mr. and Mrs. David Rose	his daughter Abigail
A relative not the bride's parent hosts	Mr. and Mrs. Arthur Davis	Their sister (or grand-daughter) Abigail Sherman*

* The bride's surname is given because it is different from the name of the hosts.

A deceased parent is not mentioned in an invitation although the name may appear in newspaper announcements.

Invitation Spelling Rules

No, it's not "i before e except after c." We know you remember that! These are the starchy rules for any printed invitation:

1. No abbreviations are permitted, except for the honorifics Mr., Mrs., Ms., Dr. and Jr. Military titles, when used, should be spelled out.
2. All numbers, except for very long addresses, are spelled out.
3. The time of the ceremony is spelled out. Half hours are styled as "half after" the hour.
4. The day and date are spelled out: "Sunday, the eleventh of June."

TITLES

If either or both of the parents have titles, such as Justice, Rabbi, Doctor, Senator, etc., their titles may be used in the invitation, as "Rabbi and Mrs. Jonas Goldsmith" or "Mr. Samuel and Doctor Martha Sherman."

If the bride has a professional title, her parents do not use it in the invitation since they refer to her by her given name only, but if the couple themselves issue the invitation (see below), the title may be used, as:

Dr. Abigail Sherman

and

Mr. Daniel Goldsmith

announce their marriage, etc.

Sometimes a bride or groom who is well-known by a professional name may wish to include it in the invitation or announcement. This is done by putting it in parentheses under the full name, as:

Daniel Goldsmith

(Danny D'Oro)

THE BRIDE'S OWN INVITATION

A bride may send out invitations in her own name when she lives independently or has no close relatives to act as hosts. The formal wording is:

The honour of your presence

is requested at the marriage of

Miss Abigail Sherman

to (or "and")

Mr. Daniel Goldsmith

on, etc. . . .

משמח

THE COUPLE'S OWN INVITATION

When a couple are hosting their own wedding, they may use the same form, or write:

Miss Abigail Sherman

and

Mr. Daniel Goldsmith

request the honour of your presence

at their wedding

on, etc. . . .

WHEN THE GROOM'S PARENTS ARE THE WEDDING HOSTS

There are some rare occasions when the groom's parents may be hosting the wedding—if the bride is an orphan, perhaps, or her family lives in a remote foreign country and will not attend. The invitation would then be worded:

Mr. and Mrs. Jonas Goldsmith

request the honour of your presence

at the marriage of

Miss Abigail Sherman

to their son

Daniel Goldsmith

on, etc. . . .

Note the use of "Miss" before the bride's name.

If the bride's parents will be present, but the groom's family has made all the arrangements, you may decide on the traditional formal style presented earlier in this chapter, using the names of both families.

Invitation Spelling Rules (continued)

5. It is not necessary to put the year into the date. If you do, it must be spelled out, as either: "One thousand nine hundred and ninety-eight" or "Nineteen hundred ninety-eight."

6. Spell out the complete name of the synagogue, hotel or club.

7. Give the full street address, using no abbreviations; spell out numbers.

8. A response may be requested by the abbreviation "R.S.V.P." or the phrase "Please reply." If no enclosures are being used, this request may be put in the lower left corner of the invitation, with the address for the response note.

ENCLOSURES

In Jewish practice it is not customary to invite guests to the ceremony only, since feasting and rejoicing are an integral part of the wedding ritual. Special invitations to the reception are usually not needed. If the reception will be held in a place different from the ceremony and the address is long, you may need to enclose a separate card—so that the invitation will look its best.

Separate reception and dinner cards are used when you divide up your guest list and invite everyone to a buffet reception—either, in traditional weddings, at the bride's or groom's table (*tisch*) before the ceremony, or, at other weddings, at a buffet following the ceremony—and then invite a smaller group of guests to a dinner afterwards.

Have these cards made up in the same typeface and ink as the invitations on matching card stock. You enclose them with the invitation. They may read either:

> *Reception*
> *immediately following the ceremony*
> *The Plaza*
>
> *R.S.V.P.*
> *90 Central Park West, New York, New York 10025*

(Note that the address of the place should be given if it is not a very well-known hotel or synagogue)

or:

> *The pleasure of your company*
> *is requested at dinner*
> *immediately following the ceremony*
> *Lakeshore Country Club, Glenwood*
> *Please reply*
> *100 East Chestnut Street*
> *Chicago, Illinois 60611*

משמח

RESPONSE CARDS

Once frowned upon by the "etiquette ladies," response cards are now very widely used because of their convenience, both to your guests and to you as a help in keeping track of your replies. The expense of printed envelopes and first-class stamps will prove to be a worthwhile investment. Even though a few of those invited may be inconsiderate enough not to respond, think of all the other phone calls you won't have to make! There are even some very informal invitations that include a reply postcard—although this may save postage, it's hardly classy, wouldn't you say?

Choose a deadline date for responses about three weeks before the wedding date, so that you have time enough to call the non-responders and give a final head count to your caterer.

When you use a response card, it is not necessary to put R.S.V.P. on the invitation.

TRAVEL DIRECTIONS

A printed card with travel directions to suburban or country locations is often enclosed. The caterer can usually supply these to you.

PAPER AND INK

How original do you want to be? How much money do you want to spend? Purists feel that only engraving or thermography on off-white or ivory papers in black ink is correct for a formal invitation. In slightly less formal styles, there are infinite variations of colored inks and papers from which to choose. Just remember that extras like colored envelope linings, oversize bordered cards, metallic inks and special monograms, decorations and die cuts run the cost way up. Prices can range from three dollars to twenty dollars or more—*per invitation.* You could be spending a good deal of that money on your honeymoon or on something special for your new home.

And be sure to ask, before you opt for purple or aqua or rainbow paper: Is there coordinating ink available for addressing? How much more will it cost to mail an oversize invitation printed on heavy card stock? When you multiply your postage costs by two

~

Coding Your Responses

THERE WILL INEVITABLY BE A FEW PEOPLE WHO RETURN THE CARD TO ACCEPT YOUR INVITATION BUT FORGET TO WRITE IN THEIR NAMES. TO AVOID THE HEADACHE OF TRYING TO DECIPHER WHO THE MYSTERY GUEST IS, YOU CAN CODE YOUR RESPONSE CARDS. YOU GIVE EACH CARD A PENCILED NUMBER INSIDE THE ENVELOPE FLAP AND PUT THE NUMBERS NEXT TO THE GUEST'S NAME ON YOUR ADDRESS LIST. IT'S WORTH THE INITIAL TROUBLE TO ERASE ONE MORE MIND-BOGGLING ITEM FROM YOUR LONG LIST OF LITTLE NAGGING DETAILS.

~

hundred or more, you can see how a small amount adds up. Keep in mind that the very finest, most elaborate invitations not only cost more than you want to think about, but the delivery time is about six weeks after you've given final approval.

INFORMAL INVITATIONS

You can save a neat little bundle by not using formal invitations if your wedding is a small one (under one hundred guests) or if you need the invitations on short notice. Your mother can even telephone relatives and friends and invite them in person, but it is always better to put the date, time, and place on paper. You should plan on giving people at least two weeks' notice, and the usual four weeks is better.

WORDING FOR INFORMAL INVITATIONS

Informal invitations are correct as long as they have a look you're proud of. The simplest? A handwritten note on a fine piece of stationery, using the best black or blue-black ink. Unless you're hosting your own wedding, you use the names of your parents as hosts. The note could read:

> Dear Mildred and Jack,
> Our daughter Abigail will be married to Daniel Goldsmith at our home on Sunday, March 12, at twelve noon. We [or Samuel and I] would be delighted to have you join us at this joyful ceremony and at the luncheon immediately following.
>
> Cordially yours,
> Martha and Samuel
> [Or Martha]

You sign the family name only when writing to those guests who are not intimate acquaintances or relatives. If handwriting thirty or forty notes is too much of a chore, you can have your original body of text photocopied onto fine paper and personalize each invitation with a salutation and your signature. Just be sure you have matching envelopes and ink before you start.

Here is an informal note using the names of both sets of parents. This invitation was printed in a cursive script that resembles handwriting, on a fine card, saving a great deal of penmanship exercise.

Note that it does not need personalization.

> We invite you to join us in celebrating
> the marriage of our children
> Abigail
> and
> Daniel
> on Sunday, March 12 at 12 noon
> at The Esplanade
> 400 Shore Parkway
> Brooklyn, NY
> Martha and Samuel Sherman
> Myra and Jonas Goldsmith

Still another variant:

> It would be our pleasure to have you share in the
> joy of a special time in our lives
> when our daughter
> Abigail
> will be united in marriage to
> Daniel Goldsmith
> on, etc.. . .
> Martha and Samuel Sherman

Note the even left margin here instead of the centering of each line.

If you're having a breezy, informal wedding in an unconventional setting, you can be as original as you like on these invitations.

INFORMAL R.S.V.P.

You do want a response, don't you? Reply cards are not used with informal invitations. You may end with just the R.S.V.P. or "Please reply," assuming that your guests will find your return address in the heading or on the envelope flap. Or you can give a phone number under the R.S.V.P. line. Just be sure you have someone assigned to answer the phone or put a welcoming message on your answering machine.

POSTAL REQUIREMENTS

RETURN ADDRESSES

Post office regulations and good sense tell us that a return address is required. Although this should be in the upper left corner of the front of the envelope, the post office will probably not refuse your mail if you put the return address on the back flap.

You may use the socially correct embossed return address. If you use an invitation stationer, you can order a die and have this done for you by the stationer, or you can buy the embosser and do it yourself. How strong is your grip? You have to press hard to get a clean, legible imprint.

Transparent self-sticking calligraphy-style labels are an attractive alternative for informal invitations. Be sure you allow enough time for your label order or your die order to be completed and delivered to you, whichever style you choose.

PROPER POSTAGE

If you did not check out the proper postage at the time you ordered your invitations, do so now. Assemble the invitation and all its enclosures, have it weighed at the post office and find out what the proper postage will be. Even the most elegant invitations will not be delivered if they bear insufficient postage.

The base first-class postal rate applies to a maximum thickness of ¼ inch and a maximum size of 6⅛" by 11½" for one ounce or less. Some invitations when fully assembled are oversize and overweight.

ADDRESSING INVITATIONS

Before you begin the work of addressing your invitations, or turning them over to a service to address them for you, run down this checklist:

- ❑ Is your address list in order? Check for correct spelling of each name.
- ❑ Did your order enough invitations (including keepsake copies)? You should have one for each couple on your list, plus one for each single name.
- ❑ Did you pick up all the envelopes (extras in case of mistakes and two sets, glued ones for the mailing envelope and unglued ones for the inside envelope)?
- ❑ Did you pick up all the enclosures? ❑ reception cards ❑ reply cards ❑ travel directions?

Do you have

- ❑ matching ink for addressing
- ❑ extra pens so friends can help
- ❑ return address labels or an embosser
- ❑ stamps—for reply envelopes and mailing
- ❑ a moistener for envelope flaps?

Now you are ready to begin. If you have decided to have the envelopes addressed by a professional calligrapher or a professional addressing service, the finishing touch for an elegant invitation, you now turn over your address list, return labels, invitations and enclosures and your stamps (or the cash needed for them, if the addresser will supply them) and have the whole job done for you. A pleasant luxury—but costly!

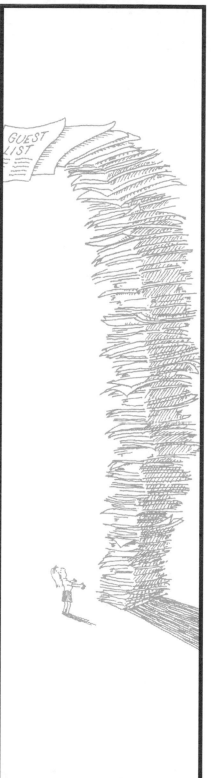

Postal Checklist

ENVELOPE SIZE: _____
WEIGHT: _____

FIRST CLASS DOMESTIC POSTAGE:
$_____ X _____ = $_____
(NUMBER OF LETTERS)

OVERSEAS POSTAGE:
TO _____
$_____ X _____ = $_____
TO _____
$_____ X _____ = $_____

STAMPS FOR REPLY CARDS:
$_____ X _____ = $_____

CASH NEEDED FOR TOTAL
POSTAGE $_____

IF YOU HAVE PROPER ID, THE POST OFFICE WILL TAKE YOUR CHECK.

YOU CAN ORDER SPECIAL COMMEMORATIVE STAMPS AND YOU CAN EVEN HAVE THEM DELIVERED TO YOUR HOME.

If you are going to tackle the addressing yourself, you can have your fiancé or your bridesmaids or friends help. A cheerful assembly line around the dining room table for writing addresses, folding, inserting, labeling or embossing, and sealing and affixing stamps makes the addressing chore go faster—and it's lots more fun! Plenty of munchies and coffee help, too. Just have the food served on a table far, far away from those expensive invitations. And for each invitation, do have the same handwriting on the inside and outside envelopes.

ADDRESSING PROTOCOL

1. Send a separate invitation to every adult couple and every single person on your list, and also to family members over eighteen living at home. (All the grown sisters and brothers living at home can receive one joint invitation, though.) The expression "and family" is not used.
2. All addresses must be handwritten, *never* typed, or, perish the thought, on computer labels.
3. No abbreviations are used, except for Mr., Mrs., Ms., Dr., and Jr. Use initials only if you can't discover someone's full name.
4. The word "and" is spelled out.
5. A correctly addressed outside envelope will look like this:

> Dr. and Mrs. Martin Singer
> 1400 Chestnut Street
> Chicago, Illinois 60611

Note the preferred indented form, very elegant on a large envelope. The block form (with all lines starting at the left) is also correct.

6. The inside envelope carries only the surname, centered, as:

> Dr. and Mrs. Singer

THE RIGHT TITLE—INSCRIBING THE ENVELOPES

Name Situation	Outside Envelope*	Inside Envelope
Dr. and Mrs.	Full names and address	Dr. and Mrs. Singer (no address)
Including young children	No "and family"—children are included on inside address	Dr. and Mrs. Singer Jonathan and Eliza
Family members over 18: two sisters	The Misses (or Misses) Julia and Alison Grant (on one line)	The Misses Grant
two brothers	The Messrs. (Messrs.) David and Jonathan Grant (on one line)	The Messrs. Grant
a brother and a sister	Mr. Paul and Miss Alice Grant (on one line)	Mr. and Miss Grant
Live-togethers	List names in alphabetical order, one under the other: (Miss or Ms.) Grace Ross Mr. Edward Taylor	Ms. Ross Mr. Taylor (no "and")
Married woman using own name	Mr. Stephen Black and Ms. Marian Weiss (both names on one line, joined by "and")	Mr. Black and Ms. Weiss
A widow	Mrs. Aaron Davis	Mrs. Davis**
A divorcée	Ms. (or Mrs.) Pauline Gold	Ms. (or Mrs.) Gold**
Two doctors	Drs. Paul and Edna Bloom	The Doctors Bloom

* The full address goes under the full name in each case, following the example on p. 134.

** When you invite a single person to bring a guest, you write "and Guest" on the inner envelope.

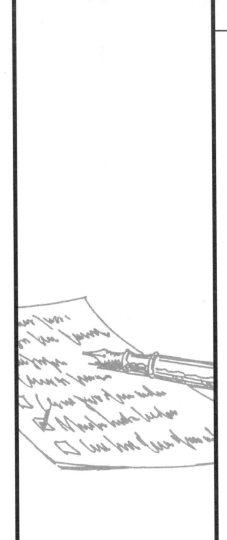

ASSEMBLING INVITATIONS

This chore is for the neat and nimble-fingered. You will receive your invitations flat, but scored for folding, with a pack of tissues to place over the type (this keeps them from sticking together).

1. Use a ruler or some other stiff, straight edge if you want your fingers to last through this process. Fold the invitation sharply along the score line with the text side out, unless you have planned to use facing Hebrew and English pages. Fold over any fancy additional flaps you may have ordered.

2. For smaller invitations, now place a protective tissue on top of the text, or between the two facing pages. Insert the invitations in the inner envelope (remember? no glue) with the fold up and the text side facing up as one opens the envelope. A single card invitation is inserted in the same way.

3. Fold large-size invitations in half once more, with a tissue in the middle. If there are no enclosures, go ahead and insert them in the envelopes with the fold up.

4. If there are enclosure cards for the reception or dinner, place them in the envelope on top of the tissue-covered text in the smaller size, or inside the second fold on the larger size, with the type facing up.

5. Now insert the folded large-size invitation, with its enclosure in the middle, in the envelope.

6. Put first-class postage stamps on the reply card envelopes, then put the reply cards under the flap with the print side up, ready for use by your guests. Put this kit and the travel directions (if any) in the inner envelope too.

7. Now close the inner envelope and put it inside the outer envelope with the inscribed side up as one opens the flap. Check to be sure everything that's supposed to be there is there. Seal the envelope.

8. Put the stamps on, after you've separated out the foreign mail. Sort the U.S. mail into local and out-of-town. Make sure the foreign mail has the right postage on it.

Bravo! You're ready to take the mail to the post office.

ANNOUNCEMENTS

The use of announcements is optional. If you decide to use them, you send them only to relatives and friends who were not invited to the wedding. As we have noted above, some families send everyone an invitation to serve also as an announcement.

You order the announcements at the same time as the invitations, and have them made up in the same typeface and on the same quality paper.

In the text, the year must be given, written out. The name of the synagogue or temple may be given and the city or state, if you wish. The announcement would read:

Mr. and Mrs. Samuel Sherman
have the honour of announcing*
the marriage of their daughter
Abigail
to
Mr. Daniel Goldsmith
on Sunday, the eleventh of June
Nineteen hundred ninety–six
New York, New York

* This line may also read "have the honour to announce" or "announce the marriage of."

ADDRESSING ANNOUNCEMENTS

Follow the same protocol as for addressing invitations, but cheer up— there's only one envelope, so there's no inside address to fret over!

Insert the announcements with the fold up, type facing up as you open the flap of the envelope.

You should prepare these when you do your invitations, but announcements are not mailed until a day or two after the wedding. Entrust that chore to your mother and mother-in-law. They'll love it.

CHECKLIST FOR NEWSPAPER ANNOUNCEMENTS

❑ Deadline date _____

❑ Will you use a photo? _____

❑ Photo regulations _____

_____

_____

_____

_____

_____

❑ Address to mail copy to _____

_____

_____

❑ Attention of: _____

❑ Fee, if any _____

❑ Can we order extra copies of the paper on the day the story appears? _____

_____

_____

_____

If you use a photo, identify it by taping a cover sheet on it giving the name of the bride ____married to ___ on_____ and a photo credit. For extra insurance, *lightly* write your name in pencil or felt-tip pen on the back of the photo, together with the name of the photographer for photo credit. If you do not want to be photographed in your wedding gown before the wedding, use your engagement photo, or any other picture of yourselves that you like.

משמח

NEWSPAPER ANNOUNCEMENTS

You can cover the same ground with a newspaper announcement. As with engagement announcements, check with the newspapers you want to use. Many have forms you fill out, making your life simple. Many charge for the announcement as a kind of ad, with an extra charge if you want your picture in the announcement. Local papers usually print every announcement notice they receive in time for their deadlines.

Some newspapers will allow you to use your own press release; however, big-city papers, such as the *New York Times*, will publish the item only if the family has some social, scholarly or artistic prominence. The story will not be published till the wedding has taken place. Check to see how much advance notice is needed. Follow the form of the wedding stories they have published in making up your own. You must include the name, address and phone number of the person issuing the story so the newspaper can verify the facts.

You call the society editor of the newspaper you plan to use for the forms or any other information you need.

SOME SPECIAL PROBLEMS IN WORDING ANNOUNCEMENTS

Shall you mention:

A Previous Marriage?
Yes. As:
"Ms. Taylor's previous marriage ended in divorce."
"Mrs. Berlin is the widow of the late Charles Alter of Denver."

Children of a Previous Marriage?
As you choose. As:
"He has two children by the marriage, Alice and Jeffrey."

Or

"She has one child by the marriage, Gabriel Alter."

Deceased Parents?
Yes. As:

~

Keeping Track of Your Replies

HERE'S A HINT: IF YOUR REPLY CARDS WERE DELIVERED IN A BOX, KEEP THE BOX. AS YOUR CARDS COME IN, DROP THEM IN THE BOX, SORT THEM ALPHABETICALLY AND CHECK THEM OFF ON YOUR LIST. WHEN THE TIME COMES TO COUNT THEM, YOU WILL HAVE THEM ALL IN ONE PLACE.

AND A HINT FOR THE VISUAL-MINDED: SOME PEOPLE TAKE THE ADDED STEP OF COPYING ONTO ONE LONG SHEET THE LAST NAMES OF ALL THOSE INVITED (IN ALPHA-BETICAL ORDER), POSTING THE SHEET ON THE WALL OR THE BACK OF A DOOR AND USING THIS AS A CHECKLIST. YOU CAN CROSS OUT THE NAMES OF THE "REGRETS" AND PUT A CHECK NEXT TO EACH "ACCEPT," THEN SEE AT A GLANCE HOW MANY REPLIES HAVE COME IN AND HOW MANY PEOPLE YOU HAVE TO PHONE.

~

"Miss Sarah Brown, daughter of Mr. (or Mrs.) Martin Brown and the late Mrs. (or Mr.) Brown."
Or, when a widowed mother has remarried:
"...married to Mr. Paul Silver, son of Mrs. Joseph Marcus of Chicago and the late Walter Silver of Denver."

Both Parents, When They Are Divorced?
Yes. As:
"Mr. Robert Lavin, son of Mrs. Mildred Lavin of New York and Mr. Arthur Lavin of Baltimore."
Or when the mother has remarried:
"Miss Marian Bloom, daughter of Mrs. Peter Abel of Albany and Mr. Harry Bloom of Buffalo."
When the remarried couple are named as announcing the wedding:
"Mr. and Mrs. Peter Abel announce the marriage of her daughter, Marian Bloom, to . . . The bride is the daughter also of Mr. Harry Bloom of Buffalo."

The Bride Keeping Her Own Name?
Yes. As:
"The bride will retain her own name professionally."

A Hyphenated Name?
Yes. As:
"The couple will use the name Bloom-Lavin."

The Address of Your New Home?
No, no, a thousand times no! If you announce plans for a wedding trip this is an open invitation for thieves to rob a newly furnished, unoccupied home. Exception: If you will be moving out of town, you may give the location, but not the street address. As:
"Mr. and Mrs. Lavin will reside in Denver."

CREATE YOUR OWN ANNOUNCEMENT

_____

_____

_____

_____

_____

_____

_____

_____

_____

_____

_____

_____

_____

_____

_____

_____

_____

_____

_____

_____

CHAPTER 10

WHAT TO WEAR

No Body's Perfect!

DON'T GIVE UP WHEN YOU LOOK AT YOURSELF IN THE MIRROR—THERE ARE MANY WAYS TO CAMOUFLAGE "FIGURE FAULTS" AND FIND THE GOWN THAT DOES THE MOST FOR YOU. THE GOWN SHOULD HAVE THE PERFECT FIT—NOT YOU! TRY THESE IDEAS:

FULL-FIGURED. A V-NECKLINE, WITH A BASQUE WAIST AND LONG, FITTED SLEEVES, IS MOST FLATTERING. WEAR HEELS AND A HEADPIECE THAT ADD HEIGHT. EMPIRE AND PRINCESS GOWNS CREATE A LONGER SILHOUETTE AND MINIMIZE THE WAIST.

WIDE HIPS. CHOOSE A FULL, BUT NOT A GATHERED SKIRT, WITH A BASQUE WAIST. AVOID RUFFLES AND BIG BOWS. LOOK FOR SHOULDER DETAIL TO DRAW THE EYES UPWARD.

Jewish tradition is quite relaxed about wedding attire. Wouldn't it be nice if *you* could be, too? While you are searching for the perfect dress that will not break the bank, reflect on this: Jewish brides have dressed in an amazing variety of apparel through the ages. While Ashkenazi (East European) brides have adopted the white gown and diaphanous veil common to European Christian weddings, Sephardic brides have worn wildly colorful costumes with veils decorated with a fringe of golden coins. The groom's dress has also varied. The only customs observed everywhere are the requirements of modesty and the desire to avoid excessive display that would shame poor guests.

Wearing bridal white is a custom that, over the years, has taken on almost the force of law. The bride's white dress and veil and the Orthodox groom's white *kittel* symbolize the spiritual purity with which the couple approach this important moment in their lives. Since the white attire has no connection to virginity or youth, it is appropriate for a bride of any age. On the other hand, you can dress in any colorful outfit you like.

THE WOMEN IN THE BRIDAL PARTY

All the dresses worn by the mothers, the bride's attendants and the bride herself should meet the basic Jewish requirements of modesty: no deep décolletage, no off-the-shoulder styles, sleeves of at least elbow length, and no miniskirts. Though a lace pantsuit may seem very chic to your maid of honor, it is really not appropriate for a woman to wear pants (even lace ones) when she is part of a religious service.

In Orthodox and some Conservative synagogues, all married women must have head coverings. These can range all the way from wide-brimmed tulle and lace hats to a bow, a few flowers and a wisp of veiling. In Reform practice, hats are not required. Unmarried women may go hatless in all denominations.

HERE COMES THE BRIDE

Before you get bogged down in the specifics of time of day and degree of formality, remember this basic principle: You are supposed

משמח

to enjoy your own wedding. Any outfit that constricts you or is uncomfortable or difficult to wear, whether it's a stylish waist-nipper that's too tight or a pair of shoes that pinch and burn, is O-U-T—out!

YOUR VEIL

A veil is always part of your outfit; its length and fullness will depend on the gown you choose. It must be made up with a face veil for the ceremony. And of course, you'll need a headdress to hold the veil in place. If you like, go for one reminiscent of the crowns worn by brides and grooms in ancient days. Or you can opt for just a few flower sprays, or go all the way through the choices of headdress to pearl or rhinestone tiaras. Just bear in mind that the headdress should not be so elaborate that it overshadows the gown, or be so imposing that your charming face disappears under it.

Wreaths of real flowers seem an attractive idea. In real life, however, they are heavy to wear and may wilt alarmingly in close quarters, no matter how much air conditioning there is. And watch those garden settings—your wreath of blossoms may attract all the bees for miles around! For a floral effect in your headdress, go for silk flowers. Light and pretty, the good ones really fool the eye.

If you opt for a full, long veil, have it arranged with Velcro on the headdress, so that you can easily remove it after the ceremony and keep the "crown" or the wreath on for the reception if you wish.

TYPE OF GOWN

By your choice of gown, you decide the degree of formality for the rest of the party. You may wear a long dress at any hour of the day and in any setting, but long veils and trains are suitable only for the most formal of weddings and the largest houses of worship.

For home and garden weddings, and in spring and summer, simple styles in sheer or lacy fabrics are most appropriate. For a daytime wedding, you may opt for a street- or ballerina-length dress. Long sleeves eliminate the need for gloves and add a finished look to the outfit. Your veil may be shoulder-length with a simple lace cap for the

---

No Body's Perfect! (continued)

FULL BUST. SWEETHEART NECKLINES, PORTRAIT COLLARS AND THE RIGHT BRA MINIMIZE THE BUST. HIGH NECKLINES ARE LESS FLATTERING. WEAR A LONG-LINE BRA WITH UNDERWIRES OR A ONE-PIECE BODY SHAPER.

PETITE. LOOK FOR SIMPLER STYLING, SO THE DRESS DOES NOT OVERWHELM YOU. AVOID EXCESSIVE BEADING AND LACES. SHEATHS AND SOPHISTICATED STYLES WORK BEST. ADD A HEADPIECE THAT WILL GIVE EXTRA HEIGHT.

SMALL BUST. START WITH A PUSHUP OR PADDED BRA. USE BOWS AND FLOWERS AROUND THE BUST AREA TO ADD SHAPE.

משמח

IN HER AUTOBIOGRAPHY, BARBARA CARTLAND, THE POP-ULAR ROMANCE WRITER, TELLS HOW SHE BEGGED PARACHUTE SILK FOR HER DAUGHTER'S WED-DING GOWN DURING WORLD WAR II, AND POOLED ALL THE CLOTHING RATION COUPONS SHE COULD GET FOR THE NECESSARY UNDERGARMENTS, STOCKINGS AND SHOES. HOW FORTUNATE THAT WE DON'T HAVE TO USE SUCH STRATAGEMS TODAY! THERE IS A WORLD OF CHOICES IN FABRIC OUT THERE.

FOR FORMAL GOWNS:

SATIN, TAFFETA, CRÊPE DE CHINE AND PEAU DE SOIE ARE ALWAYS IN SEASON. THE BEST QUALITY IS DISTINGUISHED BY A CREAMY TEXTURE AND HEAVY FEEL. LACE IS ALSO GOOD AT ANY TIME OF THE YEAR, EITHER AS TRIM OR AS THE ENTIRE GOWN. SINCE IT IS SO SHEER IT WILL REQUIRE LINING.

AT WINTER WEDDINGS YOU CAN GO FOR BROCADE, BEADED FABRICS OR VELVET. WATCH OUT FOR VELVET, THOUGH—THE SMOOTH, PLUSHY KIND HAS A REGRETTABLE TENDENCY TO

shorter dresses, fingertip or floor length for long dresses. Using a pouf of tulle for the face veil will add an airy look to a fingertip veil.

For a semiformal late afternoon or evening wedding you may use a sweep train—one that trails just a few inches on the floor. The veil should be floor length or just as long as the back sweep of the dress.

For a formal evening wedding you can go all out with a bouffant gown with a train and a full veil to match. The train should not be too long for the place you've chosen—cathedral length, which runs about twenty-two inches behind you, belongs in a cathedral, not in the little *shul* around the corner! The best choice in long trains is one that is detachable, by the magic of Velcro, so that you are free to move around after the ceremony and are not burdened with carrying it over your arm or bunched up in a bustle behind you.

If you've found a dress you adore but the neck is too low or the sleeves too short, a fine store can have a seamstress add lace or tulle; a very sheer yoke can be made more modest by lining it, and sleeves can usually be added. Just remember that alterations are expensive. When you find out what it will cost to modify the dress, your love of that dress may vanish.

Bridal shops in Orthodox communities specialize in styles that meet the requirements of modesty without alterations. The long sleeves do away with any need for gloves, which are just a nuisance during the ceremony.

Select the bra and slip you intend to wear with your dress and wear it to your fittings. The right bra, especially, can make a big dif-ference in the way a dress fits. If the style calls for a crinoline or stiffened underskirt, that usually comes with the dress, though it may be an expensive extra that you just have to have.

THE BRIDE'S HANDBAG

You will not carry a handbag during the procession or the ceremony, but you will need a bag, perhaps even two. You will want a small, dressy white bag (a beaded one is especially pretty) in which to carry your personal things—lipstick, mirror, comb, tissues for the tears of joy and the like. Leave this in the bridal room during the ceremony.

Some bridal dressmakers will also make up a drawstring bag to match your gown which you use for the safekeeping of the many envelopes containing money gifts that will be presented to you at the reception. If you don't fancy this, pass all the gifts you receive along to your father or your husband to keep safe in an inside jacket pocket.

SHOES

Decide on your shoes early on. They should be silk or satin, dyed to match the dress exactly (not all whites are the same). Choose a pair you can stand in comfortably (you'll be on your feet for hours!), and break them in by wearing them around the house before the wedding.

When it comes to hose, beware of white stockings! They never look right because, once they're on your legs, they never match the dress and shoes. Instead, go for the sheerest champagne, nude or pale blush color you can find and have an extra pair to take with you on the big day, in case of disasters just before the ceremony.

HEIRLOOMS—"SOMETHING OLD"

Should you wear Great-Aunt Tillie's wedding dress? Not unless you love it and it fits—and is a classic style that doesn't look outlandish. If you absolutely hate it, or it will need a great deal of alteration to make it fit, thank her most graciously for her offer and "regret" sincerely. Perhaps you can use part of the bridal outfit—the tiara or the beautiful lace veil she's treasured all these years.

Some families have ornate silver or ivory-bound prayer books or Bibles that are used for weddings. With a floral marker these can serve as your bouquet and make very effective heirloom additions to your ensemble without forcing you to adopt a style you don't like.

"SOMETHING BORROWED"

In ancient times betrothed girls wore borrowed finery at the joyful celebrations announcing their engagements just after Yom Kippur. In modern times, it is still a *mitzvah* to lend a wedding gown to a

---

Which Fabric? (continued)

CRUSH AND SHOW SHINY MARKS. "CRUSHED" VELVET HAS A TEXTURE ADDED THAT ELIMINATES THESE PROBLEMS. BUT IT IS HOT TO WEAR AND NOT VERY SLENDERIZING.

FOR INFORMAL DRESSES, SILK MAKES THE SOFTEST, PRETTIEST SUITS AND DRESSES, YEAR-ROUND. A VERY SHEER, FINE WOOL IS A GOOD CHOICE IN THE COOL MONTHS.

AH, SUMMERTIME! THIS IS WHEN YOU CAN WEAR ORGANZA OR MOUSSELINE DE SOIE, EMBROIDERED NET OR SUMMER LACE. FOR GARDEN WEDDINGS, WHICH ARE USUALLY MOST INFORMAL, YOU CAN CHOOSE FROM DOTTED SWISS, ORGANDY, EYELET BATISTE OR MANY OTHER COTTON OR LINEN FABRICS. WATCH OUT FOR THE CRUSH FACTOR ON ORGANDY AND LINEN.

TO AVOID DAMAGING OR STAINING YOUR GOWN, BE SURE THAT DRESS SHIELDS ARE SEWN IN UNDER THE ARMS.

bride, so you need not hesitate to wear one that belongs to a relative or dear friend.

In view of the high cost of elaborate wedding gowns, many brides today consider renting their gowns, in those communities where they are available. If you do rent a gown, be careful not to select a dress that is far too opulent for the wedding style you have chosen and be sure it fits properly without too much alteration.

BUDGET BEAUTY

There are many ways you can be beautifully dressed, in perfect taste, and still save hundreds of dollars. From a practical point of view, you're only going to wear the dress for one evening out of your life, so why spend a king's ransom on it?

Upscale consignment shops often have beautiful gowns for sale at a fraction of the new cost. At good shops the dresses will have been cleaned before being offered for sale. Check them carefully for stains (especially under the arms) that dry cleaning did not remove, examine the hemline carefully for any tears and make sure of a fit that does not call for extensive alterations. Taking a dress in a bit is not hard, but letting it out can be treacherous because the old seam line will show. A fragile fabric such as organza may tear as you open the seam.

Discount houses and large bridal specialty shops advertise clearance sales from time to time, offering gowns at rock-bottom prices. Women have been known to line up at dawn waiting for the doors to open so they can stampede in to snatch a bargain. The try-on situation may be primitive, and of course, there are no returns. If you can brave the crush and fight your way to a gown you like, that fits, you will have accomplished a budget wonder. Beware, however, of bogus sales—if the gowns are advertised at bargain prices but shown by appointment only, you are probably being invited to a "bait and switch" operation.

If you want something sprightly and a little less formal, shop through the prom and bridesmaid dress racks in department stores. The best buys are offered at clearance times. You may find just the

משמח

right thing in a white formal and dress it up a bit more, if you like, with some extra lace or fancier buttons. Informal dresses for country or garden-style weddings abound in regular dress departments.

Next we come to the do-it-yourself department. If you, your mother, or a friend are handy with a needle, you can make your own wedding dress. A simple style that depends for its effect on generous use of fine material in a full skirt is really not hard to sew. It's the fancy extras—ruffles, sequins, lace trims, feather boning and all that fussy stuff—that complicate the job and add to the cost, just as they do to a store-bought dress. You can try on a few gowns in a good store to see what you like for yourself, then go out and get the pattern and fabric and tune up your sewing machine. Before you commit to this, however, try to assess whether your sewing skills are up to the task. Many people begin their dresses and end up having to engage a professional seamstress to finish the job—and their services can be quite pricey.

You will find a wide variety of styles, most of them rather simple to make, in the Simplicity and McCall's pattern books. Vogue patterns are rather more complicated, but for an accomplished dressmaker they are not overwhelming. Most full-skirted dresses with long sleeves use about seven to ten yards of fabric, sheath styles about four. Expect to spend anywhere from $10–$50 a yard for fabric, with the less expensive silks starting at about $15. However, you may be able to spend far less if you find a suitable remnant.

If you want a bit of glamour, visit a few trimming shops and revel in the lace insertions, pearls, sequins and flowers available. Many of these decorations can be glued on with an iron or using a special backing.

The most effective part of your costume—your diaphanous, floating wedding veil—is also the easiest to make yourself. Tulle veiling is unbelievably inexpensive when you buy it off the bolt. The trick to a soft, romantic effect is yards of double veiling, gathered to a soft puff and attached to a tiara, a wreath or a lace cap. Although you can sew a lace edge to the veiling, it floats more lightly if left unfinished.

Don't Hang It!

MANY BRIDAL SHOPS ADVISE BRIDES NOT TO HANG THEIR DRESSES IN THE CLOSET BECAUSE GRAVITY WILL TAKE ITS TOLL ON FINE FABRICS AND DRAPING. KEEP YOUR GOWN FOLDED, WITH AS FEW FOLDS AS POSSIBLE AND WITH TISSUE INSIDE THE FOLDS, TO KEEP IT FROM CREASING. IF YOU TAKE IT OUT OF THE BOX TO SHOW IT, TRY TO FOLD IT IN DIFFERENT SPOTS WHEN YOU PUT IT BACK.

FOLLOW THIS PROCEDURE WHEN YOU PUT YOUR GOWN AWAY AFTER THE WEDDING.

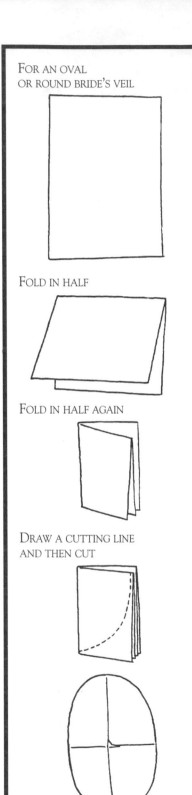

FOR AN OVAL
OR ROUND BRIDE'S VEIL

FOLD IN HALF

FOLD IN HALF AGAIN

DRAW A CUTTING LINE
AND THEN CUT

To cut a round or oval veil, fold the veiling in half, and then in half again, and cut across the corner to a template you have decided on for the shape. Make a shorter face veil the same way.

Some pattern books have designs for men's ties, vests and cummerbunds, so you can help your menfolk save some precious dollars and still look elegant.

No matter how you decide to go about finding the wedding dress of your dreams, give yourself plenty of time—start looking as soon as you set a date.

USING A BRIDAL SALON

There are shops that specialize in bridal wear and offer to coordinate the outfits of the whole wedding party. If you know the salon has been in business for a long time and is reliable, or you can get recommendations from brides who have used their services, you might decide to buy your dress there. The extra cost may be worth it to you in terms of energy and time saved. *However*, remember that you will be buying from a model or a catalog and will not be trying the actual dress on until it is made for you. You may be "sweet-talked" into spending much more than you intended to, when the salespeople gush away about the dress that is "you, darling, exactly you." The accessories they sell you—underthings, shoes, and the like—can probably be bought for much less, from a bigger selection, in other stores.

If alterations are involved, they are usually astronomically expensive. And isn't it strange that when you shop for a "civilian" or non-bridal dress, size 10 fits perfectly, but the bridal gown always needs another fitting? Unless you have an unusual figure, the right dress for you should not need much alteration beyond sleeve length and hem adjustments. And if it's truly custom-made, even those should not be necessary.

Bridal salons often require tremendous lead time, sometimes as much as four to six months, to have your dress made, but require a sizable deposit, as much as 50 percent down, with your order. Your money sits in the shop's bank account while you are waiting impatiently for the first sight of your dream gown. You may even find, to

your dismay, that the dress that is delivered is not like the model you were shown, but is made of inferior materials or has much less beading and trim. If your big day is close, you may be forced to accept the inferior dress or to shop madly for a ready-made dress. In short, you should never choose something custom-made unless you know the firm is super-reliable.

If you're using a salon on a personal recommendation, negotiate a deal for a price that includes any alterations needed and have a complete, specific description of the gown (not just a catalog number), the set price and delivery date put in writing.

COMPLETING THE PICTURE—HAIR, NAILS, MAKEUP AND JEWELRY

Of course you want to look your best on your wedding day. Most brides seem to gain an extra radiance on the day that gives truth to the old saying that "all brides are beautiful." It follows that you don't have to strain for a startling "new look" or an experimental hairdo.

Consult with your hairdresser, perhaps bringing in the headpiece you plan to wear, and try out the suggested style before the wedding day. If you're going to make a radical change in length or color, do it well before you start down the aisle.

If you've always worn your nails long, this is the time to go for a soft pastel color. Crimson, gold or silver three-inch claws are just too far out for one who is supposed to be a "blushing bride," the picture of modesty.

That also means go easy on the makeup. Remember that you will be adorned with flowers and veiling and that a softly colored makeup looks best with white. No theatrical eyelashes or crimson-gash lips, if you want to look your best.

Some brides wear no jewelry on their wedding day, except for the engagement ring, which is worn on the right hand for the occasion, so that it can be put on over the wedding ring after the ceremony. Pearls and simple diamond or gold earrings are also appropriate, especially if they are the gift of your bridegroom.

Shop with a "Buddy"

YOU REALLY WILL NEED A CANDID SECOND OPINION WHEN YOU GO THROUGH A MAZE OF STORES AND TRY ON DOZENS OF DRESSES. TAKE JUST ONE PERSON WHOSE TASTE YOU TRUST WITH YOU, PREFERABLY THE SAME PERSON, ON EACH SHOPPING TRIP (IF SHE HAS THE STAMINA). DON'T TAKE YOUR MOTHER, UNLESS YOU ARE REALLY ON EXCELLENT TERMS WITH HER AND SHE HAS THE ENERGY YOU NEED FOR THIS KIND OF SHOPPING. BUT DO ASK HER TO LOOK AT THE DRESSES ONCE YOU HAVE NARROWED YOUR SELECTION DOWN TO TWO OR THREE FINALISTS. ANY REPUTABLE SHOP WILL HOLD A SELECTION FOR YOU TILL YOUR MOTHER CAN COME AND SEE IT.

משמח

ENTER THE MOTHERS

Since both mothers will take part in the procession, they should coordinate their outfits, at least as to length and degree of formality. Styles may vary to suit the age and figure of each woman, but the overall look should harmonize, especially when it comes to the headgear, which is required in all but some Conservative and all Reform services. Since hats are so becoming, most mothers enjoy adding them to their outfits. They will be worn for many hours on the wedding day, so it's best to choose a comfortable lightweight hat style.

Don't ever suggest they go shopping together! The size a woman wears, how much she has paid for her dress and how she looks standing in the fitting room in her slip are highly personal and best kept private at the outset of this relationship.

SHOES AND HANDBAGS

The mothers should choose shoes dyed to match their gowns or a dressy contrast, such as gold or silver. They should also make sure they are comfortable for long hours of standing, and break them in before the wedding day. Your mother will want a handbag appropriate to her dress, but it is not carried in the procession, under the *huppah* or in the receiving line (if you have one). Leave the handbag in the bride's room until the reception begins, or give it to a relative to hold.

JEWELRY

Mom is not a prayerful bride, so she can pile the family jewels on, as long as they're real or very fine costume jewelry.

THE BRIDE'S ATTENDANTS

As the bride and star of the show, you select the color and style of the dresses for the bridesmaids and maid of honor, though you may want to take one or two of them along on a preliminary shopping trip. It's best to choose a simple style and a color combination that will be flattering to all. The length should match that of your bridal gown.

מ‎שמח

The neckline should be modest. If your attendants really want a more décolleté, sleeveless look for the reception, look for a matching jacket or little cape to be worn during the ceremony.

The bridesmaids do not necessarily all have to dress alike. You're not outfitting a musical comedy chorus. Settle on a complementary color scheme and a few harmonizing styles and let your friends choose the dress each one thinks is most flattering to her. Better yet, announce your color range—all pinks, for example, shading from light blush to fuchsia—assign a shade to each bridesmaid, and let each one select a dress she likes for herself. You should mandate the hemline and dyed-to-match shoes and a hosiery color—nude is best—so all the legs and hems match. Since your attendants pay for their own dresses and shoes, they will be truly grateful if they can invest in a dress they will be more likely to wear again after the wedding.

For an informal daytime wedding, there are many less expensive "garden"-style dresses to choose from. Pastel sheers printed with tiny flowers, each dress a little different, can create a charming effect.

The maid or matron of honor usually wears a more formal gown in a contrasting color, but check to make sure it harmonizes with the mothers' choice of colors.

Though they need not wear head-coverings if they are single, it makes for a more finished look if your attendants are all turned out alike. Select a simple headpiece with this in mind.

Once you've decided the details of color and length, if you settle on using a bridal shop, have all the attendants meet there at the same time to select their dresses and have the hemlines adjusted.

DO-IT-YOURSELF

You may decide with your bridesmaids that you will all make your own outfits. Select a simple style; have everyone use the same pattern and purchase the fabrics together to be sure the dresses are coordinated. Simple ballerina-length print skirts and frilly blouses (which can be purchased) or long, flowing rustic-style dresses in varying pastels can make a charming picture at a daytime wedding. The same styles in satins and lace will work for an evening affair.

~

"Themes" and Colors

ARE YOU THINKING ABOUT AN "ORIGINAL" THEME? STOP AND RECONSIDER! IT IS NOT REALLY APPROPRIATE TO GO FOR SOME FLASHY OR OUTRAGEOUS SETTING—STROBE LIGHTS, ROCK MUSIC, ATTENDANTS DRESSED AS CHARACTERS FROM MOVIES, OR MUSEUM-TYPE PERIOD CLOTHES, TO MENTION A FEW "CONCEPTS" BEST FORGOTTEN. KEEP YOUR OVERALL SETTING LIGHT, JOYFUL AND ATTRACTIVE, NOT GAUDY.

YOU GET TO CHOOSE THE COLOR SCHEME FOR YOUR BRIDAL PARTY. SETTLE ON A GROUP OF RELATED COLORS THAT WILL BE BECOMING TO EVERYONE. THAT USUALLY MEANS SOFT PASTELS FOR SPRING AND SUMMER AND RICH AUTUMN TONES FOR FALL AND WINTER, ALWAYS WITH FLORAL DECORATIONS AND SKULLCAPS FOR THE MEN TO MATCH. "BLACK-AND-WHITE" WEDDINGS ARE ALSO POPULAR, BUT TO SOME, THE SIGHT OF BRIDESMAIDS IN BLACK DRESSES SEEMS A BIT FUNEREAL FOR A WEDDING.

~

משמח

When You're Expecting

IF YOU'RE PREGNANT, YOU DON'T NECESSARILY HAVE TO SEEK OUT A CONCEALING TENT STYLE. IT ALL DEPENDS ON HOW FAR ALONG YOU WILL BE AT THE TIME OF THE WEDDING. THERE ARE MANY SIMPLE EMPIRE OR CHEMISE STYLE GOWNS THAT WILL SUIT YOU NICELY, UNLESS YOUR CONDITION HAS BECOME VERY OBVIOUS, IN WHICH CASE YOUR BEST CHOICE WILL BE A MATERNITY STYLE, MADE UP IN WHITE OR PALE PASTEL. IF YOU'RE IN YOUR FIRST TRIMESTER, YOU WILL HAVE A MUCH WIDER CHOICE. BE SURE YOUR SHOES ARE COMFORTABLE—YOU WILL BE STANDING FOR WHAT WILL SEEM LIKE AGES TO YOU. DON'T TRY TIGHT CORSETING OR CLOSE-FITTING STYLES—YOU WILL JUST BE MISERABLY UNCOMFORTABLE AND MAY EVEN DISTINGUISH YOURSELF BY FAINTING—OR WORSE!

PREGNANT ATTENDANTS

You have a dear friend or relative whom you want very much to include in your wedding party—but she's pregnant. Should you have her attend you? If she will not be on the verge of delivery by the time the wedding day rolls around—and she doesn't mind "going public" about her coming baby—then by all means, include her. It would be best not to have all your bridesmaids dress alike in this case, so that your pregnant attendant can choose a style (Empire, chemise, A-line) that is becoming. There are many beautiful maternity styles available as well. Have her pay careful attention to her shoes, since she is going to have to stand for what may be a long time for her. If she's the fainting kind, it's best to honor her instead with a reading, where she will step up to the *huppah* to say her piece and then be able to retire gracefully to a seat in the front row.

AND NOW FOR THE MEN

Theoretically, men have an easier time of it when it comes to dressing for an occasion. The groom's outfit is determined by the formality of his bride's choice. The other men in the bridal party all wear the same togs as the groom. One foray into the formal rental place and it's done. Maybe. If you decide with your fiancé to depart from conventional dress, you will discover the world of men's fantasy attire—one rental firm in Manhattan advertises sixty different styles!

We'll start with the easy choices. No matter what style you choose, all men must have a head covering during the ceremony, except in some Reform services. At traditional receptions, head-coverings are worn through the whole reception. They may be satin or brocade skullcaps color-coordinated to the bridesmaids' dresses (correct for all degrees of formality), homburgs or fedoras with business suits, or top hats with formal wear. Panama hats will do with summer wear.

BRIDE'S ATTENDANTS' CHECKLIST

To avoid confusion and misunderstandings, type out a list of instructions for each attendant. Give these out as soon as you have all of the necessary information.

If you're all buying dresses at one store or bridal salon:

Name and phone number of store _____

Name of Salesperson _____

Color_____Style # _____

Have your dress ordered by _____(date)

Pick up your dress _____(date)

Pick up your shoes _____(date)

PLEASE BREAK IN YOUR NEW SHOES!

If you are making your own dresses:

Use _____(company)

Pattern # _____

Purchase fabric at _____

Salesperson_____

On the Wedding Day _____(date, time)

Time and place where bridesmaids will finish dressing for the ceremony _____

_____

_____

Transportation arrangements from wedding to
    reception (if required)_____

_____

_____

Attach a swatch here, if you can supply it, or the name and number of fabric.

LESS-THAN-FORMAL WEDDINGS
A dark business suit with a fine white shirt and handsome tie is proper for all but the most formal occasions, day or evening. Midnight blue or black silk or fine worsted is an elegant choice.

Dinner jackets (tuxedos) are not worn before 6 P.M., but an exception may be made at weddings that begin at 4 or 4:30 P.M. and go on into the evening hours.

FORMAL ATTIRE
When the bride wears a long formal gown and veil, the groom wears:

for day weddings	morning suit, or Oxford gray jacket and striped trousers, or gray cutaway and trousers gray waistcoat and striped tie or ascot
for evening weddings	"black tie"—dinner jacket and trousers white tuxedo shirt, cummerbund or black waistcoat "white tie"—tailcoat and trousers white formal shirt, white waistcoat
for summer weddings (day)	blazer and white flannels, soft white shirt, ascot tan tropical or other light summer suit
(evening)	white dinner jacket, black formal trousers

The groom also traditionally wears a *tallit* or a *kittel* as part of his outfit.

SHOES AND ACCESSORIES
Shoes are usually black, with silk socks to match; some men choose patent leather pumps for formal wear. White shoes may be worn with a blazer outfit in summer.

Cufflinks and studs are chosen to match the outfit.

ALL-WHITE

Yes, a groom may dress in an all-white outfit, as befits Jewish solemnity. The other men of the party may dress in white, or in suitable summer wear if it is a summer wedding. For other seasons of the year they should wear business suits or formal wear appropriate to the occasion.

The *kittel* is a white ceremonial robe worn by Orthodox men for special religious occasions, such as a wedding ceremony or a Passover seder, and at the end of life under a shroud. Wearing one at the wedding ceremony recognizes the solemnity of this important event in the life cycle.

AVANT-GARDE DRESS

Original styles in formal wear are now readily available from rental outfitters. If you are choosing among the sixty styles we noted above, or even among fewer, make a thoughtful selection that will flatter all the men, bearing in mind that both fathers should wear the same style. Consider carefully whether your company of ushers, best man and the fathers, all togged out in brightly colored outfits with ruffled shirts, might not look like a TV singing group.

INFORMAL DRESS

Informal dress gives the men in the wedding party a chance to wear relaxed, colorful clothing, such as flowered shirts, matching vests and trousers of fabrics like crushed velvet, or variations on peasant outfits. The men's clothing should be coordinated carefully with the bride's choice of color, fabric and overall look. If the ushers wear a very youthful, dashing style, will the fathers feel comfortable and look right in it? Perhaps they can wear conventional dark business suits or semiformal wear and all will be pleased.

KNOWING THE RENTAL ROPES

If you are renting outfits, all the men should use the same supplier. Make the arrangements about one month in advance, so the neces-

sary fittings and alterations can be done in time. Make an appointment for all to meet at the outfitter's and be fitted at the same time.

Decide what hats you are going to wear. All should be uniform. With the newest brightly colored formal wear or colorful informal outfits, velvet or satin skullcaps are probably the best choice.

Ties or ascots for the ushers should all be alike.

Gloves are optional.

A good rental agency will provide complete coordination and all the accessories you need. Fitting should be meticulous, especially since the back of the jacket will be seen for a long time during the ceremony—and that is when a poorly fitting jacket becomes very noticeable.

Each man pays for his own outfit.

MENS' FITTING CHECKLIST

❑ Jacket neck—fits without gapping

❑ Jacket back—hangs without wrinkles or bulges

❑ Sleeves—right length and reaching to the same place on each man's arm

❑ Trouser lengths—coordinated

❑ Hats—correct size for each man

❑ Ties—choice ❑ Ascot ❑ Four-in-hand ❑ Instructions on tying provided

❑ Shirts— ❑ rented ❑ using own

❑ Separate collars (for formal neckband shirts) supplied by _____

_____

_____

_____

❑ Studs and/or cufflinks ❑ rented ❑ using own

NOTES:_____

_____

_____

_____

_____

_____

_____

_____

_____

_____

_____

_____

_____

GROOM'S ATTENDANTS' CHECKLIST

Make an instruction sheet for each usher.

1. Rental Agency _____ Phone _____
   Name of Fitter _____

2. Pick up your outfit on _____

3. Break in your new shoes!

4. Assemble at_____(place) on_____(date and time)
   for the ceremony.

5. The boutonniere goes on the left lapel. Pin it on.

6. DON'T FORGET YOUR HAT!

7. Transportation arrangements from ceremony to reception (if needed) _____
   _____
   _____
   _____
   _____
   _____

CHAPTER 11

PLANNING THE RECEPTION

Your reception can range all the way from a simple buffet at home to an elaborate three-part catered extravaganza. Only the size of the place and the size of your purse need limit you, since lavish hospitality is traditional at Jewish weddings. The bride-queen and the groom-king rate the very best their families can serve as part of the rejoicing.

PRE-CEREMONY BUFFETS

At Orthodox weddings, there are separate receptions before the ceremony for the bride and the groom. Some refreshment must be offered to all who come to the wedding to rejoice with the couple and their families. At its simplest, cake and wine are served. Other sweets, fruits and nuts, and liquor may be added.

At elaborate catered affairs it was once customary to serve a full smorgasbord with an open bar before the ceremony, on the theory that guests must be kept from fainting away with hunger before the "action" began. The result was a delayed ceremony, with guests entering the sanctuary half-sloshed and too replete with food to pay much attention to the proceedings. Most rabbis have done away with this practice and now start the ceremony promptly—within fifteen minutes of the published time. Make sure your guests understand that there is no leeway for the old-fashioned "Jewish four o'clock"— which used to mean any time before six.

When you know guests are arriving after a long trip from many distant points, you can arrange to have soft drinks offered to those who arrive early. Don't allow yourself to be talked into offering more.

THE RECEIVING LINE

The receiving line is slowly falling into disuse except at the most formal of weddings in liberal congregations and those occasions when there will be a buffet and cocktail reception for most of the guests and a small private family dinner afterward. No food may be served until all have passed through the line—which can make for a tedious time for the guests and too much fatiguing standing, smiling, and making small talk for the wedding party.

WHERE TO STAND

When you do have a receiving line, it is arranged just outside the sanctuary or the ballroom this way:

Bride's mother (first)
Groom's father (optional—but usual)
Groom's mother
Bride's father (optional—but usual)
Bride
Groom
Maid or Matron of Honor
Bridesmaids

Ushers and the best man do not join the line. Fathers often choose not to stand in the line (especially in awkward situations resulting from divorce), but instead circulate among the guests, see that champagne or some other drinks are available and, together with the ushers, see that guests are introduced to each other (a great opportunity for matchmaking, which is always in the air at weddings).

WHAT TO SAY

You don't have to memorize a long script. Your face may ache after a while, but the important thing is to smile and smile. Your guests will congratulate you. You simply thank them cordially and add some phrases that indicate how glad you are that they could come to your

wedding. Then you turn and introduce the guest to the next person in line. No chit-chat—this is not the time for personal conversations that hold up the rest of the line.

You and your mother should take care to introduce the members of your family and your friends to the groom's mother and vice versa. If you do not know a guest's name, ask graciously. Don't ever pass anyone along the line as Mr. or Ms. "Um-m-m!" And be thankful for those guests who are thoughtful enough to introduce themselves and tell you their relationship when they know you've never met them before.

Don't even try to remember all those names. And do expect to be kissed. Some enthusiastic aunts even kiss the groom!

WHEN THERE IS NO RECEIVING LINE

At a small home or outdoor wedding, there is no formal recessional. You turn and face your guests and receive their good wishes. And then everyone moves on to the buffet or the place where dinner will be served.

When you decide to observe the seclusion (*Yihud*) custom, there is also no receiving line. You and your new husband slip away for a few blessed minutes of quiet right after the recessional, during which you can glory in the wonder of being truly married at last, and break your fast if you've been fasting—or take pictures if you've not. Meantime, there is a cocktail hour during which your parents greet the guests. After a brief interval, when everyone has been seated, you enter to a triumphant fanfare, a round of applause and congratulations and showers of confetti.

When you have taken your places, the meal service may begin. Obviously, you're not going to spend much time in seclusion—it's time to eat! Many couples find this procedure beats standing and smiling and uttering polite nothings while everyone files past in a multicolored blur.

SEATING ARRANGEMENTS

THE BRIDAL TABLE

Even if the reception will be a luncheon or cocktail buffet, you may want to have a bridal table for your wedding party, so you may be served a seated meal. If the wedding party is small, your parents and the rabbi may be seated at the same table with you.

Your parents may have a separate table, if they wish, with the groom's parents, the grandparents, the rabbi and his wife and any other honored guests. The size of the wedding party is usually the deciding factor.

The seating at a bridal table is arranged all along one side, so that guests may come up and talk with you.

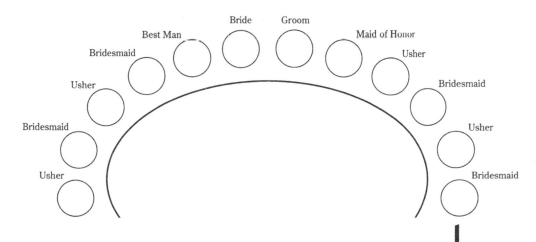

At the Parent's Table

Grandparent · Grandparent · Rabbi · Groom's Mother · Bride's Mother · Bride's Father · Groom's Father · Rabbi's Wife · Grandparent · Grandparent

At the Bride's Table

Bride · Groom · Best Man · Maid of Honor · Bridesmaid · Usher · Usher · Bridesmaid · Bridesmaid · Usher · Usher · Bridesmaid

At segregated Orthodox meals, the men and women of the wedding party are seated at separate head tables in the men's and women's sections of the reception room.

THE OTHER TABLES

Though it is usual to seat family members together, you really have to look out for the occasional friend who does not know the family, or the out-of-town relative who may not know many people, and arrange to seat them with a congenial group. If you have a large family, members of the family may be assigned to different tables where they can act as assistant hosts, seeing to it that all are introduced around.

Children are seated together at a separate table, but their parents should be asked to keep an eye on them.

MAKING THE ROUNDS

As the reception progresses and the dancing begins, bride and groom should make the rounds of the tables and exchange a few words with their guests. This is particularly important when there has been no receiving line.

You may be handed gift envelopes; offer your sincere thanks and then carefully put the envelopes away either in the inside pocket of the groom's jacket or in the bride's bag, if you are carrying one. At a home wedding, beware of putting the envelopes in a desk or sideboard drawer. Checks are easily lost in the confusion—they have been known to slip out of the back of a drawer or get stuck in the drawer lining before they have been noted in your gift record, leaving room for misunderstandings all around.

THE REPAST

We'll call it that, because it can be anything from a buffet of finger sandwiches to a full served meal. The basics apply, no matter what you serve.

~

Storm Warning

IF YOU CAN FIND OUT WHERE THE SPEAKERS ARE LOCATED IN THE RECEPTION ROOM, TRY TO SEAT YOUR OLDER GUESTS FAR AWAY FROM THEM AND FROM THE AREA WHERE THE MUSICIANS WILL BE PLAYING. THIS SHOULD PREVENT MOST COMPLAINTS ABOUT THE SOUND SYSTEM. THE SOUND IS ALWAYS TOO LOUD FOR THE OLDER GENERATION AND NEVER BOOMING ENOUGH FOR THE YOUNGER! IF YOU HONOR GRAND-PARENTS WITH SEATS AT A HEAD TABLE, THEY WILL JUST HAVE TO GRIN AND BEAR THE SOUNDS THAT TO THEM ARE JUST NOISE. CHANCES ARE, THOUGH, THEY'LL BE TOO BUSY TABLE-HOPPING TO COMPLAIN MUCH.

~

HAND-WASHING

First, in traditional circles, comes ritual hand-washing. Provide a place for this, or allow time for trips to the nearest rest rooms.

HA-MOTZI—THE BLESSING OVER BREAD

Every buffet or bridal table features a huge braided *hallah*, which is cut after the blessing over bread is said (you probably know this as *ha-motzi*). Usually Grandpa or a favorite uncle is given the honor of reciting this and cutting the bread into chunks to distribute to the guests so that all may share it. At a large catered reception, the honored guest makes the first few cuts, then the wait staff takes over, cuts and serves the *hallah*.

Some couples do this together as their first act of hospitality as bride and groom.

REJOICE, REJOICE!

Of course, everyone's happy at your wedding reception, even the women who are shedding tears—tears of joy. As it's such a *mitzvah* to increase the rejoicing, you and your guests will want to participate in all the joyful ideas you can dream up.

ON WITH THE DANCE!

You will surely have dancing, whether you hire an orchestra or a disc jockey, or just have a friend play your favorite tapes. In a formal setting there is a "first dance" with a set order. The bride and groom dance together first, usually to a waltz, and are then joined by their parents and finally the attendants. The groom dances with both mothers and the bride with both fathers, taking turns around the floor. Then it's back to the newlywed husband and wife as the other guests are invited to join the dance.

At traditional weddings, there is a great deal of spirited dancing, though there is no mixed dancing. Even at contemporary weddings, where mixed dancing is the rule, traditional circle and *mitzvah*

dances are popular, along with the *mazinkeh* dance, if either the bride or the groom is the last child in the family to be wed.

Expect to be carried on high in chairs by young and healthy male guests. Elevating the bride and groom in chairs and dancing around them in a lively circle is seen even at the most reserved, formal affairs, once the music starts. Give the musicians a list of the dances and traditional tunes you want played.

If you want to add vitality and fun to the dancing at your wedding, consider the following ideas, even if you have conventional "ballroom" dancing. All the women whose husbands' feet hurt or who are without partners will appreciate it, too. Write the list out and give it to the band leader, or have your own MC announce:

The *mehutonim* dance—The new in-laws dance together, then switch partners.

The *bubbes'* dance—For all the grandmothers at the wedding, honored grandmas in the middle.

The bachelor's *freylakh* (happy song)—For all the unmarried men in the room—any age! Circle right, circle, left . . . etc.

The maiden's *freylakh*—For all the single women there.

All couples who have been married five years or less—ladies to the right side, men to the left, clap your hands and meet in the middle, swing your partner . . . etc.

Mitzvah dances can include all the guests, who try, for at least a moment, to dance with the bride and groom. The women form a dancing circle around the bride, the men around the groom.

At Orthodox weddings, guests indulge in much clowning and hilarity to entertain the bride and groom. This custom suits any wedding reception. If you have talented guests who want to offer you the gift of their song or verse, why not appoint one of them to act as master of ceremonies? If your band or caterers provide an MC, have your appointee work with him or her to present the performers. Sometimes this pleasant duty is given to the best man. Just be sure he screens out anyone who wants to tell off-color jokes.

A DJ or MC can also offer you karaoke time, when guests can stand up and sing. If you can include some oldies and Yiddish

משמח

favorites, you will have all the old-timers vying for a chance to sing for you.

TOASTS AND FUN

A champagne toast to the new couple is standard. It's offered by the best man after champagne has been poured for all. He may call on fathers, grandfathers and others to offer their congratulations. But it's best if this is not a stiff, starchy "hear, hear" kind of moment, but one that allows for jokes and clowning around. People don't send telegrams any more, but you can add a lot of laughs by "reading" e-mail supposedly sent to the bride and groom.

At a small wedding, you can name a toastmaster for each table and ask him or her to say a few words of greeting and welcome, tell a happy anecdote about the bride or the groom or the way they met, and so forth. Just be sure to tell everyone you choose before-hand, so they will not be completely unprepared when it's their turn. Go over the list of toasts with the best man and write out the names in the order they are to be called on—to avoid embarrassing lapses of memory.

CUTTING THE CAKE

The wedding cake is cut when dessert is served. The bride makes the first cut, assisted by the groom, using a flower-and-ribbon-decorated cake knife. The couple shares the first slice, with the bride usually feeding the groom a bite or two. Then, if you have a caterer, the cake is taken off to the kitchen to be cut and served by the wait staff.

At a home wedding or a partially catered affair, ask a friend or the person in charge of serving to cut the cake. This is also best done in the kitchen after you have made the first cut.

Wedding cakes are often an extravagant necessity. You will prob-ably find yourself persuaded to order a much larger cake than you really need, so as to have three impressive tiers. Save your hard-earned dough (pun intended!). A cake can be made with a false bottom layer frosted to match, and you can plan from the start to

How to Cut the Wedding Cake

CUT VERTICALLY THROUGH THE BOTTOM LAYER TO THE EDGE OF THE SECOND LAYER (1). THEN CUT WEDGE-SHAPED PIECES AS SHOWN BY (2).

WHEN THESE PIECES HAVE BEEN SERVED, DO THE SAME WITH THE MIDDLE LAYER. CUT VERTICALLY AROUND AT THE EDGE OF THE TOP LAYER (3), THEN CUT PIECES AS SHOWN BY (4).

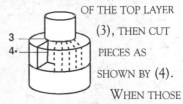

WHEN THOSE PIECES HAVE BEEN SERVED, RETURN TO THE BOTTOM LAYER AND REPEAT THE CUTS (5) AND (6).

THE REMAINING TIERS MAY BE CUT INTO DESIRED SIZE PIECES.

Toasted to a Tee

TOASTS, WHETHER SERIOUS OR JOKING, ARE AN IMPORTANT PART OF THE WEDDING RECEPTION. LIKE ANY OTHER RITUAL, TOASTING HAS ITS ETIQUETTE. IT HELPS TO SORT THINGS OUT IN THE MIDST OF MERRYMAKING. FOR EXAMPLE:

- TO MAKE A TOAST, STAND UP, TAP ON YOUR GLASS TO GET THE CROWD'S ATTENTION (DON'T USE SO MUCH FORCE THAT YOU BREAK THE GLASS!) AND GO TO IT—SAYING SOMETHING LIKE "LADIES AND GENTLEMEN, I HAVE A TOAST TO MAKE," OR "I HAVE A FEW WORDS TO SAY."
- THE "TOASTEE"—THE PERSON BEING TOASTED—DOES NOT DRINK AT THE END OF THE SALUTE, BUT SIMPLY SMILES AT THE TOASTER.
- A WEDDING TOAST SHOULD NOT TAKE LONGER THAN THREE MINUTES—MORE THAN THAT AND IT'S OVERDONE! THE TONE CAN RANGE FROM THE SERIOUS AND SENTI-MENTAL TO THE HUMOROUS.

have the top tier made as a fruit or spice cake that will be taken off and wrapped for the freezer so that you may enjoy it on your first wedding anniversary.

You will probably still have leftover cake. (It seems to grow secretly in the kitchen!) Arrange to have it wrapped and taken home, where your parents can serve it during *sheva brokhes*, if you will be observing that custom, or put it in the freezer to use for your own first hospitality in your new home.

During the time the cake is being served, you and your husband make the round of the tables, greeting all the guests. Parents usually circulate at this time also.

GRACE (*SHEVA BROKHES*)

Seven days of feasting after a wedding have been a tradition among the Orthodox since biblical times. These are usually held in a different household each day. At each meal during these days, the Seven Wedding Blessings (in Hebrew, *sheva berakhot*) are added to the Grace after Meals, so the feasting came to be called, in colloquial Yiddish, *sheva brokhes*.

The first time these blessings are said at the wedding feast is marked by a special ritual. It is an honor to be asked to lead the Grace or to recite one of the Seven Blessings. Decide in advance who is to be so honored at your reception and give a list to the person who will lead the Grace. This is a task your father can carry out. At modern traditional weddings, this ritual is followed only at the first wedding meal. (See page 80 for the text of the blessings.)

Special Grace booklets (*bentshers*), some lavishly illustrated, that contain the text in both Hebrew and English can be

imprinted with the names of the bride and groom and the date of the wedding. They are given to the guests as keepsakes. You get these at the same place that makes your imprinted skullcaps—a Hebrew bookstore or your caterer. You may want to combine the text with other passages, such as your vows to each other, or a translation of the marriage contract or your special readings, in a wedding booklet.

LEAVE-TAKING

When the wedding runs on to a very late hour, you may be wishing everyone would leave, but no one should go until the cake has been cut, and at traditional weddings, until the Grace after Meals has been said. The bride and groom do not leave until Grace has been completed and most of the guests have left.

If the wedding is being held in the evening at a hotel, you may want to reserve a room there and start your wedding trip the next day. Often this is part of the "package" offered by a hotel caterer.

WATCH THE CLOCK!

If you will be paying for music or service by the hour, be sure to have the caterer or a close relative remind you when the over-time is about to begin. Decide then whether you want to continue the music or food service. If everyone, including you, is having a wonderful time, play on! If you think it's time to close the party down, have the band play the traditional good-night numbers. If you've ordered a Viennese dessert table, you can be pretty sure the party will run overtime, so grin, eat your crêpes and cakes and enjoy!

Toasted to a Tee
(continued)

THE ORDER OF THE TOASTING CAN BE:

- BEST MAN TOASTS THE BRIDE.
- GROOM TOASTS THE BRIDE.
- BRIDE TOASTS THE GROOM.
- FATHER OF THE BRIDE TOASTS THE COUPLE.
- BRIDE TOASTS HER GROOM'S PARENTS.
- GROOM TOASTS HIS BRIDE'S PARENTS.
- FATHER OF THE GROOM TOASTS THE BRIDE.
- MOTHER OF THE BRIDE TOASTS THE COUPLE.
- MOTHER OF THE GROOM TOASTS THE COUPLE.
- EVERYONE ELSE WHO HAS A WISH TO OFFER—GOING AROUND THE TABLES PER-HAPS, AS SUGGESTED ABOVE.

AND SO ON, AS LONG AS THE CHAMPAGNE AND THE GOOD WILL HOLD OUT!

CHAPTER 12

THE BUSINESS SIDE
OF YOUR WEDDING

RECEPTION
−$2000 to ?

BAND
or
DJ
−$600
to $2500

USHERS
GIFTS
(PENS)
−$35

BOUTONNIERES
−$15 ea.

HUPPAH
−$500

TUXEDO
−$60
a day

BRIDAL
BOUQUET
−$100

BOUQUETS
−$175

BRIDESMAID'S
GIFTS
(NECKLACES)
−$35

LIMO
−$75
a day

RING
−$600 to ?

BRIDAL
GOWN
−$825

PHOTOGRAPHER
−$725

Your budget and the size and style of your wedding will shape your decision about catering, so you don't have to agonize over it like Hamlet. Certain other limits will be defined by tradition and community custom.

MEETING *KASHRUT* REQUIREMENTS

The requirements of the Jewish community and those of observant family members will also define your choices. Traditional practice mandates kosher food and wines; most synagogues will allow you to use only the resident caterer or the few they approve as properly observing the dietary laws.

Some more liberal congregations may allow you a choice of caterers, but may restrict the menu to dishes not in themselves forbidden (*tref*): that is, you cannot serve pork or shellfish, or milk and meat at the same meal. Sometimes, all meat foods are prohibited. So many people are vegetarians these days that that may not be such a hardship.

Hotels and clubs usually have their own banquet services, both kosher and non-kosher. Restaurants vary. If you have your heart set on the rooftop terrace of a five-star hotel and it is either not kosher or the kosher menu is out-of-sight expensive, you can usually arrange for a vegetarian, dairy or fish meal. In such a setup, be sure you specify:

No shellfish or swordfish
No meat stocks (as in aspics or soups)
No meat garnishes (such as bacon bits)
No meat or seafood fillings for crêpes, egg rolls, quiches, curries and the like.

Choosing a theme, such as a Mediterranean, Indian or Chinese feast, can make non-meat meals original and festive.

SUPERVISION OF AN OUTSIDE CATERER'S *KASHRUT*
If a place outside a synagogue represents itself as kosher, ask what supervision is being given.

How Much Help Do You Need?

FOR A SMALL HOME WEDDING, YOU MAY NEED ONLY SOME EXTRA HELP, RENTED FURNISHINGS AND SOME OR ALL OF THE FOOD PREPARED BY PARTY COOKS FOR YOU. YOU AND YOUR MOM DON'T WANT TO SPEND THE DAY IN THE KITCHEN, DO YOU? YOU NEED AT LEAST THIS "BARE BONES" HELP.

FOR AN ELABORATE PARTY AT HOME OR IN A RENTED VENUE THAT DOES NOT HAVE A RESIDENT CATERER, YOU MAY HAVE EVERYTHING CATERED IN AND SERVED FOR YOU. FOR A LARGE FORMAL WEDDING, YOU WILL NEED THE FULL SERVICES OF THE BEST CATERER YOUR BUDGET PERMITS.

Ask: (1) Is the kitchen under the supervision of a recognized rabbinical authority? (2) Is a *kashrut* supervisor (*mashgiah*) present during the food preparation and service?

Part of the higher cost of kosher food service derives from this necessary supervision. Be sure you are getting it, if you are paying for it.

WINES

Check the requirements of the synagogue before you order your wines. Some permit only certified kosher wines (including champagnes). Liquors (scotch, vodka, etc.) do not require certification.

IT'S A MERCEDES—WATCH YOUR STEP!

Your wedding is probably one of the largest expenditures your family or you will make until you buy your first home—and weddings aren't sold on a "small down payment/monthly installment" plan. A small home or partly catered wedding can run into four figures; if you go for a fully catered, formal affair with more than one hundred and fifty guests, you can spend as much as you would on a luxury car. When you're interviewing caterers and florists and auditioning bands, think of your wedding as a service you are buying instead of as the emotional high point of your life to date, and you and your family will be better able to make businesslike decisions.

You may be debating lace tablecloths versus high-fashion colors in linen, or dreaming of orchids floating in waterfalls, but your parents (or you and your fiancé) will be signing a contract with the caterer, which is an ironclad business deal. So let's be practical. Approach the discussion with a clear budget in mind and a good approximation of the size of your guest list.

Any cancellation, changes or last-minute additions will cost additional money, usually large sums. There has probably never been a change in plans resulting in lower costs after a contract was negotiated! And even with a contract, brace yourself for an inevitable cost overrun. Sales taxes, an item sometimes overlooked, add a hefty amount to the already large wedding cost.

HOME WEDDINGS CHECKLIST
(with Some Catering Help)

Go back to Chapter 6 (not Square One!). The checklist on page 89 will help you review your home setting once more and decide on the degree of outside help you want. In addition to that checklist, go over these points with any service you consider:

1. Who will make the wedding cake? _____

_____

What kind? _____

How will it look? _____

_____

_____

_____

_____

_____

2. Who will supply (if not from home): _____

	Source	Cost
Coat racks and hangers	_____	$ _____
Beverages, ice, and tubs to put them in	_____	$ _____
Punch bowl, ladle and cups	_____	$ _____
Serving utensils, dishes and glasses	_____	$ _____
Tables, chairs, bar, etc.	_____	$ _____
Delivery charges for rented equipment	_____	$ _____
Ice and beverages	_____	$ _____

3. Is serving help available? _____

Cost basis:_____ persons _____ per hour _____ per day _____

4. Is cleanup help available? _____

Cost basis:_____ persons _____ per hour_____

5. Who will dispose of trash? _____

_____

How? _____

_____

Cost? _____

CATERING SERVICE

Name _____

_____

_____

Phone _____

Total Estimated Cost $ _____

Name _____

_____

Phone _____

Total Estimated Cost $ _____

EXTRA HELPERS:

Name _____

Phone _____

Name _____

Phone _____

Name _____

Phone _____

When you decide to have catering help in your home, have the service you select look over your kitchen and serving area. What is adequate for Mom and her sister may not work for a professional caterer. Check out particularly your appliances, electrical capacity, storage and serving facilities. If your space isn't quite right, caterers may suggest using their refrigerated truck for storage and their professional-size appliances. If your oven's too small to heat food for your crowd, either go for a cold spread, or see what the caterer can do when he or she supplies a microwave setup.

When you get the cost estimate, add one-and-a-half times more for all the items you forgot, changes you make or other unforeseen contingencies.

WHAT TO ASK A FULL-SERVICE CATERER

For "comparison shopping," you will need a neat small notebook or a batch of index cards in an envelope, and a file folder with pockets. You will be given quotes in dizzying profusion, presentations with pictures, menus and other assorted promotional material. Put all that in your trusty file folder, then fire away with these questions. *Write down the answers* in your notebook on a page for each venue, or on the cards, one for each place. See the section "How to Comparison Shop" later in this chapter.

1. Will mine be the only wedding, or will there be other functions at that time? How many other affairs can be held at once?
2. If there are other parties, what provisions are there for the proper reception of my guests and privacy for my function?
3. What rooms are available and how will they be set up? (Look. And while you're looking, check out the rest rooms, too.)
4. Is there a separate rental fee for the room? What services and equipment are included in the fee?
   ❏ furnishings ❏ tableware ❏ candles ❏ cake table and service ❏ piano and dance floor ❏ coat checking ❏ bar setup ❏ valet or free parking

5. What choices are there in table settings and room decor? Can we see samples of settings?

6. What menus are offered? What is the cost of each? Will guests be offered a choice, or do we select one set menu?

7. What types of meal service are offered?
   ❑ captain-served buffet $_____

   ❑ French service (platters passed) $ _____

   ❑ white glove $ _____

   ❑ standard sit-down dinner $ _____

8. Can you provide for guests with special dietary needs?
   ❑ vegetarian ❑ kosher ❑ diabetic

9. Hors d'oeuvres—what are the offerings? _____
   Hot _____
   Cold _____
   passed about by wait staff before dinner $ _____ per guest
   (for)_____hours
   set up as a smorgasbord or buffet $ _____ per guest

10. Children's meals—charge per person $_____

11. Meals for disk jockey, band, photographer $_____

12. Are gratuities for wait staff, bartender and attendants in coatroom, parking lot, etc., included?

13. Is the catering service covered by liability insurance, especially for accidents that may result from drunk driving after the reception?

14. What is done with leftover food? (Ask to have it boxed up for your mothers to take home or give to a local charity. You paid for it; make the most of it.)

15. Suppose we have to cancel because of some unforeseen problem. What is the refund policy?

16. Can we taste the food? Can we see the place when it is set up for a wedding? (To do this you come early and do not stay. In all fairness, don't ask for this unless you are really

משמח

A Wedding Reception That Almost Wasn't

ONCE THERE WAS A FAMILY THAT RENTED A LOVELY CLUBROOM FOR THE WEDDING RECEPTION AND HIRED AN INDEPENDENT CATERER AND MUSICIANS AND FLORISTS AND EVERYTHING. BUT WHEN THE GUESTS BEGAN TO ARRIVE AT THE CLUB FROM THE SYNAGOGUE, THEY FOUND THE BUILDING DARK, THE CATERER SITTING FORLORNLY IN HIS TRUCK FULL OF FOOD AND FLOWERS, AND THE BAND NAPPING IN THEIR VAN. WHAT HAPPENED?

A TOTAL FAILURE OF COMMU-NICATION! THE PERSON WHO HAD THE KEY HAD NOT BEEN NOTIFIED TO COME AND OPEN THE HALL AND NONE OF THE SERVICE PEOPLE KNEW WHERE TO REACH HER. FORTUNATELY, A GUEST WHO WAS AN ALUMNUS OF A NEARBY COL-LEGE SAVED THE DAY BY CALLING THE DEAN AND GETTING PERMIS-SION TO USE THE COLLEGE SOCIAL ROOMS FOR THE RECEPTION.

interested in the place. You will be wasting everyone's precious time if you're just satisfying your curiosity.)

17. What is the policy on price increases? (When you reserve far in advance, food prices may go up before the wedding date. New taxes may be imposed.) When can we get a set price, with protection from price increases?

18. Liquor—Cost of open bar service $_____ per guest for _____ hours
What drinks will be served?_____
Is punch included?_____Soft drinks?_____
Can we provide our own liquor? Bar setup charge $_____ (includes mixers, etc.)

Can we specify the brands we want the caterer to serve?_____

Types of beverage service:

open bar before dinner $_____per guest_____per hour

wine steward and bar cart during dinner $_____

champagne and wine service only $_____

cocktail hour, then bottles per table during dinner $_____

19. What planning and hospitality assistance is offered? _____consultant_____host_____maitre d'

20. Who will provide the florist for room decorations, bouquets? Centerpieces $_____ Bouquets $_____

Can we use our own florist?_____

21. *Hallah* and wedding cake: Included? Charge if not $_____

Can we see samples of the cake? Taste? Provide our own cake?

22. Desserts—What desserts are on the menu, besides wedding cake?

Viennese table (lavish dessert buffet) $_____
Menu_____

Can we box up and take leftovers home?

23. Price basis: Dinner—Per guest $_____ × number of guests = $_____

Per hour of bar and buffet service $_____

"Package" price $_____ (includes _____)

שמח

24. Overtime: When does it begin? _____ Charge per hour
    $_____

25. Guarantee of Guests: Is there a minimum number? Charges for less than minimum?
    Provision for exceeding the head count?
    Date when guarantee must be finalized _____

Synagogue Questions (additional):

Is there a separate fee for the use of the sanctuary and *huppah*? $_____
Rabbi's fee $_____(if not included)
Cantor's fee $_____(if not included)
Choir, organist $_____
Bridal room setup $_____ (should be included)

Hotel Questions (additional):

What is the ceremony setup?
Who will officiate? (Check ceremony details.)
Is there a special hotel room rate for out-of-town guests?
Does the rate include a complimentary bridal suite?

ECONOMIZING

When you have recovered from sticker shock after you get a few price quotes, it's time to consider how you can have a wedding that will please you and avoid mortgaging the future.

ELIMINATE *TCHOTCHKES*

What's a *tchotchke*? A cute, trivial novelty or souvenir item no one needs. You will be offered monogrammed matchbooks, personalized napkins, fancy menu booklets complete with tassels, a wide choice of favors for your guests, monogrammed glasses for you and your husband's first toast, monogrammed sort-of-silver cake knives to cut the cake, blue garters and so on and on through whatever fantasies novelty purveyors can think of next. These fripperies can add up to a surprising

---

A Wedding Reception That Almost Wasn't (continued)

THE UNSCHEDULED ACTIVITY FOR THIS WEDDING WAS HAVING THE GUESTS LEND A HAND IN THE SETUP OF TABLES, CHAIRS, TABLE-CLOTHS, CENTERPIECES AND BAR. AFTER THE BRIDE AND HER MOTHER FINISHED THEIR QUIET HYSTERICS IN AN IMPROVISED BRIDAL ROOM, A VIBRANT, JOYOUS GOOD TIME WAS HAD BY ALL— PRECISELY BECAUSE OF THE IMPROMPTU AIR THIS EMERGENCY HAD GIVEN TO THE OCCASION.

MORAL—KNOW WHO HAS THE KEY! SEE TO IT THAT ALL YOUR SERVICE PEOPLE CONNECT WITH EACH OTHER. AND DON'T CRUMPLE WHEN THERE'S AN EMERGENCY! THERE'S ALWAYS SOME SOLUTION, THOUGH IT MAY NOT BE EXACTLY WHAT YOU IMAGINED WHEN YOU MADE YOUR PLANS.

How Much Liquor Do We Need?

CHAMPAGNE. CHAMPAGNE CAN COST ANYWHERE FROM $60 OR MORE PER BOTTLE FOR THE BEST DOWN TO $4 FOR THE KIND YOU GET WHEN IT'S OFFERED "FREE WITH YOUR DINNER." ABOUT $10 A BOTTLE WILL GET YOU SOME VERY NICE SPARKLING WINE (IT CAN ONLY BE CALLED CHAMPAGNE IF IT COMES FROM THE CHAMPAGNE DISTRICT IN FRANCE) THAT NEEDS NO APOLOGIES. IF YOU'RE JUST USING IT FOR THE TOAST TO THE BRIDE AND GROOM, FIGURE THAT EACH BOTTLE WILL YIELD SEVEN GLASSES. IF YOU'RE SERVING ONLY CHAMPAGNE THROUGH THE RECEPTION AND DINNER, FIGURE THAT EACH GUEST WILL HAVE THREE OR FOUR GLASSES DURING THE EVENING.

amount of cash before you're through. Resist the fascination of your linked initials or first names. Your guests will carry away the memory of your happiness and their rejoicing without all this junk.

When you get down to a serious discussion with the caterer, after he or she has told you how wonderful the affair will be, ask how you can economize. This is the point in the negotiations to mention the sum you had in mind and ask how the caterer can work within that budget.

A change of day and hour will affect the price; so will the menu choice. Chicken is less expensive than prime rib, and more healthful, too. Many people do not eat red meat at all now, so don't feel you must go for the most expensive item on the menu.

Don't be intimidated by comments from the caterer on "elegance" or "once-in-a-lifetime" celebrations. Don't react to the implication that you can't afford or are too miserly to have your wedding in this top-drawer establishment. Your budget is what you regard as prudent. And if the caterer starts to work you over with "might-as-wells," remember that you might as well have that extra money in your bank account rather than the caterer's.

Regardless of the size and price of the function, it is the caterer's responsibility to make it as perfect as possible.

HOW TO COMPARISON SHOP

You can start your search for the ideal caterer by recalling weddings you have enjoyed recently and asking friends for their suggestions and comments. Visit the places you are considering, go through all the questions listed above in your preliminary conferences and *write down the answers.* And note carefully whether the people you will be dealing with are courteous and responsive to your wishes.

If you like a catering hall and the prices quoted, go back to see a wedding or a formal dinner in progress, especially if you have never been to a party there. If you are considering a restaurant or a country club, it is a good idea to have dinner there on a Saturday or Sunday, when presumably the kitchen and staff are setting forth their best, at their busiest. Check—How crowded are the public rooms?

משמח

Will your party have adequate privacy and quiet if the rest of the place is full? What ambiance is projected by the clientele the place draws, the physical setting and the quality of service? Carefully check the maintenance of the rest rooms on a busy evening.

If a place seems like a good possibility, have the caterer give you a preliminary estimate in writing, spelling out the details of menu, service and everything else you've discussed. Then compare your various estimates and impressions before you commit yourself.

REFERENCES

If you are not familiar with a caterer's work, or he or she is new in the business, ask for references—the names of those who have used the facilities recently. This is most important when you are planning almost a year ahead. You will be asked to give a sizable deposit, and you'll want to make sure the caterer will still be in business when the date arrives!

You can also ask the caterer what other professional services he or she would recommend (florist, photographer, musician and the like). If you like the caterer's work, try to use the people the caterer recommends. Things will probably go more smoothly when the professionals are accustomed to working with each other. But if you are not obligated to use these suppliers, feel free to shop around.

THE BOTTOM LINE—
SUMMARY OF BUSINESS DETAILS

SIGNING THE CONTRACT

The catering contract you sign is a legal document. Ask to take it home and study it before signing it. The contract should state:

1. Specifically, all foods selected; for example, particular vegetables; not "cheese" but "Jarlsberg" or "Brie"; specific cuts of beef, etc. Also the number and kinds of hors d'oeuvres, the specific champagnes, wines, beers and liquors.

How Much Liquor Do We Need? (continued)

THE HARD STUFF. ASSUME THAT EACH GUEST WILL HAVE THREE OR FOUR DRINKS. A FIFTH OF SCOTCH, GIN OR VODKA WILL GIVE YOU 25 ONE-OUNCE DRINKS, OR 18 ONE-AND-A-HALF-OUNCE DRINKS. A CASE, CONTAINING TWELVE FIFTHS, WILL YIELD 300 ONE-OUNCE DRINKS.

BEER. ON TAP, HALF A KEG WILL GIVE YOU 260 EIGHT-OUNCE GLASSES; THAT EQUALS SEVEN CASES OF BEER IN BOTTLES OR CANS.

NONALCOHOLIC CHOICES. PROVIDE THE USUAL SODAS AND JUICES, SOME SPARKLING GRAPE JUICE THAT LOOKS JUST LIKE CHAMPAGNE, AND NONALCOHOLIC BEER AND WINE. MORE PEOPLE ARE DRINKING LESS ALCOHOL THESE DAYS.

CATERING COST COMPARISON CHART

CATERER	MENU	SPECIAL FEATURES	FAULTS	NOTES
Phone: Contact:				COST P/P $_____ TOTAL COST $_____
Phone: Contact:				COST P/P $_____ TOTAL COST $_____
Phone: Contact:				COST P/P $_____ TOTAL COST $_____
Phone: Contact:				COST P/P $_____ TOTAL COST $_____
Phone: Contact:				COST P/P $_____ TOTAL COST $_____

If a change of date or time will change the price, make a new row of facts for that caterer.

Cost P/P: per person; Total Cost includes all the extras.

משמח

2. The hours of service (if the caterer is coming to your home, the time of arrival and departure).
3. Whether or not there can be a future price increase. Try for a written limit, for example: "No more than a 10 percent increase because of market conditions."
4. The rooms to be used, with notice to you to approve any change, should it be necessary.
5. All the service details you agreed upon after discussion.
6. Terms of payment.
7. A cancellation clause outlining refunds if some change of plans becomes necessary.
8. For a home wedding, that you keep all uneaten meals and leftover foods, properly packaged for refrigeration or freezing, and that all garbage and trash will be taken away at the end of the party. (You may also request that the caterer at a formal affair package all the leftovers for you, and if you are supplying the liquor, that all bottles be returned to you, full or empty. Some people number the bottles to be sure they've gotten them all back.)

CANCELLATION INSURANCE

For weddings booked long in advance of the actual date, it's smart to pay the fee for insurance to cover the loss resulting from a cancellation or postponement forced by a drastic change in plans. Ask whether the caterer supplies this or whether you must buy it independently.

You should be covered for the loss of your deposit and for the loss of the entire fee. Check the conditions allowed for cancellation or changes in your plans.

No one is immune to accident, illness or other family emergencies. May you have a good policy—and never have to file a claim on it!It is possible to buy insurance to cover nonrefundable deposits if the ceremony is postponed or canceled because of a death in the immediate family or a disaster like the arrest of the groom. Since the cost of weddings sometimes runs into five figures, it may be worthwhile to consider such a policy. But if you are not spending a

~

The Cash Bar

A CASH BAR, WHERE YOUR GUESTS PAY FOR THEIR DRINKS, MAY BE SUGGESTED TO YOU AT SOME CLUBS OR RESTAURANTS AS AN ECONOMY MEASURE. YOUR ANSWER MUST BE—*NEVER!* THIS IS AGAINST THE FUNDAMENTAL IDEA OF A JEWISH WEDDING RECEPTION, WHICH IS TO REJOICE, REJOICE TO THE FULLEST. IF YOU HAVE TO SAVE HERE, SERVE ONLY BEER AND WINE, OR CUT DOWN YOUR OPEN BAR TIME, BUT NEVER, NEVER ASK YOUR GUESTS TO PAY FOR ANY PART OF THE HOSPITALITY EXTENDED THEM. THAT'S WHY YOU EVEN PAY THE PARKING AND COATROOM STAFF TIPS.

~

CATERING COSTS AND DEADLINES

Caterer Selected _____

Phone _____ Contact _____

Total Price, including taxes, tips and extra charges $ _____

Terms of Payment:

Deposit $_____ Payable on _____ Refundable until _____

Additional Payments $_____ Due _____

$_____ Due _____

Final Payment $_____ Due _____

Form of Payment: ❑ Cash ❑ Check ❑ Credit Card

Deadline Dates:

Finalizing menu due date _____

Preliminary head count due _____

Final exact number (the "guarantee") due _____

Seating plan for dinner due _____

Note: Try to leave a large final payment to be made on the date of the affair, so that you have some leverage if you are not satisfied with some aspect of the service. In general, if you are working more than three months ahead, the largest part of the total should not be paid too far in advance.

huge sum on your wedding, the cost of the insurance may not be worth it.

The insurance company won't pay if either of you just gets cold feet and wants to call the whole affair off, and the probability of a postponement or cancellation due to some unhappy event is fairly low. So think twice before you buy cancellation coverage. If you have a cancellation clause in your caterer's contract, you may be able to recoup your deposit if the room can be rebooked and the band can find another engagement.

You should also check into what coverage you have from your homeowner's personal liability policy for accidents or damage resulting from too much celebrating.

Weigh the cost of the additional insurance against your possible losses—then decide. You may wind up saying "I don't" to the insurance agent.

RECORD-KEEPING

Use the cash flow chart at the back of this book to enter all the sums you are committed for and the amount of cash or checks you will need to have on hand on the day of the wedding. Include the cash you will need to tip delivery people, drivers and other help on the days immediately preceding the wedding and the wedding day itself. Remember—banks are closed on Sunday! And automatic teller machines have withdrawal limits.

EXTRAS

Extras are an inevitable fact of life. Expect them and be prepared to take them with good humor if they are reasonable. If you think you are being gouged on the day of the wedding, pay something and give the classic response—"So sue me!" about the rest. Just remember that it will cost money to mount a lawsuit, and that if you should lose your case, you will have to pay court costs. You can probably reach a fair settlement a day or so after the wedding, when heads are clearer and nerves not flaring.

~

Checklist—Budget Cuts

CONSIDER THESE COSTLY FRILLS— DO YOU NEED OR WANT:

COST

A FLORAL *HUPPAH* $_____

FULL FLORAL DECORATIONS IN
   THE SYNAGOGUE $_____

WHITE GLOVE "FRENCH" SERVICE
                      $_____

ROLLING BAR CART THROUGH
   THE DINNER SERVICE
                      $_____

FULL SMORGASBORD BUFFET JUST
   BEFORE DINNER $_____

"VIENNESE TABLE" AFTER
   DINNER $_____

DESSERTS *AND* THE WEDDING
   CAKE $_____

WEDDING FAVORS OTHER THAN
   SKULLCAPS (*YARMULKES*)
                      $_____

TOTAL EXTRA COSTS
                      $_____

~

YOUR LIABILITY AS A HOST

Rejoicing with the bride and groom does not have to mean drunken reveling. But it does sometimes happen that a few guests go beyond the limits of common sense and wind up really smashed. With recent court decisions, this has become a serious problem for both hosts and caterers. Be aware of your responsibilities.

Liquor may not be served to anyone underage, even at a home party. Courts have ruled that the hosts were financially liable when teenagers who were served liquor at parties in their homes became involved in auto accidents or criminal matters. Caterers and restaurants have been held to the same rule.

Adult guests who are too drunk to drive but do so, and have an accident after being served drinks at your party, are also your responsibility and liability. As a good friend you should call a taxi or find someone else to drive the car in these cases. Caterers and bartenders are also liable in this situation.

Better yet—try some of these ways to limit alcohol consumption by all the guests at your reception:

- Limit the cocktail reception before dinner to about an hour.
- Ask the bartender to pour one-ounce drinks or three-ounce glasses of champagne.
- Err on the side of strictness and allow no alcoholic drinks to be served to underage youngsters. Nonalcoholic wine and beer can always be offered instead.
- Look into having no bar, but tray service instead. You select a few of the most popular drinks—champagne, Manhattan and Martini cocktails, or red and white wine, for example. The wait staff circulates through the company, offering these drinks from trays. You can keep everyone happy and keep the liquor consumption down by limiting this service to the time before dinner, while dinner is being served, and a few intervals after dinner. It's smart to stop serving well before the end of the party, to give people a chance to sober up. Coffee alone won't do it.
- Have plenty of soft drinks and punch available.

If you make it very clear that you wish the alcohol consumption to be kept down, reliable caterers will be happy to cooperate, especially since they are even more accountable than you should there be an unfortunate accident, be it a bad fall or an auto crash.

DEALING WITH THE FLORIST

Flowers add grace and beauty to any wedding. They can also be so expensive as to become a very large item in your budget. If you don't level with the florist and tell him or her how much you would like to spend on this, you will be offered floral decorations everywhere, up to and including the rest room, the wedding limo and the bride's garter belt (to surprise the groom, a florist's magazine unblushingly suggests).

Start by deciding what flowers you must have. Check with your synagogue. Some favor only large arrangements for the *bimah* (platform before the Ark), and do not allow a floral *huppah*, in the interest of keeping the spiritual significance of the ceremony uppermost.

Reject any suggestions to rent synthetic flowers or a plastic arbor to use as your *huppah*. This is always tacky, no matter how "lifelike" it is supposed to be. Better use just a few beautiful flowers and let them stand out as ornaments.

You or your friends can do the flowers yourselves, from blooms purchased wholesale. Just be sure your florist will guarantee the freshest delivery the day before and that you have enough proper containers and an adequately cool space to store your completed arrangements.

BASICS

1. The bridal bouquet, matched in formality and style to your gown.
2. Corsages for the mothers and grandmothers.
3. Boutonnieres for the groom, fathers and grandfathers.
4. Floral arrangements for the synagogue *bimah* (platform)—these are your gift to the congregation.
5. Centerpieces for the bridal table and buffet table.

משמח

Adding Elegance to Economy

WHEN YOU OPT FOR THE ECONOMY OF A WEDDING AT HOME OR IN A RENTED NON-CATERED SPACE, YOU NEED NOT SACRIFICE THE ELEMENTS OF ELEGANCE. SPLURGE ON HIRING THE BEST HELP FOR THE DAY, RENT FINE LINEN, CHINA, SILVER AND GLASSWARE, SERVE GOOD WINES AND CHAMPAGNE, FILL THE HOUSE WITH MANY CANDLES (A SIGN OF REJOICING) AND FLOWERS (WHICH CAN BE FROM FRIENDS' GARDENS).

RENT PROFESSIONAL AUDIO EQUIPMENT FOR THE MUSIC. USE RECORDS OR TAPES AND THE TALENTS OF GIFTED FRIENDS.

TO RETAIN YOUR SERENITY AS BRIDE (AND YOUR MOTHER'S SERENITY, TOO), BE SURE TO DELEGATE THE TASKS OF RECEIVING GUESTS AT THE DOOR, OVERSEEING THE HELP, SERVING FOOD AND DRINK, RUNNING THE SOUND SYSTEM, AND CLEANING UP.

IF YOU HAVE A SUITABLE PLACE FOR IT AND LIKE ORGANIZING THINGS YOUR OWN WAY, SUCH A WEDDING RECEPTION WILL BE A WARM AND ORIGINAL PARTY. YOU CAN REALIZE YOUR PERSONAL DREAMS FOR YOUR WEDDING WITHOUT TOTALLY FRACTURING THE FAMILY FINANCES.

PLEASANT USUAL ADDITIONS
1. Bridal attendants' flowers.
2. Boutonnieres for ushers and best man.
3. Garlands for *huppah* poles.
4. Centerpieces for each table.
5. Floral arrangement for the bride's home.

EXTRAS (SOME EXPENSIVE, SOME NOT)
1. Entrance and reception room floral decorations, palms, fountains, etc.
2. Aisle decorations.
3. Floral *huppah*.
4. Outdoor lighting, ornamental plants and fountains for a garden wedding.
5. "Breakaway" centerpieces that come apart into small bouquets for the guests to take home. Discuss with the caterer how this should be handled.
6. "Thank-you" flowers sent to the parents the day after the wedding—a thoughtful and gracious gesture from an appreciative honeymoon couple.

TSEDAKAH
In the Jewish tradition of *tsedakah*, consider giving all the flowers to a hospital or nursing home after the reception. Have this announced to your guests at dinner, before they start taking the flowers apart to take home.

CHOOSING A FLORIST
Ask your friends, your caterer or your synagogue for recommendations. Observe as you attend functions yourself; ask who has done the flowers, if you are impressed by them.

Ask the florist to give you the names of people whose weddings he or she has done recently and check with them. Were they satisfied? Was everything delivered as promised?

Ask to see samples of work done. Look around the shop itself. Is it neat? Attractive? Do you see good flowers in the cooler and on display? Are the people you talk to friendly, courteous, receptive to your ideas? What design suggestions do they make when you discuss your color scheme?

Although the concept of "seasonal" flowers has changed with the spread of air-delivered flowers from all over the world, if you can work with whatever flowers are most abundant at the time of your wedding, you will find they are probably less expensive. If your wedding date coincides with Mother's Day, Valentine's Day or Christmas, be prepared to pay a bit more, as these are peak times for flowers, and do place your order as early as you can, because flowers become scarce then, too.

Have a preliminary proposal made in writing, or take notes. Consider your plan carefully before placing your order.

PRESERVING YOUR BOUQUET

Some florists are equipped to preserve and mount the bridal bouquet in a glass dome or framed arrangement. This may cost as much as your bouquet! If you really want this keepsake, check out the kits and books available that will show you how to preserve flowers yourself. The directions can even be found in some microwave cookbooks. You could mount a small garland of the dried flowers arranged around your wedding invitation for an interesting memento.

YOUR WEDDING CAKE

If you are having your reception catered by a kosher establishment, you will have no problem finding a baker, because you will not be allowed to use any baker but the caterer's own, or one he or she recommends as being unquestionably kosher. (That baker will also supply the wedding *hallah*.) Your only choices in the wedding cake will be the filling, the icing and the decoration. Ask to taste a sample. Many of these cakes resemble white or yellow flannel in taste and texture, and are topped by too thick, too sweet sugar icing. Some, though, can be very good.

FLORIST CHECKLIST

Name of florist_____

Phone _____

Address _____

_____

Contact_____

ORDER: CHARGE TO: BRIDE   GROOM

Bride's bouquet

   color and type of flowers _____

   _____

   style _____ $ _____

Mothers' flowers (for both mothers)

   color and type of flowers _____

   _____

   style _____ $ _____

Wedding party

   Matron/Maid of honor

     color _____

     style _____ $_____

   Bridesmaids

     number _____

     color _____

     style _____ $_____

   Flower girl baskets

     number _____ $_____

   Boutonnieres

     Groom

     Best Man/Ushers

       number _____ $ _____

ORDER: CHARGE TO: BRIDE   GROOM

   Fathers/Grandfathers

     number _____ $ _____

Ceremony Decorations

  Platform (*bimah*)

    Style_____ $_____

    Other decorations (list)

    _____

    _____ $_____

  Huppah

    Style _____ $_____

Reception Decorations

  Color scheme _____

  Bridal table _____ $_____

  Buffet table _____ $_____

  Centerpieces

    number _____ @ _____ $_____

Other room decorations

    _____

    _____ $_____

Subtotals	$_____	$ _____ *
Sales tax	$_____	$ _____ *
Grand total	$_____	$ _____ *
Deposit	$_____	$ _____
Balance	$_____	$ _____

Date Due _____

Payable by ❑ cash ❑ check ❑ credit card

Enter these figures in the cash flow chart.

  *Note: This division of expenses is traditional, but the two families may agree to share the cost of the flowers in other ways. Be sure all the parties understand what the share is. You may want to have the orders made out and signed separately, and the bills presented separately.

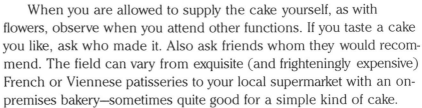

When you are allowed to supply the cake yourself, as with flowers, observe when you attend other functions. If you taste a cake you like, ask who made it. Also ask friends whom they would recommend. The field can vary from exquisite (and frighteningly expensive) French or Viennese patisseries to your local supermarket with an on-premises bakery—sometimes quite good for a simple kind of cake.

Start looking early on, about three months before the wedding date, if you have that much time. If you will be ordering from a baker (not your caterer), do the smart thing: Before you make a commitment, purchase a small layer cake in the flavor and frosting you fancy, take it home and have the family give it the taste test.

Special-order cakes take time to make, especially if you want something "custom" in the decoration. You can choose cake frosting in the colors of the reception or decorated with original motifs that have personal significance. Just bear in mind that every special item adds to the cost. Allow at least two weeks, although some bakers say they can make up a fairly standard cake for a short-notice wedding in three to four days.

You need not limit yourself to the conventional white or yellow cake. There are fruit-flavored (strawberry, raspberry, lemon) and liqueur-flavored (such as Amaretto or Kahlua) white or yellow cakes. You can choose almond, nut, mocha, spice or even chocolate cake. Fillings can be fruit or flavored creams (nondairy for kosher cakes). Use your imagination, but watch the costs.

HOW BIG A CAKE?

In a good, moderately priced bakery, a cake yielding about one hundred servings will cost between $150 and $200, plus any extra charges you run up for fancy ornamentation. The cakes are usually made in graduated round tiers, ranging from a small 8-to-10-inch top layer to a 16-incher in a four-tier model that will serve about 125 people. Once you have made the first cut in the cake, it will be whisked away to be cut up. Here is one trick where you can save, especially if you have more than a hundred guests. Have a nice, moderate-size show cake and order enough matching sheet cake to

QUESTIONS FOR THE BAKER

How far in advance do I have to order the cake? _____

What choices do you offer in cake? _____

_____

_____

Fillings? _____

_____

_____

Icing? _____

_____

_____

Ornamentation? _____

_____

_____

How big a cake do I need? _____guests_____tiers—sizes _____

How much will it cost? Choice A _____ B _____ C _____

Can I see samples? Taste? (for a caterer's baker) _____

Can you deliver to_____

_____

_____(address)?

Charge? _____

Will you set the cake up at the reception site?_____

Payment terms: Deposit $_____ Balance $_____ Due _____

(Try for payment on delivery—to ensure promptness and proper setup.)

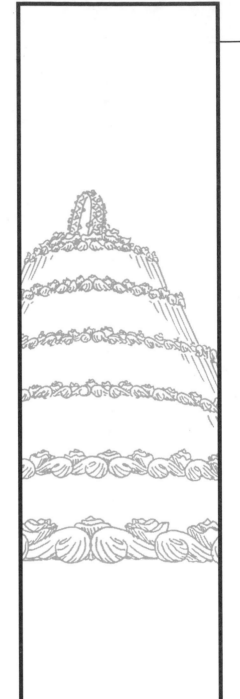

feed the whole crowd. None of your guests will know the difference, but your expense sheet will. And it's all too likely that your caterer is doing this, unbeknownst to you, anyway.

FOR DO-IT-YOURSELFERS

If you're having a home wedding, or a self-catered function in a rented hall, you can make your own cake—if you, your mom or a friend are fairly experienced bakers. You can work this in easy stages. A few weeks before the date, bake a tier every few days, until you have the three or four you need; wrap each one and store it in your freezer. You can make each tier a different flavor, if you like. Unless you have taken a cake decorating course, stay with a good white frosting (Royal, which is made with egg whites and dries like a hard shell, will keep your cake fresh-tasting, even if you frost it several days ahead) and then decorate very simply, with a few butter cream roses and swirls, or spun sugar ornaments you can buy at cake decorator supply houses. Edible silver shot lends glamor, and fresh flowers are truly lovely. Lily of the valley, with its flat green leaves and fragrant blossoms, orange blossoms, violets or tiny roses will make a beautiful cake without too much stress-inducing demand on your skill. And let purists howl—you can prepare a very creditable cake with top-quality cake and frosting mixes. A little liqueur improves these short cuts.

Check boxes of cake mix carefully. Many are kosher, but all except angel food cake will be dairy. Frosting mixes are generally dairy. To make a *parve* (neutral, neither dairy nor meat) cake, substitute a kosher *parve* margarine for the butter in the recipe; use fruit juices instead of milk or cream. The many kosher cookbooks now on the market have cake recipes that you can adapt for a wedding cake, using the tips in a booklet obtainable from the Betty Crocker customer service department. Another helpful booklet on using cake mixes to make a wedding cake is published by Pillsbury Wedding Cakes, P.O. Box 550, Minneapolis, MN 55440, or call 1–800–767–4466.

You can find simple but good recipes in standard cookbooks, with clear directions that explain every step of the process. Cake

שמח

decorating books will show you many examples of this art, but most require a great deal of skill and equipment. Use them for ideas only!

THE MUSICIANS

"If music be the food of love, play on!" Shakespeare, as usual, had the words for it. Music is a very important part of any wedding, both to enhance the ceremony and to accentuate the jubilation at the reception. When you have a choice of musicians, seek recommendations from friends and relatives and the caterer. Check also whether the synagogue can provide a choir or organist for the ceremony.

Make time to go out and audition the bands at work. It can be part of your overall examination of a place you are considering. Some band leaders will offer you audition tapes. These are not always truly representative of the sound you will be getting. When bands are busy, during the height of the wedding or holiday party season, you may get the leader's name over a group of pickup musicians who may or may not be as great as you want your music to be. That is why you must see the group at work.

YOUR CHOICES

Your music-makers can range from an instrumental soloist or a classical trio for a small reception to a full-size dance orchestra for a large one. Continuous music costs more, but it is worth it for the added liveliness it brings. So are strolling musicians during dinner. You will need three or four pieces for up to a hundred guests and five or six for a larger group. Some band leaders base the required size of the band on the size of the reception hall.

When you are deciding on the type of music you want, remember that you will have people of varying ages and generations at the reception. Neither all heavy metal rock or all quiet classical will make everyone happy. Be sure your musicians can play a variety of styles—ethnic, "society" (dance music) and rock, so that everyone has a chance to dance and rejoice at your wedding.

Very popular musicians are booked up well in advance, especially at holiday times, so start looking and listening early.

Where Can You Find Jewish Music?

YOUR SYNAGOGUE LIBRARY, LOCAL JEWISH BOOKSTORE AND A LARGE WELL-STOCKED RECORD STORE CAN ALL GIVE YOU SHEET MUSIC TO PLAY OR RECORDINGS TO LISTEN TO.

IF YOU HAVE ACCESS TO A COMPUTER, YOU CAN FIND SOURCES OF JEWISH SHEET MUSIC AND RECORDS IN THE JUDAISM SECTION OF AMERICA ONLINE OR OTHER ONLINE SERVICES. AMERICAN ONLINE ALSO HAS A JUDAICA STORE FROM WHICH YOU CAN ORDER SOME OF THESE ITEMS. WHEN YOU GO ONLINE YOU WILL ALSO FIND LISTINGS FOR PHOTOGRAPHERS, ARTISTS WHO WRITE *KETUBAHS*, AND OTHER WEDDING PURVEYORS. AND OF COURSE, YOU CAN SEARCH THE WORLD WIDE WEB FOR ALL KINDS OF SPECIALTY ITEMS.

SHEET MUSIC IS PUBLISHED BY, AMONG OTHERS, TARA PUBLICATIONS, PAUL ZIM PRODUCTIONS, AND KAMMEN MUSIC. THEY ALSO HAVE RECORDINGS FOR SALE.

MUSIC CHECKLIST

Does the sound at the live party equal what you heard on the tape? _____

_____

How do the musicians dress and behave at work? _____

_____

What ambiance do they project? _____

_____

What types of music do they play? _____

_____

Do they know the traditional music you may want? _____

_____

Will they undertake to learn it if you provide the sheet music? _____

_____

Will they play for the ceremony as well as for the reception? _____

_____

What special features do they offer as entertainment? _____

_____

_____

Will the band leader act as master of ceremonies? _____

What do you think of his or her choice of humorous material?_____

_____

Does the band get everyone up and dancing at the party you observe? _____

_____

Will the band play requests and ethnic material?_____

_____

(See Chapter 5 for appropriate music for a Jewish wedding.)

מש מח

DETAILS OF THE MUSIC CONTRACT

You will be signing a legal contract for the music. It should specify the date, time and exact location of the reception and:

1. Number of players (the leader may count as two in some union contracts) _____
2. Fee per player $_____
3. Number of hours of music for this fee (allowing a half-hour for setup)_____
   Time_____ to _____
4. Overtime charges begin_____
   Charge per hour $_____ Minimum overtime $_____
5. Taxes (in most states music is not taxable) $_____
   Union pension and welfare fund surcharge $_____
   (usually a percentage of the total price)
6. Terms of payment
   Total cost $_____ (before overtime)
   Deposit $_____
   Balance due $_____(payable on the day of the wedding, not before)

   Enter these figures in the cash flow sheet at the back of this book.

7. Cancellation clause—for your protection, state costs if you have to cancel.
   Musicians selected—Name of Band_____
   Leader_____Phone_____

USING A DJ

There's nothing like a good live band to put pep into your party. The operative word is *good*. Your budget may not permit hiring the musicians you really want, or the available groups in your area may not be suitable for a wedding where the guests will be of all ages and generations. You can then turn to recorded tapes and CDs.

In this situation, hiring an experienced DJ with professional equipment is the best solution. The best way to find one is by word of mouth, or through your own experience in attending functions at which

Storm Warning!

BE SURE THE BAND LEADER KNOWS THE EXACT TIME AND LOCATION OF THE RECEPTION AND HOW TO GET THERE. YOU DON'T WANT A LOST BASS PLAYER AND A DRUMMER AND THEIR EQUIPMENT WANDERING ABOUT LOOKING FOR YOU.

IMPRESS THE NEED FOR PROMPTNESS. THE BAND SHOULD BE FULLY SET UP AND TUNED BEFORE THE GUESTS ARRIVE. AND ON THE RIGHT DAY AND TIME!

CHECK OUT THE ELECTRICAL SETUP AT ANY UNCONVENTIONAL LOCATION OR YOUR HOME. ELECTRIC INSTRUMENTS NEED POWER AND PROPER OUTLETS TO FUNCTION. IF IN DOUBT, HAVE THE LEADER DO A SITE CHECK.

a DJ has provided the music. Most DJs also act as a master of ceremonies. Check out their acts carefully. Watch out for the ones who specialize in insults, foul language and double entendres. And did the DJ have the guests up and dancing at the affair you auditioned?

Ask about the DJ's record library. Does he or she have the selections you especially want played at your reception? Will he or she get certain special ethnic numbers you want? Will you be charged for the discs or tapes (which the DJ will keep)?

Your agreement with the DJ should include:

Date, time and place of the reception (and how to get there, if necessary)
Hours of music_____Charge $_____
Overtime charges per hour $_____

If you really have to economize, you can ask a reliable friend or relative to work the tape or compact-disc player, give him or her the record library you want to use, and hope for the best. If your sound system is not really adequate, you can rent sound equipment for the day. Make sure you and your friend know how to work it.

PRETTY AS A PICTURE: PHOTOGRAPHERS

Your wedding pictures are a precious record, preserving not only the appearance but also the emotions of this important day in your lives. Hiring the best professional photographer you can afford will ensure you against the disappointment and regret that come from poor pictures.

FINDING A PHOTOGRAPHER

To select a photographer, get recommendations from friends and the caterer. Look through your friends' albums and visit several studios. Examine the work carefully. Look for crisp and careful composition. Do you see good use of lighting, varied backgrounds? Is the color clear, natural-looking and not garish? Are the "candid" shots in good taste? This is a very individual matter, so if you don't want pictures

משמח

of the groom putting the blue garter on the bride's leg, or the bride smearing the groom's face with the wedding cake, steer clear of photographers who like such shots.

You can also see examples of photographers' work at bridal fairs and photography shows. Be warned that the photos in the portfolios presented may not have been taken by the person who will actually be taking pictures at your wedding. If you decide to interview a photographer, ask who will be assigned to your sessions and ask to see that person's work. If they can't or won't do this, they are probably going to use a "pick-up" approach, taking anyone available from their "stable" (list) on the day. Steer clear of such places; the results can vary from beautiful albums to a mess.

Good photography runs into money. Get references; ask for the names of former clients and ask them if they were satisfied with the work, the photographer's attitude on the job and the "value" factor—did they feel they got what they paid for?

The best studios tend to be booked up well in advance, so start early on this search. It's best to stay with studios that specialize in wedding photography; they have the experience and the equipment to handle on-site picture-taking, which is quite different from studio portraiture.

SMILE! YOU'RE ON TV!

Do you want a video of your wedding? Don't jump to answer yes before you think this through. Camcorders are such common possessions that every conceivable event is now immortalized on videotape. The question is how often, after the first few weeks, you are going to pop the tape into your VCR to watch the proceedings once more. You can leaf through an album or look at a group of framed pictures far more easily without all the gadgetry. On the other hand, videos will show you, the bride and groom and stars of the show, how things really looked that day, as compared with the posed quality of formal portraits. You will also get the sound of the occasion and the feeling of the whole group as they rejoiced with you.

~

When a Friend Takes the Pictures

BE CAREFUL! RELYING ON A CAMERA-BUG FRIEND AS YOUR ONLY PHOTOGRAPHER IS NOT WISE, UNLESS SPECIAL CIRCUMSTANCES MAKE IT DIFFICULT TO HIRE A PROFESSIONAL. (FOR EXAMPLE, IT MAY WELL BE PROHIBITIVELY EXPENSIVE, IF NOT IMPOSSIBLE, TO FIND A PERSON WHO IS WILLING TO HAUL HIS EQUIPMENT OUT TO YOUR SUNRISE WEDDING AT A DESERTED BEACH!) WHEN A FRIEND OFFERS, IT IS TEMPTING TO ACCEPT; WHEN YOU KNOW ONE OF YOUR FRIENDS IS GOOD WITH THE CAMERA, IT IS TEMPTING TO ASK. BUT IT CAN BE AN IMPOSITION ON A GUEST, WHO MAY FEEL THAT THE PRESSURE TO GET A PERFECT PICTURE SPOILS HIS OR HER ENJOYMENT OF THE PARTY. MOREOVER, AS MANY A BRIDE HAS DISCOVERED TO HER REGRET, CHAMPAGNE AND CAMERAS DO NOT MIX WELL.

YOU CAN PLAN TO HAVE A MINIMUM NUMBER OF PROFESSIONAL SHOTS AND HAVE YOUR FRIENDS' CANDIDS SUPPLEMENT THEM. BE SURE THE AMATEURS KEEP OUT OF THE PROFESSIONAL'S WAY. UNPLEASANT ARGUMENTS MAY RESULT IF THEY DO NOT.

~

In choosing a videographer, apply the same criteria that you would for a photographer. His or her pictures should be clear, crisp and in proper, natural color. Some photo studios may also offer video services. That will have you dealing with only one supplier, which tends to make things easier. You can also try the old reliable word-of-mouth. If you're going with a friend's recommendation, ask whether the videographer became an intrusive "spectacle director," ordering the guests around in and out of the picture. Avoid this, of course.

For the best results, you will want the videographer to use the latest equipment, to have editing and dubbing machines, microphones and lights for special effects. Will there be more than one camera? How many assistants will there be? Ask to audition sample tapes. They should be cable-quality productions.

An award-winning video won't be cheap. Special effects and elaborate video formats run into a great deal of money. In the end, your budget and what you feel is most important will decide these matters. The least expensive setup uses one camera and does not provide for editing afterward. Much of the footage may turn out to be boring, but if this is all you can afford, you will still have your videotape record and you can always fast-forward over the boring spots. (With this as your safety, you might consider asking your uncle to do the taping on his camcorder while you spend your budget on professional stills.)

PLANNING THE PICTURE-TAKING

Once you've decided on the photographer and the videographer, sit down with them and discuss your desires and expectations. This is the time to discover whether they are courteous, open to your ideas and creative. There are certain shots that are traditional; go over these with the photographer and decide which ones you want, which to eliminate and which you might want to add. If you want pictures of people who are not in the wedding party, make out a list of the guests and events you want to capture on film.

Traditional formal pictures include:

PORTRAITS

- ❏ Bride and groom—official portrait
- ❏ The entire wedding party
- ❏ Bride, groom and family members
- ❏ Bride with both parents
- ❏ Groom with both parents
- ❏ Bride with in-laws
- ❏ Groom with in-laws
- ❏ Bride and groom with grandparents or other special relatives

These are usually taken right after the ceremony, while everyone is still fresh and unrumpled.

CEREMONY PHOTOS

Most synagogues will not allow picture-taking in the sanctuary during the ceremony. For the most serene, dignified ceremony in other venues, you should not permit it either. Using a zoom lens from a position at the doorway, a skillful photographer can get most of these shots. The ones at the *huppah* can be posed afterward while the bride and groom are observing a brief seclusion.

- ❏ Each member of the wedding party as he or she enters to go down the aisle
- ❏ The groom and his parents, as they enter
- ❏ The bride and her parents, as they enter
- ❏ The wedding party grouped at the *huppah*
- ❏ The wedding vows
- ❏ The ring ceremony
- ❏ Any special ceremony events, such as circling the groom, lighting candles
- ❏ Participants who are honored with readings
- ❏ The kiss
- ❏ The walk back as a married couple

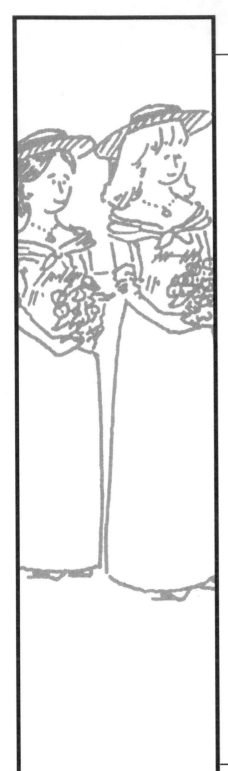

INFORMAL OR CANDID SHOTS (OR SCENES TO BE USED IN A VIDEOTAPE)

❑ The bride and her parents arriving at the ceremony
❑ The groom arriving at the ceremony
❑ Bride and bridesmaids getting ready before the ceremony
❑ The bride giving flowers to the mothers and grandmothers
❑ The bride giving a boutonniere to her father
❑ The groom and best man putting on boutonnieres
❑ Putting on the veil—the *b'deken* if you're following tradition
❑ The groom signing the *ketubah*, also the bride signing if it's a modern or equalized contract
❑ The bride and groom entering the reception room
❑ The first dance
❑ Cutting the cake
❑ Shots of the invitation and the *ketubah*
❑ Table shots—greetings and comments from guests (for a videotape)
❑ Cutting the *hallah*
❑ Saying Grace at the end of the meal
❑ Anything else you think you may want

Be sure to ask how many pictures will be taken—a good photographer plans to shoot about three times as many as you have opted for, to give you the widest possible choice.

After you've gone over all of this, the photographer and the videographer should understand what you want and be able to come up with suggestions for the best package or standard deal—how many albums, how many photos to be framed, etc. Some packages include frames, parents' books, and black-and-whites for newspaper announcements. Ask for the exact price for the photos you have ordered and also the charges for any additional reprints of individual photos people may request; the same for additional copies of the videotape.

You should have a copy of your videotape made as a "safety," just in case something happens to the original. Though you can run off extra copies of your photos on a color copy printer, they will never be as clear and sharp as the originals, or copies made by the

photographer. Some photographers may raise questions about the rights, as they claim the images are their property.

Among the extras that studios offer are thank-you cards with a picture of the bride and groom. It seems like a very nice, personal touch, if your budget allows for it, but, let's face it, most people glance at them and throw them out, so why not just send a nice handwritten note on good stationery?

BRIDAL PORTRAITS

Though you can arrange to be photographed in your gown at the time of the final fitting, so that you have a bridal photo for newspaper announcements, most brides wait until the wedding day for this picture. Not only is it hard for bridal salons to get your dress finished in time for an advance picture-taking session, but many brides feel a deep reluctance about wearing the dress before the wedding day. Apart from this feeling, you know you will look your best on your wedding day with that special bridal radiance. You can use your engagement picture or any other portrait you like for newspaper announcements.

THE PHOTOGRAPHY CONTRACT

You will be signing a contract for services that can range from $400 to $4,000. Get a fixed price up front so you know what expenses you are running into for pictures and can plan sensibly.

The contract should specify:

Date, time and place of photo sessions
__photo albums, consisting of ____pages @ $_____per album
Total $_____

__additional photos _____ @ $_____ each   Total $_____
__extra albums ____pages @ $_____per album
Total $_____
___number of pictures to be taken at the wedding
___number of proofs to be shown to you

Specify that you will choose the pictures to be included in the finished work.

Time when photographer will arrive_____(allowing enough time for pictures you want before the ceremony)

Time when photographer will leave_____

Cost if slides are made and only the pictures you want are printed   Total $_____

Negatives to be kept by_____

List parts of "package deal"—(If selected) _____, _____, _____   Total $_____

Terms of Payment:

Deposit $_____

Balance $_____ due_____*

*on completion of satisfactory work

Enter the money figures in your expense records at the back of this book.

Photographer selected_____

Address_____

Phone_____

Contact_____

A BICYCLE BUILT FOR TWO? TRANSPORTATION ISSUES

Though some couples may have arrived at their weddings on bicycles, on motorcycles or in hot-air balloons, you will probably be much happier to use a sleek white limo complete with bar and TV—if the budget can stand it.

Coordinate your need for cars and drivers. Check out the limousine services available to you and inspect their cars. Referrals from friends are your best guarantee of reliable service. Reserve your date and time well in advance, then double-check during the week before the wedding to make sure your reservation is still in the computer. Any driver or company you hire should be fully licensed and insured.

Be sure the drivers have the correct addresses and times for their pickups as well as their destinations. If the reception will be in a different place from the ceremony, be sure the car pool drivers know the address and above all, how to get there. Give the drivers a list of their passengers.

Arrange for payment of hired drivers either before or after the wedding. Some livery companies add a tip for the driver to the bill, some do not. Ask—you will want to tip a driver who has performed well, but if you are not completely happy, you certainly don't want to tip twice! If the driver owns his or her own limo, you do not tip.

You can do with just one hired car for yourself and your parents. If you have to move from the ceremony location to the reception, you use the same car to travel there as a couple, while the parents share the car used to drive the groom and his parents to the ceremony.

Order your transportation to get you and the groom to the synagogue or hall an hour ahead of time, to allow time to finish dressing and to take pictures. Arrange for your bridesmaids to arrive at least a half hour early if they are to dress together and be in your photos.

If you can't arrange to hire wedding transportation, seek out your friends and relatives who have cars they would be willing to let you use. They will probably offer to drive. All you ask is that the cars be clean. Thank your friends with a little gift, a tank of gas and a car wash you pay for.

COMMON SERVICE PROBLEMS (AND HOW TO AVOID THEM)

CONTRACTS

You need a proper contract or letter of agreement for each service you are ordering, even stationery (which, for a large wedding, can run into real money). If the service provider does not have a contract form, write out the specifics of your order in duplicate and have both copies signed by the two of you. Keep one copy and give him or her the other.

TRANSPORTATION CHECKLIST

Make a copy of this list for the car service, then give each person in the wedding party a card with the name and phone number of the driver and the time of the pick-up.

Bride and Parents

Driver_____Phone _____

Time to be at house* _____

Address _____

Transfer to reception** _____

Address _____

Fee $_____

Groom and Parents

Driver_____Phone_____

Time to be at house* _____

Address _____

Transfer to reception** _____

Address _____

Fee $_____

*Time this to arrive one hour before the ceremony for photos and paperwork.

**For the trip to the reception, the bride and groom ride together, while the parents share the car used to transport the groom and his parents.

Bridesmaids (to ceremony and transfer to reception)

Name _____

Driver_____Phone _____

Address _____

Time to be at house_____*

Name _____

Driver_____Phone _____

Address _____

Time to be at house_____*

Name _____

Driver_____Phone _____

Address _____

Time to be at house_____*

*Time this to allow the bridesmaids to arrive at the synagogue or hall at least a half hour before the ceremony.

Car Pool (for guests who may need a ride)

Driver _____

Passengers _____

_____

_____

_____

_____

_____

_____

_____

Driver _____

Passengers _____

_____

_____

_____

_____

_____

_____

Note: If you have guests arriving from out-of-town, don't try to meet planes or trains. Offer them the names of car services, directions for public transportation, or the names of willing friends. There is tension enough for both immediate families without this added responsibility on the wedding day.

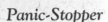

Panic-Stopper

FOR THE GROOM AND THE FATHERS: MAKE A NOTE OF THE CASH YOU WILL NEED ON THE WEDDING DAY FOR TIPS AND MISCELLANEOUS OTHER SMALL EXPENSES. TO CUT DOWN THE STRESS ON THE WEDDING DAY, THE GROOM MAY PUT THIS SUM ASIDE IN AN ENVELOPE AND GIVE IT TO THE BEST MAN TO HOLD FOR HIM AND DISBURSE AS TIPS FOR DELIVERY PEOPLE, PORTERS, LIMO DRIVERS AND THE LIKE. DON'T FORGET TO TAKE ANY CASH THAT'S LEFT WITH YOU ON YOUR HONEYMOON TRIP. YOU'LL NEED IT. (SEE CHAPTER 22 FOR A GUIDE TO TIPPING WHEN YOU TRAVEL).

FOR THE BRIDE: MAKE A SEPARATE LIST OF ALL THE SUPPLIERS' NAMES AND PHONE NUMBERS ON CARDS FOR YOURSELF AND YOUR MOTHER. GIVE YOUR FIANCÉ AND HIS MOTHER A CARD WITH ONLY THOSE NUMBERS THEY WILL NEED, SUCH AS THE ONES FOR THE FLORIST, THE LIQUOR STORE, AND THE DRIVERS. THEY SHOULD NOT CALL ANY OF THE OTHER SUPPLIERS YOU WILL BE DEALING WITH, BUT RATHER CLEAR ANY SPECIAL REQUESTS THEY MAY HAVE THROUGH YOU OR YOUR MOTHER.

The contract or letter should specify exactly the merchandise or service ordered, the delivery date and the full price. It should state that there will be no additional charges, BUT that if there are some prices, such as the market price of flowers, that may fluctuate, there should be a limit specified on the total extra charge. Learn the phrase "not to exceed X amount."

Make sure the provider signs the contract. Some less reputable places have the bride and groom sign, then do not sign themselves. Technically, this is not a valid contract and they are not bound to the details.

Put down as small a deposit as possible, especially for any custom-made items, such as your gown, your printing or your flowers. This gives you some leverage if the company does not perform to your satisfaction. Be sure there is a cancellation clause with reasonable fees for a cancellation months in advance.

For photography contracts, add a clause stating that you will owe no money and all deposits will be refunded if the photos do not turn out right, or if the photos you specified were not taken. Negotiate the price of additional prints.

For flower contracts, make sure you specify the substitutions you will accept if unusual or out-of-season flowers are not available. Make a note that you will adjust the balance due if the flowers are not fresh, or the arrangements fall apart because they are not securely fastened.

It shouldn't be necessary, but in your music contract it is prudent to include a clause stating that the musicians must arrive on time, properly dressed. "Grunge" may be okay at a rock concert, but not at your wedding!

CHAPTER 13

WEDDING GIFTS

The tradition of giving wedding gifts not only helps a couple set up their first household but also enables the guests to add to the rejoicing that accompanies the start of their life together. Everyone who attends the wedding is expected to give a gift. Often people you've invited who cannot attend send you gifts as well.

Though both guests and newlyweds sometimes calibrate their gifts to the scale of the affair (big wedding, big gift, small wedding, not-so-big-a-gift), you really should not participate in this kind of comparison. A big check from that rich uncle in Australia whom you've never met should not be compared to a small but specially selected gift from your graduate student pal or your great-aunt who is living on a small pension. Which gifts come from the heart of the giver, from the desire to start you two off on a happy life together? One of the best reasons for not showing off your guests' generosity by displaying the gifts at a home reception is to prevent invidious comparisons.

Above all, if you or your parents throw an ostentatious wedding you can't afford, with the idea that cash gifts will enable you to recoup the cost, think again. You may, but what if you do not? And who gets to keep the cash, you or Mom and Dad? There is also, within some tightly knit communities, a competitive spirit that enters into the planning which can make things turn rather ugly. One-upmanship in the hospitality area can take a couple and their parents to ridiculous extremes of extravagance. Enjoy the generous impulses that cause your guests to give you gifts, and do your best not to be mercenary or materialistic about the gifts themselves.

SAFEGUARDING YOUR GIFTS

Wedding gifts of money are a Jewish tradition. You're not going to keep these in the cookie jar or under the mattress, so plan with your fiancé to open a joint account for the deposit of your checks and cash gifts. Also arrange for a safe-deposit box for any bonds you may receive. The gifts will start showering into the bride's home before the wedding day, so make your bank arrangements well before the date.

"The envelope." On your wedding day this refers to the ones containing checks or cash that will be handed to you as you make the rounds of the tables, greeting your guests. Though the envelopes are given to you, you should arrange with someone (your father or mother or your trusty brother or sister) to hold on to these for you till you can check them off on your gift list and get to the bank to deposit them. In the excited haze that surrounds you while you're center stage, it is all too easy for you or your new husband to mislay or lose some of those envelopes.

Though it is rare at Jewish weddings, some people will bring gift packages to the reception. Arrange with the caterer to have a locked area where these presents can be kept until it is time to take them home. Ask your maid of honor or the best man to take charge of these gifts and watch to see that the cards do not become separated from the gift boxes. That, plus the danger of breakage, is the reason that you do not open these packages at the reception.

Your floater insurance policy should cover all your gifts while they are in transport and after you bring them to your new home.

THE "WISH LIST," OR, HOW TO GET WHAT YOU REALLY WANT

After all the jokes you hear about receiving six food processors, four coffee makers, and table linens in impossible colors, you will appreciate the idea of making up a list of things you and your fiancé really want for your new home. Give this list to your mother or your maid of honor. Include your silver and china patterns and your color schemes for table, bed and bath linens. There is no need to be shy about expressing your true desires. If a guest didn't want to be sure of giving you something you will enjoy, he or she wouldn't ask!

Your list-keeper should note who is giving what, to avoid duplications as much as possible.

If you would truly prefer a monetary gift, your family may very properly suggest this alternative, *if asked*. Your mother can tactfully mention that you don't yet know just where you will live, or that you are moving to a distant area, or that you plan to pool the cash gifts to make a major household purchase.

THE BRIDAL REGISTRY

In essence, a bridal registry does what your mother or maid of honor would do—tells people what items you have said you would like and makes a note of the gifts purchased for you to avoid duplications—all by computer magic. Some registries even note who bought what for you, so that if a card is lost or a gift does not arrive, you or the giver can easily track the vital information.

Should you register? From a practical point of view, it will save your well-wishers worrying time (about what to give and shopping time to find it). You will stand a much better chance of receiving things you really need to set up your new home. And, let's face it, it's much, much easier to return or exchange a gift you absolutely hate or can't use when everything comes from the same source.

SELECTING A REGISTRY

You start by selecting stores that offer a registry service and carry a large selection of good stuff, quality items in colors and styles you like. The best choices for most people are department stores, since you can centralize your list based on their wide array of merchandise. Specialty stores are a possibility, but they may make life difficult for your guests, who will have to hunt around for them. If your people live in many different cities, a store that is part of a national chain, like J. C. Penney or Macy's, is a wise choice because your list will be posted in all their stores.

The next step is to shop the store carefully, as if you were really buying everything yourself. Pick out china and silver patterns, colors for the bedroom, bathroom, kitchen and table linens. Decide what appliances you'd like. Look at decorative objects such as mirrors, vases, trays and other bibelots. Some stores will send you around with a registry consultant who will help you with suggestions and make up your list. At others, you will be given a list to check off and add to as you make the rounds.

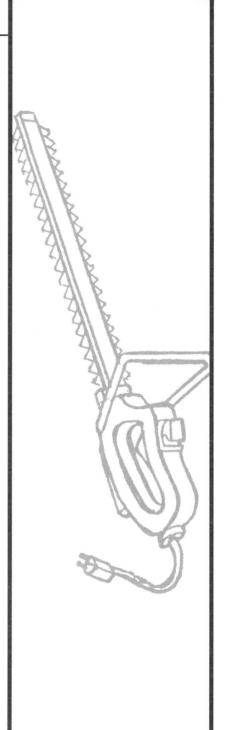

YOUR FIANCÉ'S CHOICES

You may have to dragoon him into it, but try to have your fiancé go along with you on some of these shopping trips. After all, he's going to live in the house too, and he will have some favorite items and some decor he can't abide. And did you know that Home Depot, Builders Square, Ace Hardware and other home improvement sources now offer you registry service? So, too, do the sporting goods giants, like L. L. Bean, Paragon, Land's End, REI, Campmor and others, from whose catalogs you can select as gifts just about any sporting or outdoor equipment the two of you can imagine. Big music and video outfits, like Tower Records, are getting into the game, as well.

PRICE RANGES

In choosing a store and in adding items to your list, don't just go for the upscale or the pricey that you know you could never afford or live up to. Try to have some moderately priced, practical things in the mix, as well as fine china and crystal. Chances are you'll use a set of fine stainless steel cookware (which can cost a mint) for many more years than you will a set of Lenox china cups and saucers; what's more, your less affluent friends can team up to give you the pots and pans without each going broke in the process. And just imagine this: You list the finest sterling silver flatware, where a teaspoon costs twenty dollars, or Royal Doulton dinnerware at over two hundred dollars a place setting because only the best will do for you. Then you receive only one or two place settings or a few odd serving pieces. What are you going to do? Fill out the set yourself? Dine in solitary splendor with your two settings?

Your guests are going to spend what they feel they want to spend, not what you seem to demand through a registry list of high-ticket items. If everything on the list is in a price category your guests regard as too rich for their pocketbooks, they are going to be resentful about giving you a gift—when it ought to come freely from their hearts because they genuinely want to make you happy.

CHECKING THE REGISTRY'S SERVICE

The registry's real service to you comes after you have made up your list. The store prints out a computerized list for everyone who asks, and keeps it up to date by striking out presents that have already been sent. A guest can order by phone and credit card and have the gift wrapped and sent by the store. Some stores will send catalogs to guests who request them, so that they can order by mail.

It's important to have the registry list your fiancé's name along with yours and the date of the wedding. There may be more than one bride with the same or a similar name in the computer; and some of your fiancé's guests who are using the registry may not be too familiar with your birth name. A comprehensive listing always helps to avoid mixups.

WHEN TO REGISTER

When to register is a tricky question. If you're going to have a big engagement party or several showers, you may want to register as soon as your engagement is announced. However, if the wedding is more than six months away, the store might not keep the items on your list in stock that long. Certain categories, such as fine china and crystal and good linens, are fairly stable in a store's inventory; but unusual, boutique-type ornamental or luxury items may disappear after each big clearance sale. Discuss this inventory matter with the registry consultant. Will they special-order a gift for a guest and send you a card telling you it's on order? Just as you may want to update your list from time to time, the store should inform you about any changes in the stock of items you want.

Updating is important also because some of your guests, after they find out what patterns or appliances you have listed, may go out and shop for them at discount stores and send them to you on their own. Unless you let the store know that you have already received a food processor or coffee maker, the item will not be taken off the list. That's how some duplicate presents are born.

משמח

MORE THAN ONE STORE?

Should you register at more than one store? If your guests will be coming from many different parts of the country and you don't fancy the stores with branches in many different cities, you may want to use several different stores in varying locations. You may also want to use both a large department store and a boutique or a store that specializes in one category, such as athletic equipment or home improvement materials, or fine arts (like the Metropolitan Museum of Art shops).

Some stores will offer you incentives to list with them in the form of discounts on things you yourself buy after you register with them, or "point credits" based on the gifts bought from the list that you can use later to buy items you were not given or to fill out a set and so on.

EXCHANGING OR RETURNING GIFTS

Presents you receive from well-meaning guests who don't use your list sometimes present a problem. Either you've been given a dozen silver-plated whatsits that you know you'll never use, or a picture or a lamp so ugly you don't even want to hide it in the closet because it will haunt you.

If you know what store the item came from, it is okay to return it or exchange it yourself. You cannot ask gift-givers to do this for you. They have already gone to a great deal of trouble and expense to select a gift they sincerely hoped you'd enjoy. If you have to make an exchange, write the expected thank-you note without mentioning your intention. It's not exactly a lie to say you appreciate their thoughtfulness in sending you a gift. If they ask about it later, you can tactfully tell them you exchanged the item for a toaster or whatever it is that you really needed. You never, never hint that the gift was atrocious or in bad taste.

Even with a registry list, there may be times when you want to return or exchange a gift—either you weren't given a sufficient number of place settings to make a dinner service, for example, or

You'll Wish You Hadn't . . .

DON'T DO WHAT SOME NOT-SO-SCRUPULOUS BRIDES HAVE DONE. DON'T REGISTER FOR A SLEW OF EXPENSIVE GIFTS, FIGURING THAT YOU'LL RETURN THEM ALL FOR CASH. GUESTS WHO VISIT YOU AFTER THE WEDDING WILL WANT TO SEE THEIR GIFTS DISPLAYED OR IN USE. IT MAY BE DIFFICULT TO EXPLAIN WHY YOU RETURNED A GIFT YOU SPECIFICALLY ASKED FOR. AND BE WARNED—SOME STORES WILL GIVE YOU ONLY AN IN-STORE CREDIT FOR ANY ITEMS YOU RETURN.

ANOTHER PLOY THAT SEEMS SLIGHTLY LESS THAN HONEST IS THE PRACTICE SOME STORES HAVE OF ALLOWING YOU A "GIFT CREDIT." THE GUESTS SELECT ITEMS FROM YOUR LIST, BUT THE GIFTS ARE NOT SENT; INSTEAD, A CREDIT IS ISSUED TO YOU FOR THE TOTAL AMOUNT THAT WOULD HAVE BEEN SPENT ON ALL YOUR GIFTS, AND YOU USE THIS TO BUY WHATEVER YOU LIKE IN THE STORE. SORRY, NO WAD OF CASH WILL CHANGE HANDS! AND HOW DO YOU EXPLAIN THIS SYSTEM TO A VISITOR WHO WANTS TO SEE THE GIFT SELECTED ORIGINALLY? AND WHAT IS THE POINT OF REGISTERING IF IT ISN'T TO EXPRESS YOUR GIFT WISHES IN THE FIRST PLACE?

you've changed your mind about a pattern or color scheme. Such transactions are fair and honest, as long as you use the same store for the substitution you make. Of course, if the store closes out the stock of some item before you've accumulated the complete set you listed, you are within your rights to return what you have already received and go elsewhere with the cash to purchase what you want.

DAMAGED GIFTS

Occasionally a gift arrives in damaged condition. When that happens, it is important to save the wrappings, so you know what store it came from, or, if the giver mailed it himself or herself, whether it was insured. Deal with the store-sent gifts yourself. Just take the item back to the store for a replacement. If the store is out of town, write or call, describe the damage, and follow the store's instructions for returning the merchandise.

If the package was insured by the sender, you will have to write or call and explain what happened, so that he or she can take whatever steps are necessary to get a replacement. If the parcel was not insured, or you do not know or cannot figure out what store it came from, the only graceful way out is simply to write your thank-you note as though the gift had arrived unbroken and hope the givers will not ask to see it in use when they visit.

ANNOUNCING THAT YOU'VE REGISTERED

You can send out the cards some registries give you with your shower invitations, but it is not considered socially correct to enclose them with wedding invitations. Count on the mother-grapevine to get that information out to all who ask.

Definite No-No's: Do not allow the store to send out a mailing to your guest list, announcing your signing on with them. Likewise, never allow the store to include your name in an advertised list of brides who have registered.

THANK-YOU NOTES

Limber up your fingers and break out your best pen and stationery. For every gift you receive you *must* write a thank-you note, even if you've thanked the giver personally at the reception. Can you really remember all the people you spoke with at the reception? Will they remember your verbal thanks?

If you start writing the notes as soon as the gifts come in, you won't have so many to do after the wedding. All your notes should go out as promptly as possible, within one month after the wedding. Not to acknowledge a gift, or to be very tardy in doing so, is extremely rude and can cause serious rifts with friends and relatives. When your guests have gone to trouble and expense to salute your marriage, the very least you can do is put forth the effort it takes to respond promptly. The worst offense a new couple can commit, in some eyes, is to hold on to checks for so long before depositing them that the giver's checking account balance gets totally unbalanced.

Let's use the power of the positive. Don't think of your thank-yous as one hundred letters all at once—regard them as five a day for twenty days! Even giving yourself weekends off, you will still have a month in which to respond. And you don't have to write an essay. A thank-you note need contain only three sentences, as in the model below. There's also no reason why your husband can't share this task. The gifts were for him, too. If he's shy about writing, let him stamp, seal, check off and mail the letters for you or look up the inevitably missing zip code numbers at the post office. And if his handwriting is better than yours, he can write some of the notes, too. Working together makes the task go lightly.

A FORM TO FOLLOW

Write your notes on white, ivory or grey informal folders in blue or black ink. If you use livelier color combinations, be sure your pen matches the border or the monogram.

Never, never type your notes.

The social world hasn't caught up with e-mail yet, either.

A New Kind of Cash Gift

YOUR FRIENDLY HUD (DEPARTMENT OF HOUSING AND URBAN DEVELOPMENT) AND A FEW MORTGAGE LENDERS HAVE MOVED INTO MODERN TIMES BY RECOGNIZING THE DESIRE OF EVERY YOUNG COUPLE TO OWN THEIR OWN HOME, A GOAL THAT SO MANY FIND DIFFICULT TO ACHIEVE. (THE HOME OWNERSHIP RATE FOR PEOPLE UNDER 35 IS 58.8 PERCENT AS AGAINST A NATIONAL AVERAGE OF 65.4 PERCENT.)

HUD HAS ANNOUNCED A BRIDAL REGISTRY INITIATIVE IN WHICH AN ENGAGED COUPLE CAN OPEN AN INTEREST-BEARING SAVINGS ACCOUNT AT ANY ONE OF THIRTY FHA-APPROVED LENDERS AROUND THE COUNTRY. YOUR FAMILY OR FRIENDS CAN CONTRIBUTE TOWARD A DOWN PAYMENT.

The salutation: "Dear Aunt Martha" or "Dear Mrs. Weiss"; or if the gift has been sent by a couple, "Dear Aunt Ida and Uncle Saul" or "Dear Mr. and Mrs. Gold"; for friends, use their first names.

The three necessary sentences (and a fourth optional) after the salutation are:

1. *Thank you for the beautiful (cut glass bowl,* etc.) Or *for your generous check, bond,* etc. (Do not mention the dollar amount.)
2. *It will be just right for our living room* (or some other sentence that indicates how you will use the gift). Or, for a money gift: *We are planning to use it toward our new stereo system* (or whatever large purchase you have in mind).
3. *Daniel* (or *Abigail*) *and I appreciate your thoughtfulness.*
4. (Optional) *We hope you will visit us soon. You will see your gift* (or name the object) *in a place of honor in our new home.*

Close the note *Cordially* or *Affectionately* (for family) or *Fondly* (for friends).

Of course, you may vary the sentences as you please, as long as you cover the bases—the main points.

If your husband writes some of these notes, he mentions your name in sentence three. Whoever writes it signs it—first name only for close friends and relatives, full name for others.

PUTTING IT ALL TOGETHER—SOME MODEL NOTES

> *Date*
>
> *Dear Aunt Grace,*
> *Thank you for the beautiful water goblets. They really complete our dinner table setting. Daniel and I appreciate your thoughtfulness. We look forward to a visit from you, when we can use the goblets as we have dinner together.*
> *Affectionately,*
> *Abigail*

For a gift of cash:

> Date
>
> Dear Mr. and Mrs. Taylor,
> Thank you so much for your generous gift. It will go towards the special rug that Daniel and I have been hoping to buy for our living room. We do appreciate your thoughtfulness.
> Cordially,
> Abigail Goldsmith

PLAYING DETECTIVE

Here's this lovely platter, with no card. Who sent it? How can you thank the sender when you don't know who he or she is? You have to put your wits to work on this one. Often the sender doesn't realize there was no card and is waiting to hear from you. Just as often, the card gets lost in the shuffle.

What to do? If your mom or maid of honor was answering questions about a suitable gift, ask if they remember who offered to send a platter. If you registered, call the gift registry and ask if it can trace the giver. If you still have the wrappings, check for a return address.

Sometimes you can guess from the gift itself who sent it. If your great-aunt Martha always sends a set of pearl-handled fruit knives to the newlywed nieces and nephews, you know whom to thank. You should also let good old Mom and your mother-in-law know which gifts you can't trace. The givers will eventually call one or the other to find out whether you received their offerings.

USING THANK-YOU CARDS

It's been much frowned upon in the past, but in these busy two-career-household days, it has become more acceptable to use a printed thank-you card, always provided you add some personal expression of thanks, such as "The cut glass bowl is so lovely!" and sign the card with both your names. There are some very tasteful cards available at good stationery stores.

A New Kind of Cash Gift (continued)

THE ETIQUETTE LADIES MAY SHUDDER, BUT THIS IS BECOMING AN ACCEPTABLE WAY TO ASK FOR A MONEY GIFT. ONE BANK, AT LEAST, OFFERS CARDS EXPLAINING THE PROGRAM THAT YOU CAN MAIL OUT WITH YOUR INVITATIONS. TACKY? MAYBE, BUT BETTER THAN RECEIVING UNWANTED CRYSTAL STEMWARE OR SILVER THAT NEEDS POLISHING. IN SOME PARTICIPATING MORTGAGE INSTITUTIONS, IF YOU DECIDE NOT TO BUY A HOUSE, THE CASH BELONGS TO YOU. GET THE STRAIGHT INFORMATION BY CALLING 1–800–CALLFHA.

KEEPING TRACK OF GIFTS

You have several choices for organizing your gift record. Before you settle on any one of them, make up your mind that you *can* and *will* keep on top of this chore—a happy one, but a chore nonetheless. Enter your gifts as soon as they are received. Acknowledge them as soon as you can.

If, at the end of the wedding reception, you find yourself with a bulging bride's bag or your husband's inside coat pocket full of checks and cash gifts, put them carefully away till the next day, when you can sort them alphabetically and enter them on your list. If this clerical work will be too much for you, entrust the checks to your father and have him make a list for you—or your mother, if she's the organized one. You can go off on your wedding trip without a care if you have taken pains to secure your gifts.

You can use the columns in your bride's book for this record. This is convenient because you have full names, addresses and phone numbers before you as you work. If you have made a card file instead of the book because your guest list was so long, you can make the entries on your cards. Wherever possible, enter the name of the store the gift came from, just in case. Also enter the amount of any checks or bonds.

If you want a quick visual scan, make use of the following wall chart. If you add two columns, one to record the gift, the other to indicate that you sent your thank-you note, you can use this chart as a gift record as well.

YOUR TROUSSEAU

What's a trousseau? Let's add "hope chest" to that and answer both questions at once. The word "trousseau" comes from the French *trousse*, which means "a small bundle." It refers to the "bundle" of clothes and accessories the bride brings with her to her new home. Brides were supposed to be equipped with enough clothing, personal linen, and the like, to last a year. In today's economy that could cost you a lot more than a small bundle.

GIFT RECORD

Last Names of All Guests (in alphabetical order)	Accept/Regret	Gift (and store) For checks note amount, date deposited	Date note sent

The "hope chest" was a chest or trunk that young girls would start filling, in the good old days when everything was made by hand, with household linens edged with handmade lace and hand-embroidered with the bride's initials. They would start on this day-dream-laden exercise in their early teens and the contents of the chest would embody all their hopes about their fantasy bridegroom. With the magic of cash, check, or charge you can fill up a hope chest today in less time than it takes to write about it, once you know what you want for your new home. This could require another not-so-small bundle, which is why bridal showers were invented.

You do have to give your wardrobe and your household effects some thought, especially if you are a career person. You will be quite busy after you are married and starting to keep house as well as holding a job. It's very comforting to have planned ahead and provided for your needs before career pressures start to eat up your free time after the wedding.

Think with a pen in your hand by filling out the lists on pages 226–28. Go over your household master list after your bridal showers and fill in with the basic necessities for your home. You will probably find that people have given you many lovely "save for best" gifts and overlooked the practical items you may have listed. So now's the time to get that knife set, the steamer, the espresso pot and the dish towels and kitchen tools you'll need for every day. If you will be keeping a kosher kitchen, you will need two of everything in two different color schemes.

Major home furnishings are conventionally the bridegroom's responsibility, but most couples share this cost after they have taken account of the gifts they have received. Your mother may still follow old family ways and provide you with your pillows and a down comforter, but you will have to eke out whatever else you need.

To start your household off in comfortable fashion you will need the usual small kitchen appliances, kitchen tools, flatware, glassware, dishes and pots and pans; tablecloths, napkins, placemats and other dining accessories; at least three complete sets of linens for each bed; six bath and six hand towels; washcloths, bath mats, shower curtains and other small bathroom appurtenances. If you don't have enough

משמח

sheets, towels and the like, you'll be doing laundry every other day, not to mention coming up short if you have guests. If finances are tight, though, you can fill in any gaps as time passes.

These household items are conventionally the responsibility of the bride's family, but most of these needs, beyond the basics, are treated as joint expenses of the couple now that young women are financially independent and do not merely pass from the support of their parents to that of their husband.

As for your trousseau, the same idea governs just how extensive this will be. The older tradition is that you will start your married life with enough new or almost new clothing and accessories to last a year, the idea being to save your new husband the expense of dressing you after he has just finished furnishing your home. But again, we come to the independent bride of today. You should aim to start your new life with a wardrobe that will save you the time and cost of shopping for clothes for a good while after your wedding.

Be practical in your choice of a going-away outfit. It should suit your destination—for example, heels and suit or day dress and coat for a city hotel or a cruise ship; casual for a country inn—and be serviceable as the basis of your dress or sportswear wardrobe for at least a year. The same is true for accessories. Despite what you have seen in glamorous romantic movies, don't, for example, pick a fragile pink silk suit with shoes to match if you're never going to have occasion to wear it again in your normal everyday life.

Before you embark on a shopping spree, go over your existing clothes carefully. Chuck the stuff that isn't worth packing to move, or leave it at Mom's for the days when you come over to help with some household chore. See that all the "keepers" are in good condition—buttons and snaps sewn on, heels on shoes not run down, hems in place—and everything spotlessly clean.

Are you surprised at how large your inventory is? Remember that all of this has to fit into the closets in your new home and leave enough space for your husband's clothes and "stuff" as well.

An immutable fact of life: Stuff automatically increases to exceed the space available for storing it.

Traditional Family Gifts

YOUR PARENTS WILL PROBABLY BE GIVING YOU SUBSTANTIAL GIFTS OF CASH OR MAJOR HOME FURNISHINGS; IN ADDITION THEY MAY WANT TO GIVE YOU CERTAIN TRADITIONAL WEDDING GIFTS. ON THE WEDDING DAY, YOU OR YOUR MOTHER GIVES THE GROOM A FINE *TALLIT* (PRAYER SHAWL) OF SILK OR WOOL. IF YOU'RE HANDY WITH A NEEDLE, YOU MAY EMBROIDER A VELVET *TALLIT* BAG YOURSELF (PATTERNS CAN BE FOUND ON AMERICA ONLINE IN THE JEWISH STORE, IF NOT IN YOUR NEIGHBORHOOD) OR HAVE ONE MADE FOR HIM. OR YOU OR YOUR GRANDPARENTS MAY GIVE THE GROOM A SILVER *KIDDUSH* CUP. HIS MOTHER MAY GIVE YOU SABBATH CANDLESTICKS, HIS GRANDPARENTS A TRAY FOR THE SABBATH *HALLAH*. HEIRLOOM CEREMONIAL OBJECTS, SUCH AS A *HALLAH* KNIFE (SOMETIMES CALLED A *MOTZI-MESSER*), A SPICE BOX OR A PASSOVER PLATE ARE ALSO OFTEN PASSED ON TO THE NEXT GENERATION AS WEDDING GIFTS.

CHECKLIST OF HOUSEHOLD LINENS
AND KITCHEN NEEDS

ITEMS	HAVE/COLOR	NEED/COLOR
DINING ROOM:		
Luncheon cloths, mats, napkins		
Informal dinner tablecloths and napkins		
Formal dinner tablecloths and napkins		
Buffet runners		
Cocktail napkins		
Tray cloths		
Place mats		
BEDROOM:		
Sheet sets (three for each bed)		
or six sheets each		
Six pillowcases for each bed		
Blankets, duvets or comforters		
Blanket covers or duvet covers		
Mattress covers		
Bedspreads		
BATHROOM:		
Bath towels		
Hand towels		
Guest towels		
Washcloths		
Bath mats		
Soap dish, wastebasket, etc.		

ITEMS	HAVE/COLOR	NEED/COLOR
KITCHEN:		
Dish towels		
Dish cloths		
Cleaning cloths and brushes		
Pots and pans		
Knives and other tools		
APPLIANCES:		
Toaster		
Blender		
Food processor		
Coffee maker		
Steamer		
Microwave oven		
Kitchen timer		
Kitchen clock		
Can opener		
OTHERS:		

CHECKLIST TO FILL OUT YOUR WARDROBE

ITEM	HAVE ON HAND	NEED
Slips		
Bras		
Shapewear		
Nightgowns/Pajamas		
Robes		
Loungewear		
Shoes		
Hose		
Panties		
Jeans		
Coats, jackets		
Skirts		
Sweaters		
Sportswear		
Suits		
Blouses		
DRESSES:		
Day		
Evening		
ACCESSORIES:		
Gloves		
Handbags		
Hats		
Scarves		

CHAPTER 14

COUNTDOWN TO THE WEDDING DAY

This section of the book is designed to help you and your mother retain your sanity—that is, keep your cool—as the "to do" list gets longer and longer and more and more complicated. Check off each item as you complete it and watch the unfinished part of the list grow shorter. Try to delegate as many chores as you can, but be sure the people you choose are *reliable*. How much you ask your fiancé's family members to do will depend on your relationship with them. Just don't shut them out of the planning altogether. It is courteous to keep them informed of decisions you make. They are providing the most important part of the whole affair—the bridegroom! They ought to know what's going on.

As you make each appointment or order each service, enter the dates and appropriate cost figures in the cash flow sheet and calendar pages at the back of the book.

AS SOON AS YOUR ENGAGEMENT IS ANNOUNCED

1. Set the wedding date (check dates when weddings may not be held, pages 24–25).
2. Decide in conference with both families on the wedding style.
3. Start work on your guest list and the groom's list. Make a preliminary head count.
4. Make a reservation at your synagogue, or begin to look for a caterer and a location for the ceremony and the reception.
5. Attend weddings and other functions with a "shopper's eye."
6. Meet with the rabbi as soon as possible if there are problems because of a previous divorce or a difference of religion. Note the meeting date on your calendar page.
7. Go house-hunting or apartment-hunting with your fiancé. Set aside days for furniture shopping.
8. Decide whether you will use a gift registry, and if so, shop for one. Use this excursion as a time to formulate your ideas for your household "trousseau" or "hope chest."

THREE MONTHS BEFORE THE WEDDING
(Or as soon as you can for a less formal, more quickly arranged affair):

1. Reserve the location and the caterer. Set dates for planning conferences. Note the dates in the calendar.
2. Shop for your gown and veil and your mother's dress and accessories. Allow at least six weeks for the delivery of custom-made clothes. If you're going to make your own dress, start sewing!
3. As soon as you decide, have your mother tell your fiancé's mother what style and colors you have chosen so that she can shop. Go over the sleeve and dress length, head covering and degree of formality. Suggest several harmonizing colors for her choice.
4. Name your maid or matron of honor and bridesmaids. Remind your fiancé to choose his ushers and best man.
5. Confer with your attendants to decide on the price range for their dresses. Select the outfits you would like them to wear. Don't go shopping with more than one bridesmaid if you want to avoid confusion and conflict. If they're going to make their own dresses, select fabrics and patterns and start sewing!
6. If the wedding will be held at home, start work on the garden, house refurbishing and cleaning.
7. Visit photographers and florists; audition musicians. Engage each of these service providers as soon as you can. Set dates for conferences with each at least three weeks before the wedding.
8. With your fiancé, select your china, silver, crystal and linen patterns. Make up your home improvement, garden or camping list if you want gifts in those categories. List your choices with the bridal registries of the stores you have chosen, or give the list to your mother and maid of honor so they can tell guests what you would like. If you go for the mortgage down payment registry (see pages 220–21), set that up now.

משמח

DON'T JUST ACCEPT THE IDEA THAT MEN DON'T REMEMBER ALL THE SOCIAL DETAILS SO DEAR TO YOUR HEART. YOU DON'T HAVE TO NAG YOUR MAN ABOUT THESE NICETIES THIS EARLY IN YOUR LIFE TOGETHER. MAKE A COPY OF THIS LIST AND GIVE IT TO YOUR FIANCÉ. HAVE HIM CHECK THE ITEMS OFF IN COORDINATION WITH YOUR TIMETABLE AND ALL WILL BE WELL.

❑ ASK YOUR MOTHER TO COMPILE HER GUEST LIST, ADD YOUR NAMES TO IT AND GET IT TO YOUR FIANCÉE BY THE DATE SHE HAS GIVEN YOU.

❑ DECIDE ON YOUR BEST MAN AND USHERS.

❑ CONFER WITH YOUR FIANCÉE AND DECIDE ON THE ATTIRE FOR THE MEN IN THE WEDDING PARTY. BE SURE YOUR FATHER IS HAPPY WITH YOUR CHOICE. HE WILL HAVE TO WEAR IT, TOO, UNLESS YOUR WEDDING IS VERY INFORMAL.

❑ SHOP FOR THE WEDDING RING (OR RINGS) WITH YOUR FIANCÉE AND ORDER THE ENGRAVING.

❑ GO WITH THE MEN IN THE WEDDING PARTY TO ORDER THE OUTFITS FOR THE WEDDING AND ARRANGE APPOINTMENTS FOR THE FITTINGS.

❑ ATTEND TO THE PERSONAL BUSINESS DETAILS OUTLINED IN CHAPTER 16. DO YOU HAVE A WILL, INSURANCE? CHANGE THE BENEFICIARY ON YOUR INSURANCE IF NECESSARY.

9. Finalize your guest list. Give the groom's family a model for writing up their list and a deadline date for delivery of the list to you. Write up your own master list. (See pages 112–13.)

10. Order your invitations, the number to total a few more than your guest list, to allow for errors in addressing. At the same time, order your imprinted formal and informal notepaper and return address labels or embosser.

11. If you want special stamps for the mailing, order them from the post office now. You may need cash for this.

12. If you will be using an illuminated *ketubah*, order it now. Important—confer with your rabbi to make sure he approves of the form you have chosen and will use it in the ceremony.

TWO MONTHS BEFORE THE WEDDING

1. Get your fiancé's guest list.
2. Pick up your envelopes from the stationer so you can start addressing them.
3. Buy your wedding shoes and lingerie before the fitting for your wedding gown. Arrange to have your shoes dyed. Use a fabric swatch for color match—there are dozens of shades of "white."
4. Tell your attendants what store and which dresses you have chosen. Make a date for them to go together to order them. The matron or maid of honor should help you by keeping track of these appointments.
5. Ask the bridesmaids to meet to shop for shoes, and have them all dyed together from a fabric swatch. Buy gloves, if you are using them. Select a proper shade of hose and have the hosiery delivered with the dresses, including an extra pair or two for emergencies.
6. Make appointments for physical and dental checkups for both you and your fiancé. See your gynecologist.
7. Shop for your wedding-day gift to your new husband.
8. Locate sheet music or tapes of special music you want played.
9. Shop for and order your wedding cake, if it is not supplied by your caterer. If it is, go over the kind of cake, frosting and filling.

משמח

10. For a home wedding, order the rental items you need.
11. Locate serving and household help for your home wedding.
12. Look over your wardrobe and decide what you will need to buy for your trousseau. Shop for these items in between your other chores.

SIX WEEKS BEFORE THE WEDDING

1. Pick up your invitations. Finish the addressing, seal and stamp the sets and mail them out. Your maid of honor and your fiancé can help with this.
2. Have the maid of honor notify bridesmaids to go for their fittings when the dresses arrive.
3. Have your own fitting, wearing the shoes and underthings you will use on the wedding day. Take your mother or your maid of honor along for that critical second opinion.
4. Check: has the groom selected his best man and ushers and arranged for their outfits?
5. With your fiancé, select your wedding ring or rings and order the engraving. Remember—for the ceremony the ring must be a plain gold band.
6. Select your gifts for the bridesmaids. Remind the groom to select gifts for his party.
7. Buy insurance for your new home and a floater policy to cover your wedding gifts.
8. If you are going to change your name, start now on the necessary notifications (see page 259).
9. Attend to other personal business details with your fiancé (see Chapter 16).
10. Start preparing for your wedding trip. With your fiancé, decide on your destination and check your reservations and transportation. Look over your luggage, wardrobe, special sports needs and the like.
11. Make an appointment to confer with the rabbi, if you have not seen him before.

The Bridegroom's Checklist (continued)

☐ MAKE MEDICAL AND DENTAL APPOINTMENTS. ARRANGE FOR YOUR BLOOD TEST AS REQUIRED BY LAW.
☐ CHOOSE A WEDDING-DAY GIFT FOR YOUR BRIDE.
☐ ORDER FLOWERS FOR THE BRIDE AND THE MOTHERS ALONG WITH ANY OTHER FLORAL DECORATIONS YOU HAVE AGREED TO PROVIDE.
☐ HELP YOUR FIANCÉE WITH THE ADDRESSING AND ASSEMBLING OF THE INVITATIONS AND ANNOUNCEMENTS.
☐ CHOOSE GIFTS FOR THE BEST MAN AND USHERS.
☐ PREPARE FOR YOUR OYFRUF AND RECITING THE HEBREW VERSION OF THE WEDDING VOW.
☐ ORDER CHAMPAGNE AND LIQUORS YOU HAVE AGREED TO PROVIDE.
☐ MAKE AN APPOINTMENT FOR A HAIRCUT.
☐ CHECK OUT MARRIAGE LICENSE REQUIREMENTS AND MAKE A DATE WITH YOUR BRIDE-TO-BE TO GET THE LICENSE.
☐ MAKE YOUR HONEYMOON PLANS. MAKE RESERVATIONS AND TRAVEL ARRANGEMENTS.
☐ WITH THE BEST MAN, GO OVER THE ARRANGEMENTS FOR YOUR DEPARTURE ON YOUR HONEYMOON.

YOU, TOO, SHOULD RELAX NOW THAT ALL THE PRELIMINARIES ARE OVER. STEP OUT ON YOUR RIGHT FOOT AND HAVE A WONDERFUL WEDDING AND A HAPPY LIFE EVER AFTER.

12. Call or write the society editors of the papers in which you want your wedding announcement to appear and ask for their forms.

FOUR WEEKS BEFORE THE WEDDING

1. Check off the guest responses as they come in. File the reply cards, if you are using them.
2. Plan housing for out-of-town attendants. Make arrangements for their transportation from the airport or station and whatever entertainment you plan for them before the reception.
3. If you will need special traffic police and parking attendants, engage them now.
4. Check the marriage license blood test requirements and make an appointment to coordinate with this schedule. Remind your fiancé to get his blood test. It's fun to do this together. Safeguard the test result sheets—you will need them for your marriage license application.
5. Arrange your "ladies' luncheon" or dinner for your attendants, perhaps at the same time as the bachelor dinner. This is the time to give the attendants their gifts.
6. Your pre-wedding social engagements will be filling your calendar. Keep a careful record and give a schedule to your mother, your fiancé and those attendants who are also invited.
7. Give the musicians any special music you want them to prepare.
8. Continue working on the personal business details in Chapter 16.
9. Confer with the florist and photographer you have engaged.
10. Check out the state requirements for your marriage license— and the fee. Your fiancé will need cash for this.
11. Settle all the details of the reception with the caterer.

TWO WEEKS BEFORE THE WEDDING

1. Make your hair and manicure appointments. For a real bit of *luxe*, have the hairdresser come to your home on your wedding day to arrange your hair and your mother's after you dress.

2. Make a date with your fiancé to get your marriage license. Don't be upset if it turns out to be a tension-filled hour! It always is. To relax, go out afterward for lunch or cocktails together and toast your forthcoming wedding.
3. Select a special outfit to wear to your fiancé's *oyfruf*. Dress as for holiday synagogue attendance. Check whether your mother and father will need hats.
4. Invite relatives and friends to the *oyfruf*. Informal notes or phone calls are fine. Let your fiancé's mother know how many people you expect, if they're planning a sit-down lunch or a buffet *Kiddush* after the services.
5. Check all your suppliers and services to make sure everything is going along as scheduled.
6. Address and assemble your announcements, if you will be using them. Give them to your mother or a friend to mail a day or two *after* the wedding, not before.
7. Send out your newspaper announcements in accordance with publication deadlines. See Chapter 9.
8. Check out the non-responses on your guest list and start calling those who have been thoughtless enough not to reply.
9. Make up your seating plan for the dinner and ask your fiancé's mother to do the same for her guests. Stock up on aspirin for this!
10. Make up a request list for the musicians.
11. Give your fiancé's father a list of those in your family to be honored at the *oyfruf*.
12. Select your going-away outfit. It doesn't have to be new, but it should be suitable to the hour of the day and your destination. If you're just going back to your apartment and starting off on your wedding trip later on, casual clothes are okay.

THE LAST WEEK BEFORE THE WEDDING

It may begin to feel like the last mile, but now, when you may want to run, is the time to slow down a bit. Maybe you should all relax by having a champagne tasting session! Better yet, get a grip on

משמח

~

What the Sages Say about Marriage

NEED ADVICE ON HOW TO STAY HAPPILY MARRIED? DON'T ASK ABBY, ASK THE SAGES. FROM THEM WE LEARN THAT:

A MAN SHALL HONOR HIS WIFE MORE THAN HIS OWN SELF AND SHALL LOVE HER AS HE LOVES HIMSELF AND SHALL CONSTANTLY SEEK TO BENEFIT HER ACCORDING TO HIS MEANS; HE SHALL NOT UNDULY IMPOSE HIS AUTHORITY ON HER AND SHALL SPEAK GENTLY TO HER; HE SHALL BE NEITHER SAD NOR IRRITABLE. SIMILARLY…A WIFE SHALL HONOR HER HUSBAND EXCEEDINGLY AND SHALL ACCEPT HIS AUTHORITY AND ABIDE BY HIS WISHES IN ALL HIS ACTIVITIES.—MAIMONIDES

things by organizing carefully, taking the time to eat properly and getting to bed early as many evenings as you can.

1. Count up your acceptances. Check with your fiancé's mother for any guests who have responded to her instead of you. Do not count in any "maybes" or "no responses." Your caterer should be able to handle a few extra guests and, unfortunately, there will always be a few "no-shows" (for whom you will have to pay). Give the caterer your final count and forget about it. You have hired the caterer to worry for you.

2. Assemble in one place all the things you will need to dress for the wedding: underthings, hose, gown, veil and headdress, shoes and cosmetics. Fill your little personal handbag for the day. Wrap your gift for your bridegroom and put it with this bag. Make sure you have everything together and don't leave anything for last-minute scurrying about.

3. Make up an emergency kit for the wedding day: safety pins, bobby pins, Band-Aids, tissues, needle and thread, aspirin. Put the kit with your bridal handbag and don't forget it.

4. Estimate how much time you will need for each step in dressing on the wedding day. Then set up a time chart that will allow you to do everything slowly, so that you will *appear* calm. Eventually, the slow motion will make you feel calm as well. Arrange for someone to help you with your dress and veil.

5. Arrange for a place where the bridesmaids will dress together and let them know when you expect them to be there in order to be in time for the ride to the ceremony and photos.

6. Pack your suitcases and travel handbag for the wedding trip. Are your reservations made? Is your transportation set?

7. Gather up your going-away outfit and keep it together with your bridal outfit. Arrange to have your going-away clothes taken to the place where you will change after the reception, and delegate someone to take your bridal clothes back home after you change and leave.

משמח

ON YOUR WEDDING DAY

You're almost there! Everything's in place, so relax and savor each minute of this day.

1. Stay with a "natural" makeup and apply it carefully, since it must last for hours. Blotting and powdering between applications of lipstick make it more permanent. Use waterproof and smudge-proof mascara and eyeliner. Brides, like Miss America, often cry for joy. And don't forget your antiperspirant.
2. Wear little or no jewelry with your wedding gown. Jewelry might detract from your beauty—and every bride is beautiful.
3. Gather up some sheets of tissue paper or a clean sheet to spread in the car for the ride to the ceremony. Try to arrange the skirt of your dress so that you do not sit on it. If there is a train, spread it on the back of the car seat. If it's raining, tuck up your skirts and watch carefully where you put your dainty bridal shoes as you step in and out of the car. Don't fret! Rain on your wedding day is supposed to signify showers of money in your wedded life.

PANIC-STOPPER ON YOUR WEDDING DAY

Let's face it—things happen! You know what they say about the best-laid plans. Rule number one for you, your groom and your parents is *don't panic*! With a sense of humor and a sense of proportion, you can find a solution to any unforeseen difficulty.

- You've been dreaming about and planning this for months now. It's only natural to feel anxious and overwhelmed by the big step you are about to take. Your parents may also be feeling anxious—is this really the right thing for you? Everyone is agitated. Smile. Meditate on how much you love each other and how happy you will be when this is over. Everything will look different in the light of day, and as the events you have fretted over all these weeks begin to take shape, you will become a radiant bride, more beautiful than ever.

~

What the Sages Say about Marriage (continued)

A MAN SHOULD SPEND LESS THAN HIS MEANS ON FOOD, UP TO HIS MEANS ON CLOTHES, BEYOND HIS MEANS IN HONORING HIS WIFE AND CHILDREN.—HUL 84B

WHERE THERE IS PEACE AND HARMONY BETWEEN HUSBAND AND WIFE, THE SHEKHINAH (THE HEAVENLY PRESENCE) DWELLS UPON THEM.—

"EQUALIZE" THESE AXIOMS AS YOU WILL. BUT LET US HOPE YOU WILL FIND YOUR WAY TO HAPPINESS THROUGH THIS VERSE FROM ECCLESIASTES 9:9:
LIVE JOYFULLY WITH THY WIFE, WHOM THOU LOVEST.

~

After the Wedding (for the mother of the bride)

THE HAPPY COUPLE HAVE LEFT. BUT THE MOTHER OF THE BRIDE STILL HAS A FEW PLEASANT DUTIES, AND THE ACTIVITY WILL PROBABLY BE WELCOME TO STAVE OFF THE "POST-PARTY BLUES."

❑ CHECK TO SEE THAT YOUR INSTRUCTIONS ARE FOLLOWED FOR THE PACKING AND DISPOSAL OF LEFTOVER FOOD. DO THE SAME FOR THE WEDDING FLOWERS. THE BRIDAL CENTERPIECE WILL GRACE YOUR DINING ROOM.

❑ PACK UP AND FREEZE THE TOP LAYER OF THE WEDDING CAKE FOR THE BRIDE AND GROOM'S FIRST ANNIVERSARY.

❑ AFTER AN AFTERNOON RECEPTION, YOU WILL HAVE TO ENTERTAIN YOUR OUT-OF-TOWN GUESTS. AN INFORMAL SUPPER AT HOME FOR THEM AND THE WEDDING PARTY IS A PLEASANT WAY OF WINDING DOWN.

- Don't fret yourself into a sweat over minor disasters, upsetting everyone around you as well. Talk to the professional responsible—the florist, if the wrong flowers have come, the baker, if the cake hasn't been delivered yet, and so on. Better yet, ask a friend to assist you in dealing with any setbacks.

- Allow some extra time for every step in the proceedings, in case there is a difficulty. Don't get hysterical about a run in your nylons or stepping through the hem on your gown. Get your sister to find you a new pair of hose, or have your mother grab a needle and thread to fix your hem.

- Save your drinking till after the ceremony. Especially if you've been fasting, that legendary bottle of champagne in the limo on the way to the reception is a no-no—for *both* of you.

- Did the ring bearer lose the ring—or the best man forget to bring it? Smile—you can borrow your mother's ring or a friend's so the ceremony can go on.

- It's raining on your garden wedding—and it's cold! You have the tent set up—ask the caterer to roll down the curtains and provide some heaters. If you provide enough champagne and liquor, no one will notice the rain after awhile.

- A loud fight has broken out between two guests who've had a bit too much to drink. Breaking it up and smoothing the combatants down is a job for the best man and the ushers or friends of your husband. No need for screams or calling the police. Have the band play louder—and smile as you ask the bar to slow down on the liquor service.

- If someone is hurt during the dancing, or while you are carried about on high in chairs, quietly get first aid and let the party go on. Unless you have to call an ambulance, the chances are that most of the guests won't notice anything amiss.

- As long as you and your fiancé and the rabbi are there, the wedding can go on. That's the important thing. Everything else can be improvised if need be. Good humor, quick thinking and kindness will save the day and let the rejoicing ring out.

משמח

Now that we've talked about a few possible disasters, forget them. Take a deep breath and smile. Everything is in order. All the planning you've done is coming to fruition and all the details are being taken care of by others. Relax. Step out on your right foot and enjoy this happy day.

Mazel tov and Siman tov!
A Happy Wedding and Bright Future to You Both!

A SPECIAL GIFT—*HAKHNASSAT KALLAH*

The day may come when you will no longer want to keep your bridal outfit on the top shelf of the closet. You can accomplish a unique act of charity (*tsedakah*) and a special *mitzvah*, that of helping the bride rejoice (*hakhnassat kallah*), by giving your bridal gown, veil and headdress to a Jewish organization that will lend them to brides who can't afford to buy their own. The finery you no longer need will enhance the rejoicing of other young women who cannot buy lovely gowns for their special day, and by proxy, you will be a member of their weddings.

An added goody is that the donation to a charitable organization is tax-deductible.

The gowns you give away will not be sold, but lent more than once to many young brides. Bridesmaids' and mothers' dresses are also needed.

Dresses should meet Jewish standards of modesty—long sleeves and high necks. If you are in doubt about the décolletage, call or write before sending off your gown. Always confirm the mailing address.

Wedding dresses can be donated to the Sarah bat Leibl formal GeMaCh of the National Council of Young Israel, 3 West 16th Street, New York, NY 10011. For details, call Chana Chechik at 212–929–1525, ext. 113 or Ms. Bonya Kaufman Fuks at 718–726–2885 (days) or 516–466–7003 (evenings). These dresses will be used for brides in the area.

After the Wedding (for the mother of the bride) (continued)

❑ IF YOUR FRIENDS AND RELATIVES ARE OBSERVING TRADITIONAL SHEVA BROKHES, THE TRADITIONAL SEVEN DAYS OF FEASTING TO HONOR THE BRIDE AND GROOM, IT'S NOW YOUR TURN TO BE A GUEST. ENJOY!

❑ HAVE THE WEDDING GOWN PROFESSIONALLY CLEANED AND PACKED TO PRESERVE IT.

❑ YOU MAY WANT TO ARRANGE FOR THE PRESERVATION OF THE BRIDAL BOUQUET.

❑ MAIL OUT THE WEDDING ANNOUNCEMENTS A DAY OR TWO AFTER THE WEDDING.

❑ KEEP TRACK OF GIFTS SENT IN AFTER THE WEDDING.

Two young women who devote themselves to this act of kindness send the dresses they receive to Israel for the use of needy brides there. Contact Mrs. Judy Neiman by telephone at 718–252–2157 or write her at 1227 East 8th Street, Brooklyn, NY 11230, or Ms. Tovi Wolfson at 718–377–7883 or at 1179 East 21st Street, Brooklyn, NY 11210.

There are other local *G'mach* groups that you can find by asking your rabbi or inquiring at a Hebrew bookstore. Forming a *G'mach* is a project you might want to initiate in your sisterhood or Hadassah chapter.

For more about the *G'mach*, see Chapter 7.

PART THREE

HAPPILY EVER AFTER

CHAPTER 15

YOUR HONEYMOON

Guess what? The word "honeymoon" literally means "moon of honey." It is an expression that comes from Europe, where newly-weds drank a special honey wine for a month after the wedding.

Orthodox Jewish practice does away with the conventional wedding trip immediately after the wedding. The young couple retire to their apartment or home and are the guests of honor at seven nights of feasting, usually in a different home each night. If there is a "new face" at the table (a guest who was not previously present), the Seven Wedding Blessings are recited during the Grace after Meals (*Birkat Hamazon*). The Hebrew for the blessings is *sheva berakhot*, which became in Yiddish *sheva brokhes*, and this is what the week of feasting is called.

Many young Orthodox couples observe this custom for a night or two in their home community, then go off on a trip, either to visit other relatives who feast them in turn, or to spend the remainder of the seven nights in a kosher resort, where all the guests join in the celebration. This does away with the whole "getaway" idea one sees at other weddings.

Actually, the noisy, prank-filled getaway that happens in other communities is opposed to Jewish ideas of modesty and decorum. A newlywed couple is to be treated with respect, not chased to a car decorated with "Just Married" signs and festooned with tin cans and streamers. The consummation of their marriage is a highly private matter, not a subject for jokes. A bride and groom do not, in Jewish tradition, run away from the guests and the celebration.

SAYING GOODBYE

If you're going to throw your bouquet, pass the word on through your maid of honor to have the bridesmaids and other single women gather to catch it. Do really want your groom to toss the garter to the single men? By Jewish standards, it's not *sheyn*— "nice"—there's that modesty idea again! When the excitement of the bouquet toss dies down, you can go off to prepare to leave.

If you're not into flower-tossing (and you certainly shouldn't try it with a flower-decorated Bible!), then when the party begins to wind down and Grace has been said, you and your new husband may slip away to change into traveling clothes. Your maid of honor, who helps you dress, goes to tell your parents that you are ready to leave, so that you can say goodbye to them, thank them for the lovely wedding and join your husband, who has said goodbye to his parents and is waiting to take you off on your wedding trip or to your new home.

You should both select going-away outfits that are comfortable and suitable to the trip you are about to take. If it's a car or plane trip, neat, stylish tops and pants, with a sweater or jacket in case it turns cold, are a good choice. If you'll be arriving at a country hotel at the end of the road, dress up a bit. For a cruise, a smart casual dress for you and a sport jacket and slacks for him are appropriate. Even if you're planning to go camping in the mountains, wear casual outfits on the dressy side to keep the mood "up" for a while longer. If your destination is the big city, heels and a suit or afternoon dress are the order of the day. You may want to add a festive touch with a corsage or a few flowers from your bouquet in your hair.

The best man should have seen to placing the luggage in the car and handing over any tickets and documents you'll need to the groom. As a last-minute check:

- Do you have the tickets?
- Do you have your wallet, keys, driver's license, marriage license and any travel documents you need? These include your passports and your reservation confirmations.
- If you have friends who are given to practical jokes, check to make sure that your suitcases are still in the car, with their contents intact.

PLANNING YOUR TRIP

There is much more to arranging a honeymoon than studying glossy travel brochures and evaluating the honeymoon pitches online. Your time and money budget come first. If all you can get away for is three days, make it the best long weekend ever. Pick a swanky hotel or resort close to home. If you have a week or more, a full-scale vacation or cruise can become the trip of your dreams.

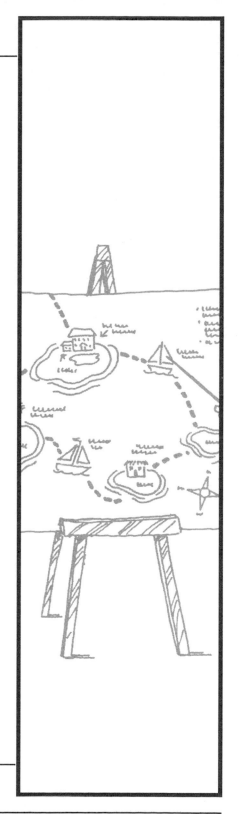

There are many ways to cut the cost of a honeymoon. Consult a good travel agent, who will be able to let you know about (and get for you) all the latest discount and package rates. If you're still students, work your student discount for all it's worth, especially on air fares. A student hostel, dormitory-style, however, is hardly a honeymoon locale. You can cut costs and get by very nicely in four-star hotels and minimum cabins on cruise ships. Whether you're in the sky suite or the cheapest inside cabin, all the ship or hotel public rooms, activities and posh meals will be available to you.

Check out the online travel services on your computer. There are often travel bargains posted there and also some travel clubs that offer big savings. The major cruise lines all have Web sites; see page 96 for a list. There is even a source on the Web for information about each ship at the Cruise Ship Center (http://www.safari.net), which gives numerical scores based on several travel guides to all the ship's amenities: food, entertainment, cabin service and more.

START EARLY

If you're getting married during the popular wedding seasons, you will find that the popular honeymoon destinations will be as solidly booked as the caterers. The wedding trip becomes one more plan you have to make long in advance of the day you will actually leave. Some of the most traveled places are Caribbean cruises and hotels, Mexico (as in Baja California, Cancún and Cozumel), and the great tourist sites in the United States: the national parks, Disneyland and Disney World, Hawaii, Cape Cod, the classic Niagara Falls, cruises in Alaska and many other places closer to home.

While you're looking at the pretty pictures, take some time to discuss carefully with your fiancé your personal ideas and preferences. What kind of activities do you both like? How much privacy do you want? How much social life do you want? Do you really just want to "crash"—rest and relax after all the hoopla of the wedding? Unless you have been living together for some time before the wedding, you will want this time to quietly get to know each other on an intimate basis. If seeing your spouse brush his or her teeth in the morning is

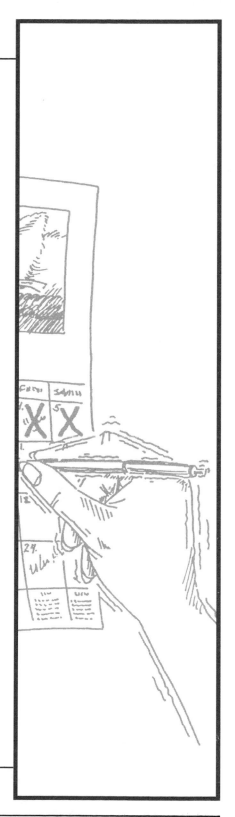

a novelty to you, you won't need too much touristy sightseeing to make this voyage of personal exploration interesting.

You can easily work out an active, sports-filled vacation—skiing, sailing, scuba-diving, hiking, or a sightseeing jaunt to a different place every day. But if you are realistic, you will realize that a grueling, on-the-bus, off-the-bus trip or one that involves long days driving to far-apart destinations is not the right prescription for a couple stressed out by wedding parties and the strain of learning to share their private everyday lives.

When you consider the cost of a trip, take careful note of what's not included. How many meals will you have to pay for? What side trips are extra, and how much? What taxes are additional? Are transfers included? Use of sports equipment? Entertainment? If you're going to a resort, will you need a car when you get there? Add a sizable amount for tips—sometimes, when you travel, it will seem that everyone has his or her hand out for one—and another sum for shopping, gifts and those unforeseen expenses that always raise their greedy little heads on a trip. In general, unless you are a very careful budget-watcher, you will probably spend half again as much as the basic trip cost on these extras—more, if no meals are included and you're stuck eating at the hotel because you have no car.

WHAT TO EXPECT FROM A TRAVEL AGENT

A good agent should be able to advise you as to the best choices, once you've expressed your needs and expectations. You do have to tell the agent explicitly what your preferences are for sleeping accommodations, meal sittings, and activities. You also have to be frank about how much you want to spend. Don't waste your time and the agent's thinking about four- and five-figure trips when your budget allows only a few hundred dollars.

The agency should handle all the connections and all the reservation paperwork and advise you as to the documents you'll need. Except for Mexico, Canada and some of the islands in the Caribbean, you will need a passport, which can take six weeks or longer to process.

You will need, in addition to, or instead of, a passport:

- your birth certificate
- your driver's license or other photo ID—for driving abroad, an international driver's license
- your marriage certificate
- proof of citizenship if you were not born in the United States

You are going to have to pay a deposit to reserve your accommodations, and pay in full for airline and cruise tickets well in advance. It's important to deal with a reputable agency. If you deal with one of those backstairs operations that advertise unbelievable rates in their tiny classified ads, you may be handing your money to someone who has no intention of providing tickets but is working a scam, or you may be the victim of a well-meaning agency that goes bankrupt before delivering your tickets and vouchers to you. So you'll have a lawsuit instead of a honeymoon. This is one time when you should not cut corners.

A good travel agent is courteous, responsive to your preferences, available by phone, a member of a professional organization and, if possible, recommended to you by people who have used his or her services and been satisfied.

WATCH THE FINE PRINT!

A Consumer Reports Travel letter mentions five widespread travel practices that it considers deceptive. Until the happy day that these extra costs are eliminated, read those beckoning ads carefully and watch the fine print for: so-called half-price air fares, which are not available unless you buy a round trip; "half-price" hotel rates, in which the base price is actually twice the featured price; European hotel listings that do not include the VAT—value-added taxes and service charges, which can add up to as much as 25 percent; cruise "port charges" that are much higher than the actual charges levied by the ports; and extra driver charges set by car rental agencies, even though the extra driver doesn't cost the rental company any more.

It's not likely that these charges and practices will be changed in the near future. In making your honeymoon plans and budgeting your expenses, just be aware that these are extra costs you must figure in, and that the only way you can check them is to read the fine print—and ask your travel agent what other charges you will incur at the hotel, on the ship, or at the car rental agency.

As with any other business agreement, read the fine print in any tour package you select. Get confirmation numbers for all your reservations and take them with you on your trip. Reconfirm your reservations 24 hours before you depart. Hotels often overbook during their high seasons; having a confirmation gives you a leg to stand on—it may even get you a bed to sleep in.

TRAVEL SAVVY

Travel light. One of the minor miseries of a trip is being stuck with more bags than you can handle in an airport or on a pier in the midst of a porters' strike. Next in order of discomfort comes having to lug an overweight carry-on bag around with you for several hours of an airport layover because you are not allowed to let it out of your sight.

Lighten your luggage by using trial or travel sizes of cosmetics and toiletries. All the bottles and cans you store on your dressing table weigh a lot—if you're carrying them around in your shoulder bag, they will begin to feel like a metric ton after the first half-hour in the airport. After you've loaded and unloaded them on an auto trip for three nights, you'll want to throw them all out.

Color-coordinate your clothes, so that one or two pairs of shoes and a minimum of costume jewelry go with everything; plan to layer blouses, sweaters and jackets for cool days. Make do with one handbag and one small clutch for dress-up. One bit of advice from every experienced traveler: lay out all the clothes you think you want to take with you—then put half of them back in the closet. If you're really in need of an item you've left at home there is a great modern invention that will supply it—it's called a "store." And what's a trip without a shopping spree or two?

THE FINE ART OF TIPPING

When, whom and how much to tip can often be embarrassing and confusing questions. In some situations you can ask your companions at the dining table in a hotel or on shipboard, or the management, but it's better to be prepared with some knowledge of the travel tipping structure. Here are some guidelines.

ON BOARD A SHIP

Room steward: Cleans your cabin, makes the bed, supplies towels, soap, ice and room service. Tip $3.50 per day per person. Tip at the end of the trip. Some also tip on the first day, "to insure perfect service"—a slogan said to be the origin of the word "tips."

Dining room waiter and busboy: Waiter, $3.50 per person per day, half that for the busboy.

Bartenders, wine steward, pool and deck attendants, etc.: Check the bar bill. On almost all ships, a service charge is automatically added, making a tip unnecessary. Other service personnel should be tipped when the service is given, at the same rate as for service ashore, usually 15 percent.

Maitre d', headwaiter: In charge of the dining room. No tip is necessary unless he has handled special requests for you.

"No-tipping" ships: Some cruise lines advertise a "no-tip" policy. People still tip for special service on such ships, but it is not necessary if you do not ask for anything "above and beyond."

AT THE AIRPORT

Porter: $1 per bag when you check in at the curb or have bags taken to check-in for you.

IN A HOTEL

Bellboy: $1 per bag, plus $1 for hospitable gestures—turning on lights, opening windows. Tip on service.

Chambermaid: $1 for each service, minimum $5 per couple per week. Tip each day; a new maid may be assigned during your stay.

Doorman: $1 per bag; $1 for hailing a taxi. Tip on service.

Headwaiter: $5 per week for special service, $2–$3 for regular service—tip on your first day.

Wait staff: 15% to 20% of the bill when no service charge is added; some add 5% when there is a service charge. Tip at each meal.

Room Service: 15% to 20% of bill in addition to the room service charge.

Other service personnel: The general rule to follow is to tip 15% to 20% of the bill, unless the person serving you owns the business. Some owner-hairdressers, for example, do not accept tips, but charge more for their services.

Note that in a foreign country, the amount to tip should be calculated in the currency of that country. It may be less or more than you would tip in dollars, depending on the exchange rate. Ask at the hotel desk, or ask the purser (aboard ship), if you are uncertain.

Adding up the tips you will have to pay out leaves you with a rather hefty bottom line. Now you can better understand why you see the pizza delivery cars driving up to swanky hotels and why many people prefer five-star motels, where there are none of the "front-end" tips associated with arriving and leaving.

CAUTION AND COMMON SENSE

Try to use traveler's checks instead of cash as much as possible. Safeguard those as you would cash, because TV ads notwithstanding, it's a headache and a bore to have to replace lost or stolen checks. Better yet, use your credit cards, judiciously, instead of cash.

Use the hotel or ship's safe. Make a photocopy of the first two pages of your passport—the ones with that hideous picture of you and all your vital statistics. Carry that around as an ID and leave the passport in the safe until you need it to go to the bank. Also leave your extra cash, your expensive jewelry and your gold watch in the safe. Never leave valuables or documents on the beach or by the pool while you swim or nap.

CARRY IT WITH YOU

While you're en route, keep all your important papers and your jewelry, camera and binoculars either in your carry-on bag or on your person. This includes your tickets, vouchers, traveler's checks, credit cards, driver's license and IDs, your checkbook, and separate lists of your traveler's check numbers, credit card numbers and checking account numbers.

In that bag you should also carry your eyewear, medications, overnight needs and birth-control materials. That same emergency and first-aid kit you tucked into your bag for your wedding should go into this bag as well. Now, if your luggage should be lost temporarily, or stolen (ouch!) you'll have the basic necessities for survival till it's found or replaced. It is also a good idea to pack your swimsuit, cap and goggles in that bag if you're going cruising, so that you can start to enjoy the pool right away, instead of losing time during the interminable wait for your luggage to be delivered to your cabin.

You don't need it! One little heavyweight you should definitely leave home is your mother's travel iron. It will get heavier every day, you will never have time to iron and it will either not work or burn out in foreign countries and aboard ship, where the electric outlets and voltage are different. It follows that you don't need any item of clothing that must be ironed. If it won't hang out in a steamy bathroom, forget it. Go for knits and all those crinkly cotton and rayon fabrics.

Do you think you could live without your hair drier? There are special travel models that are small, lightweight and adaptable to 220 volts (common abroad). You'll find the big models you use at home are just a heavy nuisance. Besides—it's your honeymoon! Are you going to spend time blow-drying your hair when you could be having cocktails in the bar or dancing on deck?

To keep your baggage load down, follow this rule: When in doubt, take it out—of the suitcase.

משמח

Pack a few days in advance of your trip, to eliminate last-minute scurrying and forgetting some essential item. Make a list of everything in your suitcase, both for insurance purposes and to keep track of your things when you pack to go home. Make sure you have enough of any prescription medications to last through the trip, enough film for all the pictures you want to take and some feminine hygiene materials, just in case.

Some experienced travelers recommend packing a complete outfit, underwear and a nightgown in your husband's bag and a set of your husband's clothes in yours, so that if one bag is lost, that traveler is not doomed to wear the same clothes until the lost bag is found or replacements for lost clothing can be bought.

Reminder: As soon as you arrive, phone your parents and his to let them know you've arrived safely and to thank them again for the splendid wedding they have given you.

COMING HOME

Happy, tanned, loaded down with gifts for everyone, you're home at last, to settle down to the simple pleasures of everyday living.

First things first—notify your family that you're home.

Select your wedding photos from the proofs that will have come while you were away.

Look over your wedding presents and return or make exchanges of the duplicates and the horrors. Start on the thank-you notes.

Finish up all the business details connected with name changes, insurance, and wills.

Invite the folks to dinner.

Have a party for all the attendants and show them the wedding and honeymoon pictures.

Storm Warning

YOU DO NOT HAVE TO DO EVERYTHING TOGETHER. ALL THROUGH YOUR LIFE TOGETHER, YOU WILL NOT BOTH WANT TO DO THE SAME THING AT THE SAME TIME. START NOW TO ACCEPT "SEPARATE TIME" WITHIN REASON AS A NORM FOR YOUR MARRIAGE. IF HE'D RATHER WORK OUT IN THE GYM INSTEAD OF SHLEPPING THROUGH THE STRAW MARKET WITH YOU, ACCEPT THAT WITH GRACE. YOU WILL BOTH BE THAT MUCH HAPPIER WHEN YOU JOIN EACH OTHER AGAIN FOR LUNCH OR DINNER, WITH STORIES TO TELL EACH OTHER ABOUT YOUR ADVENTURES ON YOUR OWN.

CHAPTER 16

THE HAPPY
COUPLE

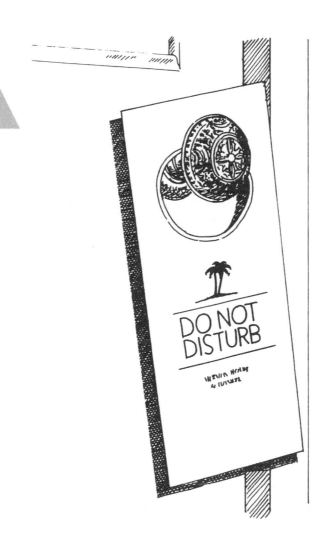

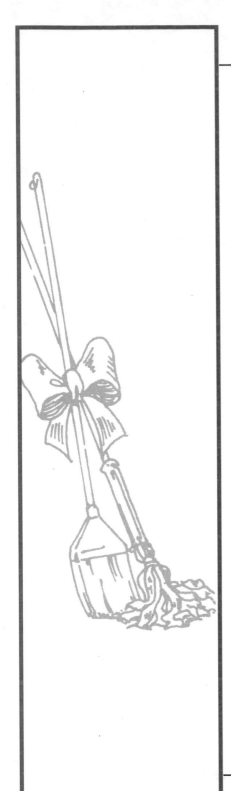

The honeymoon is over. So are all the celebrations. You've both gone back to work. But now the real work of your personal life begins—making a happy home together. Since biblical times, the bride and groom have been accorded a special status—that of "newlywed," a term applied to the first year of their life together. In Deuteronomy we read:

> When a man takes a new wife, he shall be deferred from military duty, he shall not be charged with any business. He shall be free for his household for one year and shall cheer his wife, whom he has taken. (Deut.:24:5)

This was, and still is, a time of learning all about each other, learning to live harmoniously together, sharing, for the first time, the whole year's cycle of seasons and Jewish holidays. In a time of arranged marriages, when bride and groom had not seen each other before the wedding day, this made special good sense, as the couple learned to overcome the anxieties and strangeness of their first year together.

Today's couples have modern anxieties to overcome: accommodating two different work schedules, moving to a new area for their new home, money worries and the adjustment to the mundane realities of everyday life. There is even a different kind of strangeness to overcome: suddenly life is not a date, you aren't always dressed up and looking your best, you catch cold, you bring home your problems from the office. Your formally polite relations with your new in-laws will change. Love and patience will make it possible for you to create out of this welter of conflicting elements a happy *modus vivendi*.

You have taken a pledge to create a Jewish home. Traditionally, that means it has a kosher kitchen and *mezuzahs* on the doorposts, that Shabbat and holidays are celebrated according to Jewish law, and that your sexual relations are regulated by the laws of family purity.

For liberal Jews, the definition of a Jewish home is filled with questions about the customs and rules you do or do not observe.

There may be differences between you as to just what observances and affiliations you wish to keep. This, too, is the material you work on in making your married life harmonious and meaningful.

What are some of the elements that constitute a Jewish home? They include:

- ❑ having ritual items—a *mezuzah* at the door, Shabbat candlesticks, a *Kiddush* cup and the like
- ❑ observance of Shabbat and Jewish holidays
- ❑ observance of *kashrut*
- ❑ Jewish books and music and respect for learning
- ❑ *tsedakah*—charity both within the Jewish community and in the outside world, and, in the sense of *tsedakah* as justice, supporting just causes
- ❑ *hakhnasat orchim*—hospitality, especially on the Sabbath and holidays
- ❑ affiliation with a synagogue or *havurah* and other Jewish organizations
- ❑ providing a Jewish education for your children and continuing your own

As a liberal or reform Jew, you may decide to pick and choose among these many elements to create what you consider a Jewish home. It is not a static entity and you will find your choices changing as the years go by and your life circumstances change.

WHAT'S IN A NAME?

Just your identity and your history. When you were a grade school kid, you may have played number games with the name of a boy you had a crush on, or practiced signing the name you'd have if you married him. But now, it's real. You're getting married and in these modern days, you get to choose what name you want to be called. This is a question you should decide early on in your engagement.

SHOULD YOU KEEP YOUR BIRTH NAME?

Once upon a time, convention dictated that a woman take her husband's name and keep it for the rest of her life, barring a divorce. A divorced woman had to carry a combination of her birth name and her formerly married name until she married again. And so our Abigail Sherman, a young woman who had struggled until her mid-twenties or thereabouts to become a person in her own right, would disappear, to become Mrs. Daniel Goldsmith or Mrs. Sherman Goldsmith (a divorcée) or Mrs. David Bronner (upon a second marriage), always a kind of addendum to the man under whose "protection" she lived. The persona she had established through many years of schooling and work would be erased.

Not so any more. Many women, of course, still do follow this old system of naming, but more and more women retain their birth names after they marry, both as a career choice and a feminist one. They are never known as Mrs. Daniel Goldsmith. Others keep their own name professionally and in social life are known as Mrs. Abigail Goldsmith. After a divorce, women often go back to their birth name if they had changed it when they married.

Feminist options also include the use of Ms. instead of Mrs. or Miss, eliminating any reference to marital status, which is basically a private matter. When you use Ms. you style yourself as Ms. Abigail Sherman or Ms. Abigail S. Goldsmith, never as Ms. Daniel Goldsmith.

INTRODUCING YOURSELF

When you continue to use your birth name after marriage, be careful to mention your husband's full name when you introduce yourselves at a gathering, especially if people know you and not him. Say "I'm Abigail Sherman and this is my husband, David Goldsmith." If you don't give his full name, he may be introduced around as David Sherman, to everyone's confusion.

You can inform people of your decision by putting a line in your newspaper announcement: "The bride will keep her own name." Or "The couple will use the name Sherman-Goldsmith." Or "The bride will use her own name professionally."

CHANGING YOUR NAME

If you do decide to change your name, you must have it changed on all your legal records, credit cards, licenses and identification.

A few weeks before the wedding, arrange to have your name changed by:

1. The Social Security Administration (you keep the same number).
2. The Motor Vehicle Bureau, if you drive. If you own your own car, also change the registration.
3. Issuers of credit cards and charge accounts.
4. Your bank. You will need to order new checks if you change the name on your account.
5. Your employer—and the payroll and pension departments if it's a large corporation or a government agency.
6. The voter registration board. This can wait till the next registration period comes around.
7. The registrar, if you're a student, for your school records. (This is not necessary if you've graduated.)
8. Your stockbroker to update the title on your stock portfolio.
9. Your insurance broker—for all your policies—and, the name of your beneficiary, if you are changing that, too.

Sometimes you may have to show your marriage certificate as evidence for the name change; other times you may be asked for your new address (if you're moving). In those cases, you will have to wait to make the changes until after the wedding, but you should take care of them as soon as possible.

If you're keeping your birth name, none of this is necessary.

LEGAL CONSIDERATIONS

How do you sign your name? No change is necessary if you are keeping your birth name.

If you're changing your name, you sign yourself Abigail S. Goldsmith (or, for the hyphenated, Abigail Sherman-Goldsmith), on all checks and legal papers.

If you are filing a joint tax return, but using your own name, you may also have to provide proof of marriage.

You can't use your husband's name on a legal document if you keep your own name; legal troubles may result.

Obviously, you need to pick one style and be consistent in its use.

CREDIT MATTERS

If you have not had credit cards before marriage, be sure that the charge accounts you do open are in both your husband's name and yours—make sure you are listed as Abigail S. Goldsmith, not Mrs. Daniel Goldsmith. Follow the same rule if you are changing the name on accounts you already have. This is the only way you, as a married woman, can develop your own credit record. Does it matter? Yes, indeed—in case of a divorce or the death of your spouse, you could find yourself without access to credit if you haven't had accounts before. If you are employed, you can have a charge account in your name only, and you should, for the very same reason.

Get used to the new name you have chosen. The very first place you will sign it will be on your *ketubah* or your marriage license.

STATIONERY

You will need new stationery in any case, showing your new address and your chosen name. You will need:

1. business-size (8 1/2" × 11") letter paper for everyday use
2. informals with your monogram or name. You can use your name alone, Mr. and Mrs., or both your names on one line as

   Abigail Sherman and Daniel Goldsmith

3. fine-quality letter paper, plain or with your monogram
4. return address labels
5. "At home" cards—If you use them with your invitations or announcements, they show your choice of name, new address and phone number (optional). For example:

At home
Abigail Sherman
Daniel Goldsmith
1210 Pine Crescent
Mamaroneck, New York 12345
914-555-1234

For best appearance, these should match your wedding invitation or announcement in paper and type.

MONOGRAMS

For linens and stationery, use the initial letters of your first name, your birth name and your husband's surname—the last being the largest or center letter of the monogram, as

A G S or A S G

For silver, use only the initial letter of your new surname or the three-letter style above.

For informal use only, as on paper partyware or bar glasses, you may combine the initials of your first name and your husband's.

If you are keeping your birth name, or hyphenating both names, experiment with a four-letter monogram, in which the two center initials, larger, are those of your two surnames, and your first-name initials are on either side, as

A S G D

JOINT DECISIONS TO MAKE

Deciding on the practical details of the new household you two are forming is more important in many ways than your choice of wedding gown, reception, and the like. Somewhere in the flurry of events before the wedding, if you are wise, you will make time to take care of all the matters on this list.

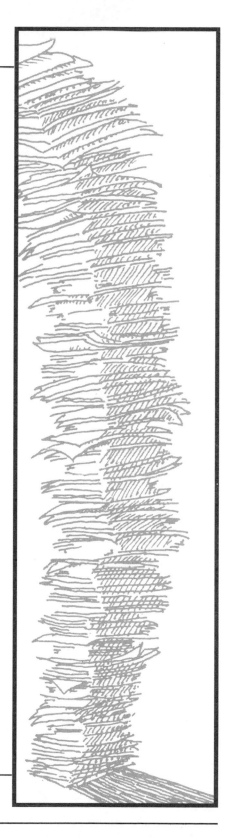

Make appointments, enter them in your calendar and *keep* them. Just as with the wedding procession itself, start off on the right foot in your new life!

1. Draw up your wills. Every person (male or female) should have a will, if only to leave everything to the spouse and appoint an executor to serve without fee.
2. Discuss life insurance for each of you. If you already have insurance, arrange to change the beneficiaries. Is the amount enough for the responsibilities of a married person?
3. Arrange joint bank accounts and a safe deposit box with entry rights for both of you.
4. Decide on your new home. Arrange to have utilities and phone ready when you move in.
5. Get home insurance and be sure it covers your wedding gifts. You may need a floater policy to cover them if they are being stored elsewhere than in your home and if their value is more than your home insurance will cover.
6. Have dental and physical checkups. Make an appointment for your blood tests.

FINANCES

It's important to reach some agreement on how you will handle your finances. At the very least, you should open a joint checking account before the wedding, in which you will deposit the checks or cash you receive as gifts. Some couples also start a joint savings account for moneys they agree to save together for wedding and homemaking expenses. The names on these accounts should be your birth name and his.

If you are both working, decide how you want to pay your bills after you are married. Making a realistic budget helps in this decision. Don't forget to set aside a sum for unexpected expenses and for vacation trips (everyone needs to play once in a while!).

Some couples keep all their earnings (and their stocks and bonds) separate and agree on who pays for what. Others have separate

שמח

accounts and also a joint account into which they each deposit money every month for all their household expenses.

APPLYING FOR YOUR MARRIAGE LICENSE

You will need a marriage license, no matter what style of wedding you decide on. You have to apply for this in person, together, at the marriage bureau in the town or county where the marriage will be performed. Usually this is in the office of the city clerk.

Call to check the application procedure and rules carefully. They differ from state to state.

Find out what the time frame is. Some states require a waiting period—ranging from a few days to a week—between the issuance of the license and the actual wedding ceremony.

Ask what documents and identification you will need to bring with you. Some states require a picture ID that shows your signature. You will also have to bring in the physician's report on your blood tests. Arrange for these tests in time to conform with local rules (check!). In some areas you must have them done very close to the wedding date.

Find your birth certificates. You will need them to obtain your marriage license and, if you are going abroad on your honeymoon, to get your passports. If you don't have your birth certificates in your files, you can obtain them by applying in person or writing to the appropriate agency, usually the board of health, in the city or county where you were born. Be advised that this takes time—don't leave it till the last few days before the wedding.

If either of you has been married before, you may have to present your divorce or annulment papers.

If you have been widowed, you may have to show the death certificate of your previous spouse.

In some states, simply indicating the exact date of the end of the marriage is sufficient. Inquire.

With all your paperwork in hand, you and your fiancé have to appear together to apply for the license. Check the license bureau hours and try to arrive well before closing time. Don't forget cash for the license fee—the groom's responsibility. The fee can be as much as $88.50 (Florida) or $125.00 (U.S. Virgin Islands).

~

Checklist for Documents

YOU AND YOUR FIANCÉ SHOULD EACH CHECK THIS LIST TWICE— ONCE TO BE SURE YOU HAVE COLLECTED THE PAPERS YOU WILL NEED—AND AGAIN WHEN YOU LEAVE FOR THE MARRIAGE LICENSE BUREAU, TO BE SURE YOU HAVE THEM ALL WITH YOU.

- ❑ PERSONAL ID (DRIVER'S LICENSE, PASSPORT, POLICE PICTURE ID, ETC.)
- ❑ BIRTH CERTIFICATE
- ❑ BLOOD TEST RESULTS
- ❑ DIVORCE DECREE OF PREVIOUS MARRIAGE, IF NEEDED
- ❑ DEATH CERTIFICATE OF PREVIOUS SPOUSE, IF NEEDED
- ❑ NECESSARY CASH FOR FEES

~

CHAPTER 17

WHEN PLANS CHANGE

May you never have to use this section! But the best-intentioned, most sincere people in the world sometimes come to the conclusion that a planned wedding should not take place. One quarrel doesn't necessarily signal a broken engagement and a scene where you dramatically fling the ring at your ex-fiancé's feet. A little patience and forbearance are in order. But if you really cannot reconcile your differences, ending the engagement, though it's painful and embarrassing, is far better than ending an unhappy marriage with a bitter divorce a few years later.

There are also those times when events beyond your control can force a change in already announced arrangements. Tough situations—tough to handle. But that's what etiquette is for; there are set procedures that can help you over these difficult hurdles and lessen the strain and embarrassment for everyone.

WHEN AN ENGAGEMENT IS BROKEN

If you and your fiancé have decided irrevocably that you must break your engagement and call off your wedding plans, you must first of all inform your parents, who can then go ahead with the necessary business of canceling contracts if they have already been set, and recalling any invitations that have been sent out. If you were making the arrangements yourself, this is your responsibility, but if it's just too much for you to face on top of your heartbreak, you can delegate the phoning and dealing to a parent, a friend or, if a really big contract is involved, your lawyer.

RECALLING INVITATIONS

If the wedding invitations have already been sent out and the wedding will not take place, all the guests already invited must be notified at once. You can do this by phone, in handwritten notes, or, if there is time, by printed cards. On your card, you write:

> *Mr. and Mrs. Samuel Sherman*
> *announce that the marriage of their daughter*
> *Abigail*
> *to*
> *Mr. Daniel Goldsmith*
> *will not take place*

You do not have to give a reason. A handwritten note could follow the same form.

If you and your fiancé were planning to host your own wedding your card could read:

> *Abigail Sherman*
> *and*
> *Daniel Goldsmith*
> *announce that their marriage will not take place*

For a less formal, handwritten note, parents could write:

> *Dear Marian and Jay,*
> *We regret that we must tell you that the marriage of our daughter*
> *Abigail to Mr. Daniel Goldsmith will not take place.*
> *Martha and Samuel Sherman*

If you are hosting the affair yourself:

> *Dear Aunt Marian and Uncle Jay,*
> *I regret that I must tell you that my wedding to Daniel Goldsmith*
> *will not take place.*
> *Your niece,*
> *Abigail*

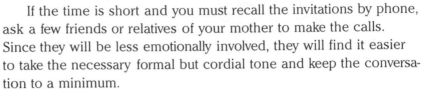
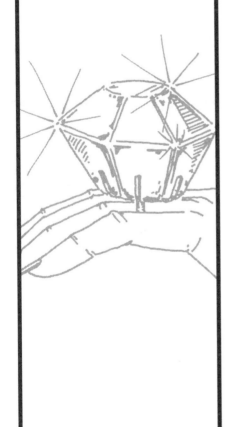

If the time is short and you must recall the invitations by phone, ask a few friends or relatives of your mother to make the calls. Since they will be less emotionally involved, they will find it easier to take the necessary formal but cordial tone and keep the conversation to a minimum.

All the caller has to say is a sentence or two, such as "This is Alice Taylor, Martha Sherman's sister. Martha asked me to call you and tell you that her daughter Abigail's wedding, which was to take place next Sunday, has been called off." Again, you need give no reason. You can diplomatically fend off gossipy inquiries by excusing yourself and saying you have so many calls to make that you really can't discuss this at the moment.

NEWSPAPER ANNOUNCEMENTS

If a formal announcement has been sent to the newspapers, your family may wish to announce the end of the engagement, but it is not always done. Lovers' quarrels are often patched up as spontaneously as they began. If the family feels that an announcement is necessary, the briefest statement is enough:

"Mr. and Mrs. Samuel Sherman of Greenwich, Connecticut announce that the engagement of their daughter Abigail to Mr. Daniel Goldsmith has been broken by mutual consent."

THE ENGAGEMENT RING

To whom does the engagement ring belong? Basically, the ring is a gift from your fiancé to you in return for your promise to marry him. Therefore, it belongs to you. But if you break your promise, even though legally you may keep the ring (yes, there have been lawsuits about very valuable rings and heirloom rings!), it is considered rather greedy to do so.

What if he is the one who broke the engagement and his promise to marry you? Keep the ring. You're the injured party. If you can't stand being reminded of this fiasco, sell it and keep the proceeds.

ENGAGEMENT PRESENTS

Although engagement presents belong to you, most women return not only the ring but any other heirlooms or valuable gifts they were given by their fiancés, just to make the decision final. Gifts from his family or his friends need not be returned.

If you have had a big formal engagement party at which you received many presents in anticipation of your being married, you really should return these gifts, since the occasion for which they were given will not take place. Your accompanying note should speak of your thanks for the sender's generosity.

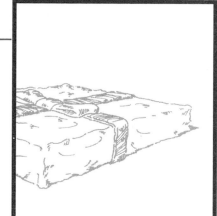

WEDDING PRESENTS

All wedding presents sent to the bride before the wedding, even if monogrammed, must be returned to the senders. You enclose a brief note, stating simply that the wedding will not take place and thank the senders for their thoughtful generosity. The groom writes to his family and friends, the bride to hers.

The bride-to-be may keep the gifts only in the unhappy situation in which the groom dies before the wedding. Even then, there's a question whether she should keep gifts that were meant for a new household that now can never be. Unless the people who sent them urge her to keep the gifts, she really should return them.

When a wedding is annulled soon after the marriage took place, any gifts that have not been opened and used should be returned to the sender, never directly to the stores.

If the marriage lasts only a short time, the gifts belong equally to the husband and wife, according to the laws of most states. However, it has been customary for the bride to keep all the wedding gifts except family jewels or heirlooms received as a gift from the groom's family. In the interest of fairness, the other gifts are sometimes equally divided between the two, with the groom keeping any that were specifically given to him. If objects of considerable value are involved, such as an art collection, you really need competent legal advice. Community property and equitable distribution of assets laws have made this a complicated problem.

Best advice—keep the peace and keep the presents in your new household!

WHEN THERE IS A DEATH IN THE FAMILY

Once you have set the date for your wedding, it need not be called off even if there is a death in the immediate family. In Orthodox tradition, it *must* not be called off. A wedding is considered such a *mitzvah* that even mourning may be interrupted to permit it to take place.

In such unhappy circumstances, the family may want to have a very quiet wedding, canceling the music, for example, and having only a small family reception instead of the lavish affair originally planned. If the invitations have already been sent out, they must then be recalled.

If time permits, a printed card may be sent out, reading:

> *Mr. and Mrs. Samuel Sherman*
> *regret that because of a death in the family*
> *the invitations to their daughter's wedding*
> *on Sunday, March twelfth*
> *must be recalled*

If the time is too short, the guests may be notified by phone or handwritten notes.

If your wedding date falls after the formal mourning period, but less than a year after the death, and you want to go ahead with your original plans, you can resolve any doubts and questions about the propriety of the reception by discussing it with the rabbi who will officiate. He will tell you what modifications, if any, you must make in your wedding plans.

Here's hoping you never need to use this information!

GLOSSARY

aliyah (pl. aliyot): a Torah honor, literally, "going up" (to the reader's desk) to read a portion of the Torah text

Ashkenazim: Jews from Eastern and Central Europe

Baal Shem Tov: Israel ben Eliezer, founder of Hasidism and a revered eighteenth-century mystic.

b'deken: the veiling of the bride by the groom before the wedding ceremony

bentsh: Yiddish for to say Grace, to say blessings

bentsher: the booklet containing the text of the Grace after Meals

bimah: the platform on which the reader's desk is located. Usually in front of the Ark, but in Sephardic synagogues it may be in the center of the room.

Birkat Hamazon: Grace after Meals

brit: circumcision, also the party given on the occasion (Yiddish—*bris*)

bubbe: Yiddish for Grandmother

erusin: the betrothal ceremony—first part of the Wedding Service

freylakh: a lively dance tune

get: a religious decree of divorce according to Jewish law

G'mach—GeMaCh: a charitable group—acronym for *Gemilut Hesed*—deeds of loving kindness

ha-Motzi: colloquial expression for the blessing said over bread

hakhnassat kallah: literally, increasing the rejoicing of the bride. Any act of charity to help poor brides. Also any merrymaking at the wedding feast.

hakhnassat orkhim: hospitality, especially on Sabbath and holidays

hallah: a braided white bread, made especially for the Sabbath, holidays and any celebratory feast—the larger, the more festive

hatan: Hebrew for bridegroom; in Yiddish, *khoson*

Havdalah: concluding service at the close of the Sabbath, using a special braided candle

havurah: fellowship; an informal group that meets for prayer, study and celebration. May exist within a synagogue or as an independent group. May be egalitarian or traditional.

hiddur mitzvah: the beautification of a ritual object

huppah: the wedding canopy

kallah: the bride

kaptsonim: poor folk, beggars. Singular, *kaptson*

kashrut: the system of Jewish dietary laws

ketubah: the marriage contract

Kiddush: the blessing said over wine; also the reception that follows at any celebration

kinyan: literally, a consideration of value—refers to the gift of a ring, in the wedding ceremony, or the gift of some material object, usually a handkerchief, at the signing of a contract

kippa: skullcap

kittel: white ceremonial robe sometimes worn by the groom during the wedding ceremony. Also worn at Festival meals.

klezmer: traditional Yiddish music for celebrations; also the musicians who play it

kosher: food and drink that meets the requirements of the dietary laws (*kashrut*)

kvell: (Yiddish) to experience joy in another's accomplishment or pleasure, especially when parents see their children reach a desired goal in life

lehayyim: "to life"—the traditional toast before drinking liquor or wine

machteniste: mother-in-law; also a new relationship to the other parents

mashgiah: supervisor of *kashrut* at a restaurant, hotel or caterer's kitchen

mazel tov: literally, "good luck"—congratulatory wish

mazinkeh tants: a joyous dance toward the end of the reception which honors parents who have brought their last daughter or son to the *huppah*.

mehuton: father-in-law; also a new relationship to the other parents

mehutonim: relatives by marriage—in-laws

mezuzah: an ornamental container fastened to the doorposts of the home, containing a scroll with the Hebrew text of the first two paragraphs of the *Shema*. May also be worn as a pendant.

midrash: rabbinic tales and explications of the Torah

mikveh: ritual bath

mitzvah: literally, a commandment; a good deed (plural, *mitzvot*)

motzi-messer: (Yiddish) a special knife used only to cut the Sabbath and festival *hallah*, often an heirloom

musaf: the additional service, said after the Torah reading on the Sabbath

nakhes: pleasure and pride in the accomplishment and virtues of one's children

nisuin: the nuptial portion of the Wedding Service

oyfruf (also **aufruf**): Torah honor to the groom (and bride sometimes) on the Sabbath before the wedding

parashah: the weekly portion of the Torah

p'rutah: the smallest coin in ancient Israel—about one cent

Sages: great Jewish scholars, authors of the Commentaries

Sefirah: the period between Passover and Shavuot when weddings may not be held

Sephardim: Jews from Middle East countries, Spain or Portugal

shammash: person in charge of the synagogue, the sexton; in Yiddish, *shammes*

Shekhinah: the holy spirit, specifically, the feminine attributes of the Divine

sheva berakhot: the seven marriage blessings, first recited under the *huppah*

sheva brokhes: Yiddish for *sheva berakhot*; refers to the week of festive meals after the wedding

sheyn: (Yiddish) literally, nice, pretty; colloquial—in the negative sense *"nisht sheyn"* equates with not fitting, not proper

shtetl: a little Jewish village in Europe

shul: Yiddish for synagogue

siman tov: literally, a good omen, congratulations, good wishes

simha: a celebration and the joy of a celebration

sofer: a Hebrew scribe

tallit: prayer shawl; in Yiddish, *tallis*

tenaim: the engagement contract; also the celebration held when the contract is signed

tisch: table, specifically, the festive table spread for the bride's or the groom's reception

Torah: the first five books of the Hebrew Bible

tzedakah: obligatory charity and just behavior intended to ensure the basic well-being of fellow human beings.

unterfirer: couples escorting the bride and the groom

yarmulke: skullcap

yihud: "union"—the brief seclusion of the bride and groom immediately after the wedding ceremony

Yom Kippur: the Day of Atonement—holiest day in the Jewish year, when all sins are forgiven

zivuk: one's preordained mate, the perfect match

Bridal Record Book
for the wedding of

_____ and _____

on

_____,

at

_____

_____.

CASH FLOW SHEET—OR, WHAT IS THIS ALL GOING TO COST?

Bride's Costs	Supplier	Total Cost	Deposit	Balance	Due Date	Cash/check/ charge	Paid— Pick-Up Date
Bridal gown							
Veil, headpiece							
Bride's shoes							
Bridal accessories							
Mother's gown							
Mother's shoes, accessories							
Synagogue Rabbi*, Sexton, choir, organ							
Reception*							
Wedding cake							
Musicians*							
Photographer*							
Video*							
Invitations, announcements, etc. Postage							
Florist Room decor Bridal flowers* Flowers for Mothers Grandmothers Bridesmaids Boutonnieres Delivery tips							
Bridesmaids' gifts							
Men's Clothes Father Brothers							
Miscellaneous: Yarmulkes* Grace booklets*							
_____ _____ _____							

Bride's Costs	Supplier	Total Cost	Deposit	Balance	Due Date	Cash/check/charge	Paid—Pick-Up Date
Rental items: List:____ ____ ____ ____ Delivery cost Tips							
Transportation for Bride/Groom Bridesmaids ____ ____ ____ ____	Driver ____ ____ ____ ____						
Wine and Liquor* Champagne __bottles @____ Beer __cases @____ Liquor __bottles @____ Wine __bottles @____							
TOTALS							

Groom's Costs	Supplier	Total Cost	Deposit	Balance	Due Date	Cash/check/charge	Paid—Pick-Up Date
Wedding attire accessories							
Attendants' gifts							
Tips to drivers, delivery persons							
Marriage license							
Honeymoon							
TOTALS							

*Optional costs that may be shared.

CALENDAR—TO DO LIST

Our wedding day is _____

(month)   (date)

The SIXTH WEEK before our wedding

_____

(month)   (date)

	Morning	*Afternoon*	*Evening*
SUNDAY			
MONDAY			
TUESDAY			
WEDNESDAY			
THURSDAY			
FRIDAY			
SATURDAY			

CALENDAR—TO DO LIST

Our wedding day is _____

(month)   (date)

The FIFTH WEEK before our wedding

_____

(month)   (date)

	Morning	*Afternoon*	*Evening*
SUNDAY			
MONDAY			
TUESDAY			
WEDNESDAY			
THURSDAY			
FRIDAY			
SATURDAY			

CALENDAR—TO DO LIST

Our wedding day is _____

               (month)   (date)

The FOURTH WEEK before our wedding

_____

               (month)   (date)

	Morning	*Afternoon*	*Evening*
SUNDAY			
MONDAY			
TUESDAY			
WEDNESDAY			
THURSDAY			
FRIDAY			
SATURDAY			

CALENDAR—TO DO LIST

Our wedding day is _____

     (month)   (date)

The THIRD WEEK before our wedding

_____

     (month)   (date)

	Morning	*Afternoon*	*Evening*
SUNDAY			
MONDAY			
TUESDAY			
WEDNESDAY			
THURSDAY			
FRIDAY			
SATURDAY			

CALENDAR—TO DO LIST

Our wedding day is _____

(month)   (date)

The SECOND WEEK before our wedding

_____

(month)   (date)

	Morning	*Afternoon*	*Evening*
SUNDAY			
MONDAY			
TUESDAY			
WEDNESDAY			
THURSDAY			
FRIDAY			
SATURDAY			

CALENDAR—TO DO LIST

Our wedding day is _____

(month)   (date)

The LAST WEEK before our wedding

_____

(month)   (date)

	Morning	*Afternoon*	*Evening*
SUNDAY			
MONDAY			
TUESDAY			
WEDNESDAY			
THURSDAY			
FRIDAY			
SATURDAY			

INDEX